Bloodtypes Bodytypes YOU and

Joseph **Christiano**, ND, CNC

SILOAM

Most CHARISMA HOUSE BOOK GROUP products are available at special quantity discounts for bulk purchase for sales promotions, premiums, fund-raising, and educational needs. For details, write Charisma House Book Group, 600 Rinehart Road, Lake Mary, Florida 32746, or telephone (407) 333-0600.

BLOODTYPES, BODYTYPES, AND YOU by Joseph Christiano, ND, CNC
Published by Siloam
Charisma Media/Charisma House Book Group,
600 Rinehart Road, Lake Mary, Florida 32746
www.charismahouse.com

Scripture quotations marked NAS are from the New American Standard Bible. Copyright © 1960, 1962, 1963, 1968, 1971, 1972, 1973, 1975, 1977 by the Lockman Foundation. Used by permission. (www.Lockman.org)

Scripture quotations marked NKJV are from the New King James Version of the Bible. Copyright © 1979, 1980, 1982 by Thomas Nelson, Inc., publishers. Used by permission.

Scripture quotations marked NLT are from the Holy Bible, New Living Translation, copyright © 1996. Used by permission of Tyndale House Publishers, Inc., Wheaton, IL 60189. All rights reserved.

Design Director: Bill Johnson
Cover design by Judith Wright
Author Photo: © Debi Harbin, www.harbinphoto.com

Library of Congress Catalog Card Number: 00-109817
International Standard Book Number: 978-1-59979-290-3
E-book ISBN: 978-1-59979-307-8

Neither the publisher nor the author is engaged in rendering professional advice or services to the individual reader. The ideas, procedures, and suggestions in this book are not intended as a substitute for consulting with your physician. All matters regarding your health require medical supervision. Neither the author nor the publisher shall be liable or responsible for any loss or damage allegedly arising from any information or suggestion in this book.

The recipes in this book are to be followed exactly as written. The publisher is not responsible for your specific health or allergy needs that may require medical supervision. The publisher is not responsible for any adverse reactions to the recipes contained in this book.

While the author has made every effort to provide accurate telephone numbers and Internet addresses at the time of publication, neither the publisher nor the author assumes any responsibility for errors or for changes that occur after publication.

15 16 17 18 19 — 19 18 17 16 15
Printed in the United States of America

Dedication

As I better understand the role genetics play in my life, I am humbled by the fact that I am only a representative of something much greater. Just as God has seen fit to extend His grace to me for spiritual life, He has also provided me with a genetic foundation for physical life. I am thankful to my parents, Joe and Helen, for passing on to me their genetics and the understanding of who my Creator is. My father has passed on to where the true meaning of life dwells, and my mother is here, still cheering me on. Thanks, folks, for giving to me. I love you.

> Don't let the excitement of youth cause you to forget your Creator. Honor him in your youth before you grow old and no longer enjoy living.
> —ECCLESIASTES 12:1, NLT

Acknowledgments

I am eternally thankful to Lori, my wife. It has been her continued support and extra "push" that have helped me to see this work completed. You are the truest example of what every man needs most in life. I love you, babe.

I want to thank the entire staff at Strang Communications and especially the Siloam health imprint for their support, vision, and expertise in making this book a success. I am appreciative for the creative and talented minds of all the team members that have made this work interactive. A special thanks goes to the editorial team at Siloam for their constant input, steady hand, and endless hours of editing and supervising, making this work enjoyable. I am grateful to Maria Gamb for her involvement in the dietary portion. Her expertise in matching and mixing the food groups, menus, and recipes for each blood type is greatly appreciated.

I appreciate those pioneers, such as Drs. James and Peter D'Adamo, who preceded me in revealing the blood-type diet theory. I thank those who have benefited by eating food compatible to their blood type and exercising according to their body genetics and have shared their testimonials in this book.

Lastly, but most importantly, I thank God, my Creator, who allows me the privilege of passing on the treasure of good health—body, soul, and spirit—to my fellow man.

Contents

TABLE OF CHARTS

Introduction

Prior to writing the first version of this book, I believed the concept or theory that linked one's blood type to diet and disease, illness, reaching one's ideal weight for life, and so forth might take some time before it would catch on. Well, for over twelve years of application both personally and professionally, I can now say that the theory for making proper food selections is now evidence-based.

Since I wrote the first version of this book, I cannot count the many people who have told me they improved their lives by applying the information it contains and changing their lifestyles. Many have said they experienced significant drops in their cholesterol and blood pressure readings. Others are saving hundreds of dollars on monthly medication costs because they have been able to reduce and/or completely eliminate taking medications. And they are delighted with the improvement in the way they are feeling. People have shared how they no longer are experiencing digestive disorders and associated discomfort—all because they started eating for their blood type and made other healthy lifestyle changes.

In addition to making food selections that are compatible to your blood type for improved illness profiles, increased energy levels, and help in reaching your ideal weight for life, I have included some additional information in this book that further unlocks the secrets to owning natural health and keeping weight off for life.

It is common knowledge as well as proven evidence that good health starts from inside. That being the case, I have added a chapter to this revised and expanded edition that addresses in great detail the value and importance of colon cleansing and detoxification for colon health and functionality as it correlates to weight loss and eliminating disease.

New Help for Weight Loss

Life is precious and was given as a gift to you—free of charge. What you do with this extraordinary gift has direct consequences on every aspect of your life.

In addition to all the positive feedback I receive via e-mail, phone calls, and mailings from those who have benefited by following the protocol outlined in my book, many people have expressed their continued concern for losing weight. Many have lost weight naturally by following the principles in this book, but others, perhaps like yourself, still need more help to achieve their weight-loss goals.

Did you know that one in three American adults (over 58 million) aged twenty through seventy-four is overweight?[1] Being overweight and physically inactive accounts for more than 300,000 premature deaths each year in the United States, second only to tobacco-related deaths.[2]

Due to the many requests of my readers, along with my personal interest in helping people lose weight and *keep it off*, I have enhanced in this revised edition the chapter dedicated to losing weight, helping you to reach your ideal weight for life. My weight-loss program focuses on enlisting help from your metabolism, learning how to rev it up so that your body can do all the work by becoming the natural calorie burner it was designed to be.

This weight-loss protocol includes everyday menus that are compatible for all blood types; that means everyone in the family can get involved. It includes temporary meal-replacement snacks that are natural fat burners to jump-start the weight-loss process and eventually lead you into eating food (blood-type compatible) to reach your ideal weight for life. It also includes a universal exercise concept acceptable for everyone at any age and with any blood type, yet with a twist that allows you to exercise correctly for your own body type.

My personal and professional experience for more than forty years in the field of health and fitness has shown me the most common denominator shared by dieters who lose weight: 95 percent of them gain all the weight back and more! Because so much emphasis is placed on dieting the weight off instead of eating foods that work in harmony with one's unique body chemistry, the failure rate remains extraordinarily high.

But that is not the whole picture. Most people do not understand the difference between hunger and appetite; therefore, they fall prey to their emotions and the impact emotions have on either success or failure of keeping weight off. To address this hidden roadblock to weight management, I have added a new chapter that points out the food triggers that can derail people who sincerely desire to lose weight and stop them from losing weight and keeping it off for life. (See my book *Never Go Back*, available at www .bodyredesigning.com.)

Life is precious and was given as a gift to you—free of charge. What you do with this extraordinary gift has direct consequences on every aspect of your life. As our world continually advances in technology, information, and new discoveries, can you honestly say that you are improving and moving in step with the areas of your life that mean the most? Consider the areas over which you have control, like personal relationships, happiness and contentment, and vibrant health and youthful functional age. Why not choose to keep in step with accurate eating and regular exercise so that you can maintain your energy, your health, and your ideal weight for life? Have you made these goals a part of your lifestyle?

As you read this book, ask yourself this question: *Does my lifestyle contribute to or take away from these vital areas of my life?* Remember, you are responsible for making the right choices!

Dr. Joe—Your Coach

As you and I establish a one-on-one relationship throughout this book, I want you to relate to me as Dr. Joe, your personal fitness and nutrition coach. My role will be to show you how to combine specific selections of exercises that are most compatible for your body type with specific food selections that are most compatible for your blood type.

So, as Dr. Joe, your personal fitness and nutrition coach, it is my job to get you to where you want to go just as quickly as possible. This interactive book will help you identify with the various mechanisms that I have designed for you as an individual, like the charts on Determining Your Blood Type (page 107) or Determining Your Body Type (page 289). Normally, if you hired me, I would ask you questions about your current level of physical activity, exercise, and involvement in some form of recre-

**I will help
you learn to
reach and
maintain your
healthy body
weight, reduce
your body fat
percentage,
improve bodily
functions,
heal your body
systems, reduce
the likelihood of
disease, control
low blood sugar,
and improve
metabolic
function.**

ational sports. I would ask you a series of background questions related to your medical history, diet experiences, and fitness goals. I would want to know as much about you as possible so I could prescribe the most beneficial strategies to reach your goals. Then I would provide you with a dietary program designed specifically to meet your individual nutritional needs.

This book will help you to develop such a dietary program. You will find that your interactive journey will place you on the exact path to meet your specific bodily needs. I will help you learn to reach and maintain your healthy body weight, reduce your body fat percentage, improve bodily functions, heal your body systems, reduce the likelihood of disease, control low blood sugar, and improve metabolic function. I will have you fill out a dietary analysis of the foods and fluids you consume and the dietary supplements that can help you experience optimal health.

We will look at the role exercise plays in maintaining good health. I will help you to determine your body genetics and to develop an exercise program to meet your specific genetic requirements. Your exercise program will be tailored to your current needs—but it will be progressive in nature to allow you to advance as you improve in health and fitness.

I will help you learn to incorporate specific exercises to redesign your current physical appearance by creating a symmetrical balance between your upper and lower body. Your program will consist of cardiovascular conditioning and anaerobic conditioning (strength training for increasing lean muscle mass and strength). Your program will be designed not only for cosmetic results but also to improve your energy level and your performance in day-to-day tasks and sports. It will aid your health by strengthening your immune system and improving your circulatory system. It will ultimately establish a solid foundation upon which you can build for the rest of your life. I want to help you not only to develop such a plan, but also to learn to be consistent in applying it to your daily life. I will show you how to properly execute each exercise. I will provide you with a way to monitor and review your progress, providing tips to keep you focused and motivated. The combination of my expertise and your willingness to commit to the plan will settle the issue of instant gratification forever. The instant gratification syndrome ultimately leads to discouragement at not being able to obtain the results you want immediately—or even close to immediately! It is my observation that there is a more valid reason for not seeing the results you want. My experience over the past thirty-five years has revealed that the primary reason for failure at following a fitness plan is due to the lack of knowledge for applying the proper dietary and exercise methodologies to reach your goal. Success will be possible when your healthy lifestyle strategy is based on your specific genetic requirements and the synergistic effects they produce in concert with one another.

This book is the closest thing to having your own fitness and nutrition coach—and a whole lot less expensive. The book is designed to work interactively with you by implementing my expertise through charts, programs, and information, plus the mechanisms that will lead you to the right sections of the book for your specific needs.

Naturally, our modified version of one-on-one training will depend on your willingness to succeed and how long you will apply the contents of what is in this book. The synergy of our one-on-one relationship through this book will take you to a new level of understanding of the importance of proper application of exercise and diet to benefit you most. Your adherence to your strategies will speed up the time for accomplishing your short- and long-range goals. It will also give you a greater sense of value in making this approach to a healthier you a lifetime of vibrant living.

From Me to You

I often refer to *instinctive eating* and *body genetics* as the fitness twins. Have you ever noticed the increased performance of your car engine when you fill the gas tank with high-octane fuel instead of low-octane fuel? The answer is obvious. The engine runs poorly on low-octane fuel. It interferes with the engine's performance. When you use high-octane fuel, your engine will perform more efficiently and smoothly. The drive will be faster because the higher octane is what your engine requires.

The same principle is true about the fuel you use in your body's "engine." By applying the higher-octane dietary and exercise strategies that are compatible to your genetics, you will enjoy the positive results sooner.

Having been an avid proponent of getting regular exercise, eating healthily, and taking nutritional supplements for most of my life, what I share in this book will come from my own personal and professional experiences over thirty-five years. My own journey for finding better ways of achieving a healthier, balanced life has caused my innate curiosity and desire to search beyond the mundane for more accurate and direct paths to optimum health.

The proof of desire is pursuit. You will never possess what you are unwilling to pursue. Desire is not what you want but is something you cannot live without.

I travel all over the country speaking and sharing the benefits that come from taking care of the body. I also work at staying in shape; I didn't just wake up one morning to discover I was in good shape—so we share the same journey. My personal level of fitness is a result of years of regular exercise, eating for my blood type, taking nutritional supplements, getting proper rest, a positive mental attitude, a zeal for life, and faith in God—my lifestyle.

But when I look at my daughters and the twelve grandchildren they have given me, I think about the positive role I can play in their lives. I value my relationship with my wife, and I know the importance a healthy body and mind have in our relationship. I look at other family members and wonder what it would be like if I were too sick to enjoy the time I spend with them.

No, maintaining my health is not a mechanical function to me. My good health didn't just happen. I have to work hard to get it—and to keep it. So will you. You will need to look beyond the sweat and discipline and focus on the really important things in your life, weighing them against an unhealthy and sickly lifestyle. Hopefully you will see the value in the principles in this book.

These new findings are important to adapt to our lifestyles so that faster results and responses for positive bodily performance can be achieved. Throughout the years I have learned to make it a point to be more open-minded and willing to accept new truths and information that become available to me. This open-mindedness can be applied to diet, exercise, personal relationships, my spiritual life—or to any area of my life. New research and studies are constantly being made available, so it would be foolish not to take the opportunity to become more informed. Such information can enhance your life and provide the impetus for continual progress.

So, if you haven't done anything to improve your health, or maybe you began and got lazy but realize it is time to take control again, I strongly encourage you to put into practice the strategies, guidelines, and new information you read in this book. Just reading about them cannot bring you a healthier lifestyle. Change will require *the will to change.*

If you are serious about redesigning your body...if you want to achieve your ideal weight for life...if you want to know a healthy way of eating...if you want to live an energetic and youthful life that is high on performance and low on maintenance...then now is the time to make your decision. The journey will never end if you will remember that you are an inspiration in constant transition. Let's take the journey together—one-on-one!

Section I

Developing a Plan for a Healthy Lifestyle

Chapter 1

Genetics—Your Foundation for Success

DNA! Genome! Cellular profiling. Stem cells. Cloning! Blood types. Body types. What is it all about? Is the existence and physiological makeup of humankind just a mixture of theories, personal points of view, and yet-to-be-proven truths? Are we dabbling into mysterious areas that should be left alone, or are we finally beginning to learn more about ourselves?

In man's conquest to survive, questions arise every day: What role do genes play in determining health, disease, longevity, bodily function, and performance? What is the origin of man—where did he come from? Do we all come from one main gene pool, or are we descendants of individual generational ancestry? Did we evolve from nothing to crawling on all fours to an eventual upright position, or did God create us? Is man degenerating because of cellular mutation, becoming less than what he started out as, or is he a result of an evolutionary process, making him far superior to what he was at the beginning of time? Why do some people enter life with blue eyes and blond hair and others with brown eyes and brown hair? Are certain body genetics designed for physical and athletic superiority while other body genetics determine the run-of-the-mill hopefuls?

Do the ABO blood types react differently to the same foods? Is there a link between red blood cells and your health?

Our genetic makeup is the foundation of all that is life.

Although phenomenal advancements have been made through modern-day discoveries in technology, science, and medicine, it will still take light-years to unravel the amazing intricacies of man. The world's best scientific minds have made amazing discoveries, but in the light of all that we still do not know about ourselves, technology seems to move at a snail's pace.

Whether you believe that God created every human being or that our existence is a result of some theoretical development of nothingness into something, the answers to our questions lie far beneath the surface—with our genetic foundation.

Our genetic makeup is the foundation of all that is life. Nothing relating to our ability to survive our environment; to fight off illness, infection, or stress; to supply our bodies with nutrition; or to make physiological adaptation is a matter of happenstance. It is no coincidence that our body is programmed with the innate ability to defend itself from uninvited invaders such as parasites, viruses, and bacteria by creating an army of antibodies.

Our genetic foundation is a mixture of trillions of cells with codes that identify, program, and link everything in our existence—from the color of our hair to our bodies' susceptibility to disease to foods that are compatible to our potential life span and capability to survive.

Some people would rather merely swim in shallow water than go below the surface to discover answers to the questions and issues of life. But there is a bottomless sea to dive into for the inquisitive and health-conscious individual who seeks knowledge of the role genetics play in our lives.

For example, did you know that...

- Gene therapy is now being researched intensively in most developed countries—for a host of very good reasons. Instead of treating deficiencies by injecting drugs, doctors will be able to prescribe genetic treatments that will induce the body's own protein-making machinery to produce the proteins needed to combat illness.[1]

- Researchers succeeded in making artificial copies of human genes that could be manipulated to produce large amounts of specific proteins. Such genes can be introduced into the human body where, in many cases, they substitute for a defective gene.[2]

- In a study that could lead to new treatments for diabetes and provide guidance on the use of genes in treating disease, scientists show that a common genetic variation increased the risk of contracting type 2 diabetes.[3]

- Australian scientists have identified a new gene responsible for controlling appetite in humans—a discovery experts say could lead to the first gene-based drug to treat obesity and diabetes.[4]

- In the not-too-distant future, scientists may be able to grow replacement organs and new blood vessels to replace clogged ones, eradicate diseases as diverse as Alzheimer's and cystic fibrosis, and tell which medication to prescribe.[5]

Gaining more knowledge and understanding about the complexities of our genetics humbles me—and convinces me of the existence of One much greater than man, with infinite creative wisdom that stretches far beyond the finite knowledge of man. The fact that man has the ability to make scientific advancements and acquire information about the genome of man serves only to prove how much greater his Creator must be.

One of the most common questions that people ask of creation scientists is this: How did such a variety of ethnic groups and diverse races arise from one human pair?

Research is revealing more and more about the origin of blood types. Much of this research points out the possibility of the emergence of all known blood types from our common ancestors, Adam and Eve. In his dissertation titled "Blood Types and Their Origin (Answering the Critics)," Jonathan Sarfati tells us:

> There is one gene in humans that controls the ABO blood type.
> There are three versions of the gene, or alleles: A, B, or O....For

The fact that man has the ability to make scientific advancements and acquire information about the genome of man serves only to prove how much greater his Creator must be.

a husband and wife to pass on all alleles to their children, they need to, between them, have the A, B, and O alleles....If Adam and Eve were genetically AO and BO, for example, their children could have had AB, AO, BO, or OO genetic makeup, giving AB, A, B, or O blood types. Indeed, about 25 percent of their children would have been of each type.[6]

There is so much more to be discovered about man and our genetic makeup—birthed in us at the moment of conception. Although scientists are discovering new things about our genetic structure daily, there is much more that remains unknown. One scientist has observed:

> Data supporting the complexity and design of life at all levels, and especially that of man, loom larger than was previously supposed—as large in fact as the enormous "gaps" in the fossil record....The further we look into the complexity to the real world of man and his living companions, the more baffling and unexplainable, at least in standard evolutionary theory, the whole complex becomes....To the skeptic, the proposition that the genetic programmes of higher organisms consisting of something close to a thousand million bits of information...containing in encoded form countless thousands of intricate algorithms controlling, specifying and ordering the growth and development of billions and billions of cells into the form of a complex organism, were composed by a purely random process is simply an affront to reason.[7]

It has taken gifted scientists years upon years to discover the things they know about man today. But it will take hundreds of more years to understand how to apply the new information.

It is when we are willing to be taught and are open to more knowledge that we continue to grow. I am growing daily in my own knowledge, particularly in my knowledge about the link between blood types and nutrition. Since I coauthored the book *The Answer is in Your Bloodtype*, I have discovered new studies about the origin of blood types. These findings lean more closely to my personal beliefs in creationism.

My purpose for mentioning this is twofold: First, I humbly

admit that no one has all the answers. But as long as we are willing to be open to greater learning and understanding, progress can be continual. Second, since I happen to believe that God is the Creator of all creation, it stands to reason that I would embrace studies that line up with my beliefs. As we learn more about the complex design of man, it just makes good sense to me that Someone greater than you or I is in charge of this whole thing.

Regardless of where you stand concerning the origins of blood type, one thing we can agree on is that eating foods compatible to our blood type and avoiding foods that are not compatible is a more accurate and individualized approach to eating than anything man has experienced.

As a naturopathic doctor, and not a scientist, biochemist, or genealogist, I'll leave the research and discoveries to them and concentrate my efforts on helping you to be healthier. My interest is to help you reach a basic level of understanding about your body so you can take care of it in a way that will contribute to living a healthier and more balanced life.

During my summer vacations from school as a kid, I remember going with my father while he worked a few hours a week for my cousin, who owned an excavation and construction company. I watched the construction workers build the foundations for new buildings, or as they called it, "pour a cellar." It was quite a process. The first thing they did was excavate the land and prepare the ground. Then they measured out the area where the foundation would be laid. After determining the proper elevations and measurements, they began to set up the forms.

Until I saw the entire process completed for the first time, it was hard to understand why they were using all those heavy planks to make a huge square in the dirt. But I learned that those planks played a very important role in the next part of the procedure. When the huge cement trucks were ready to pour the concrete, they poured it into the wood forms, which shaped the foundation of the building.

I learned that each foundation differed in size, shape, and materials. Certain job sites required the forms to be dug deeper in the ground, while other forms were extended higher. The deeper or higher the forms were laid, the thicker the concrete base or foundation would be. The design and composition of each poured foundation determined the size and weight of the structure that it could support.

Each building structure, whether a residential home, a high-rise building, or a strip mall, required a unique foundation that functioned as its basis for structure, stability, and support. Similarly, our ability to survive, support, and improve our structure will be determined by the mixture of the material found in our foundation. Our foundation, of course, is our genetics.

The amount of time and effort you put into customizing and building your "house" (your body) will help it to last for many years.

Consider yourself as a general contractor who wants to redesign or custom-build a house. In this case, the foundation of the house you want to construct, or reconstruct, is your genetics. Instead of brick, mortar, and wood, you are using the materials that comprise your body.

The amount of time and effort you put into customizing and building your "house" (your body) will help it to last for many years. By understanding the purpose of a strong "foundation" (your genetics) and by using the proper "tools and materials" (the proper nutritional and exercise applications and methodologies), you can assure a healthy, happy future.

You have a specific biological makeup that was given to you at conception. It's the genetic substance that makes up your entire existence.

I have three daughters—Amy, the oldest, and twin daughters, Jenifer and Cara. Amy's genetic foundation has given her facial features that resemble mine, while genetically Jenifer and Cara have their mother's facial features.

But your genes are not limited to your facial characteristics. Your genes not only determine if you will look more like your mom or your dad and what color your hair and eyes will be, but also how susceptible you are to certain diseases and illnesses. Your cellular profile and the way your body responds to certain foods, viruses, and bacteria are determined by your genes also.

Have you heard of infants who could not tolerate a traditional milk formula but flourished on a formula using soy milk? The infant did not reject the traditional milk formula simply because he or she was uncooperative—the formula was not compatible to the infant's blood type. How about the little boy who grew up wearing husky-size jeans because of his large buttocks and thighs? It wasn't his fault—he was born with a body type that included large buttocks and thighs. Knowing your children's blood types can help you make healthy food selections for them at an early age.

Two very important considerations can greatly help you maximize your genetic potential. These are providing your body with the best nutritional program for your specific genetics and applying the best fitness approach for your genetic structure. Let's take a look at each consideration before we go any further.

You are what you eat, but it is also vitally important for you to eat what you are!

Blood Types and Nutrition

You are what you eat, but it is also vitally important for you to eat what you are! Each of us should eat a diet that is compatible with our blood type.

We can begin to get an understanding of this important concept by taking a look at the animal kingdom. It is instinct that drives animals to eat. Lions are meat eaters—they won't be happy if you try to feed them a diet rich in fruits and vegetables. Other animals are vegetarian by instinct, and they will not eat meat. This is no accident—instinct is a protective mechanism for all animals, including humans.

Each blood type has different characteristics that allow it to eat, digest, and assimilate food best for that group. Type Os are blessed with strong stomach acid and powerful enzymes that can metabolize almost anything—even some food not recommended for them. Types A, B, and AB must be more careful in their eating habits or suffer the consequences.

What are these consequences? What happens when we eat food not compatible with our blood types? Agglutination happens, which can be explained as follows:

> Your body has antibodies that protect it from foreign invaders. Your immune system produces all kinds of antibodies to protect you and keep you safe from foreign substances. Each antibody is designed to attach itself to a foreign substance or antigen. When your body recognizes an intruder, it produces

more antibodies to attack the invader. The antibody then attaches itself to the intruder and a "gluing" effect (agglutina- tion) takes place. In this way, the body can better dispose of these foreign invaders.[8]

When it comes to eating foods that are not compatible with your blood type, this "gluing" effect can take place in the digestive system, joints, liver, brain, or blood. Continual ingesting of foods not compat- ible to your blood type can cause havoc in your body systems. This agglutination of cells, or clumping, will eventually break down the function of that particular system and lead to health problems.

One main reason why certain foods are identified as "Avoid" foods is because of the protein molecules, or *lectins*, that they contain. It is when these dietary lectins that are present in certain foods enter the host's body that problems prevail.

In my book *The Answer is in Your Bloodtype* (Personal Nutri- tion USA, Inc., 1999), I included information on the specific characteristics of each blood type in relation to nutrition. Let me give you an overview of some of these characteristics.

BLOOD TYPE O

One of the factors contributing to the longevity of blood type O individuals (besides the eradication of diseases such as typhoid, cholera, smallpox, plague, malaria, and others that still exist in third-world countries) is the fact that they survive well as meat- eaters. In his book *The Chemistry of Man*, Bernard Jensen, PhD, ND, stated, "Nearly all of the oldest people I have encountered in my travels around the world were meat-eaters."[9]

Individuals with type O blood have the thinnest blood, strongest immune systems (with the exception of some diseases), strongest stomach acid, and live the longest of all the blood types at present.

Genetically, stomach acid was designed to break down the high-protein diets on which our original ancestors thrived. As food sources changed, type Os were able to adapt to metabolizing almost any food because of this strong stomach acid.

Since the ancestors of type O were hunters, descendants carry- ing this gene tend to be larger, stronger individuals. If you were to check the blood types of most competitive bodybuilders and professional athletes, an overwhelming number of them would be blood type O. Most American Indians and Eskimos are also Os.

Because type Os have the thinnest blood of any type, they are less likely to be affected by blood clots or the buildup of plaque—making them less susceptible to heart disease, at least at an early age. They also seem less susceptible to cancer.[10]

Since the ancestors of type O were hunters, descendants carrying this gene tend to be larger, stronger individuals.

Strengths:
- Thinnest blood
- Strongest stomach acid
- Strong immune system
- Longest life span
- Metabolizes food well
- Neutralizes cholesterol
- Low blood clot risk

Weaknesses:
- Thin blood may not clot well in brain.
- Intolerant of newer dietary and environmental conditions
- Greatest threshold for abuse of smoking, alcohol, etc.

Health risks:
- Strokes
- Blood disorders like hemophilia and leukemia
- Arthritis and/or inflammatory diseases
- Ulcers
- Allergies

Nutritional profile:
- Animal protein primary source
- Foods rich in vitamin K
- Eat beef, salmon, mozzarella cheese, pinto beans, artichoke, broccoli, greens, figs, plums
- Avoid pork, wheat, corn, lentils, navy beans, cabbage, brussels sprouts, potatoes, melons, oranges

BLOOD TYPE A

As man migrated geographically to locations where meat was not readily available, environmental adaptation was required for

survival, which involved adaptation to a different diet—specifically
vegetarian. These early migrations were to places like Europe, Asia,
and Australia, regions totally different from the plentiful plains of
Africa where animal protein was abundant. These early migrators
learned to survive on fruits, vegetables, and grains. As a result,
many people with blood type A do best avoiding almost all animal
protein in favor of a vegetarian diet.

**Many people
with blood type
A must avoid
almost all
animal protein
in favor of a
vegetarian diet.**

Individuals with type A blood have the thickest blood of all blood
types. In the United States, meat and potatoes have comprised the
traditional staple diet. Type As do not tolerate either meat or potatoes
well. When Type As eat these foods that are inconsistent with their
blood type, their already thick blood agglutinates, or gets thicker and
stickier. The thick blood requires the heart to pump harder, inevi-
tably causing high blood pressure, hypertension, an enlarged heart
muscle, and an increase in heart disease. This is the major reason
why type A individuals have the shortest life span today.

Another downside for individuals with type A blood is that in
their adaptation to a vegetarian diet, over time type As began to
secrete less stomach acid necessary to metabolize meat protein. Type
As have very low stomach acid by genetic standards; while the low
acid accommodates the metabolism of fruits and vegetables, it does
a miserable job metabolizing animal protein.

A constant diet of mainly meats and potatoes provides fewer
nutrients to the body, lowers immune function, and thickens the
blood, leading to heart disease, cancer, and earlier death. For
precisely these reasons, type As are susceptible to heart disease
and cancer. The Japanese are an exception; they eat a staple diet
of fish, rice, and green tea—the perfect diet for individuals of type
A blood.[11]

Strengths:
- Adapts well to dietary and environmental changes

Weaknesses:
- Thick blood
- Shortest life span
- Affected by stress more than other blood groups
- Sensitive digestive tract

- Vulnerable immune system
- Must avoid almost all animal protein

Health risks:
- Heart disease
- Cancer
- High blood pressure and hypertension
- Enlarged heart muscle
- Decreased immune function
- Anemia
- Liver disorders
- Gallbladder disorders
- Diabetes

Nutritional profile:
- Eat soybeans and tofu, and drink green tea for anti-oxidant qualities; eat grouper, cod, and salmon; eat soy cheese and drink soy milk; eat lentils, broccoli, carrots, romaine lettuce, spinach, blueberries, blackberries, cranberries, prunes, raisins
- Avoid animal fat; meat or dairy products; meat-and-potato diet; kidney, lima, and navy beans; durum wheat; eggplant; peppers; tomatoes; cantaloupe; honeydew melons

BLOOD TYPE B

Type B blood is not as thin as type O blood, nor is it as thick as type A blood. For the most part, type Bs can eat meat in moderation without great fear of developing heart disease. Type B individuals have the ability to eat and metabolize dairy products, which both type O and type A do not tolerate well at all.

It is believed that improper foods, or the improper metabolism of specific foods, lower the immune system of Bs and make them susceptible to autoimmune diseases. Type B individuals average the second longest life span after Os. This is probably due to the fact that animal protein, which contains all those essential amino acids, is good food for Bs. Additionally, since type Bs can eat a large variety of foods, they are able to acquire all or most of their essential vitamins, minerals, and amino acids from food more easily than As and ABs.

Type Bs have the genetics to be the second most muscular, next to type O. While Bs build muscle easily, some gravitate to sports, perhaps as coaches and trainers, but the vast majority tend to pursue careers in medicine, law, science, and technology.[12]

Improper foods, or the improper metabolism of specific foods, lower the immune system of Bs and make them susceptible to autoimmune diseases.

Strengths:
- Naturally strong immune system
- Acquires most essential vitamins, minerals, and amino acids from food more easily than As or ABs
- Lives longer than As and ABs
- Second most muscular

Weaknesses:
- Some chronic medical problems such as skin disorders or foot problems

Health risks:
- Polio
- Lupus
- Lou Gehrig's disease
- Multiple sclerosis

Nutritional profile:
- Can eat meat in moderation
- Metabolizes dairy foods fairly well
- Eat lamb; venison; cod; grouper; farmer, feta, and mozzarella cheese; kidney, lima, navy, and soybeans; broccoli; cabbage; collard and mustard greens; pineapple; plums
- Avoid chicken, American cheese, ice cream, wheat, white and yellow corn, pumpkin, tofu, persimmons, rhubarb

BLOOD TYPE AB

Blood type AB individuals are blessed with inheriting the two dominant genes—A and B. Since both A and B are dominant genes, AB is the only blood type with two dominant traits.

ABs are susceptible to both A and B diseases, making them prone to cancer, heart disease, and autoimmune diseases. Research has also noticed a clear trend for women of this blood type to have many menstrual problems—such as excessive bleeding, clotting, cramping, and irregular menstrual cycles—either leading to hysterectomies or continued misery. A large number of the women who experienced menstrual problems also experienced migraine and other headaches. There is a clear pattern of hormonal imbalance that plagues this blood group. ABs are slightly more muscular than As but less muscular than Bs. It is easier for an AB to build muscle than an A, but in some cases, ABs have as difficult a time building muscle as As.

Eating properly for an AB requires guidelines similar to As, but with small amounts of animal protein. ABs should acquire their vitamins, minerals, and essential amino acids through plant and vegetable proteins.[13]

ABs are susceptible to both A and B diseases, making them prone to cancer, heart disease, and autoimmune diseases.

Strengths:
- Only blood type with two dominant traits
- Friendliest immune system

Weaknesses:
- Pattern of hormonal imbalance
- Tendency to chemical imbalance disorders

Health risks:
- Cancer
- Heart disease
- Anemia
- Autoimmune disease
- Women tend to have menstrual problems and migraines and other headaches.

Nutritional profile:
- Limited to small amounts of animal protein
- Eat turkey; cod; mahimahi; navy, pinto, and soybeans; oat and rice flours; collard, dandelion, and mustard greens; figs; grapes; plums
- Avoid chicken, duck, all pork and venison, clams, crab, haddock, lobster and shrimp, kidney and lima beans, white and yellow corn, peppers, guava, mangoes, oranges

Blood Types Determine What to Eat

In this book you will learn to eat what you are—to eat according to your blood-type genetics. With proper diet, including nourishment from the food and supplements specific to your needs, the chance of disease is greatly reduced. In fact, proper diet according to blood type, coupled with exercise, enables your immune system to be its strongest. A strong immune system can make the difference between a longer or shorter life span.

Since the body cannot repair itself without protein, protein is the key element in the equation for good health. We must all have protein; the form of that protein determines how long we will live. For individuals with blood types A and AB, animal protein from meat is unacceptable, with a few exceptions. For Bs, while meat is not particularly harmful in the short run, it contributes to heart disease and a host of other assorted ailments in the long run.

The body accesses body fat for fuel when it has burned its sugars and carbohydrates. The goal is to keep the body in an anabolic state for as many hours a day as possible. In this way the body always has the fuel it needs to rebuild and repair. Carbohydrates provide energy, but they don't fulfill the body's need to build strong bones and boost immune function.

Body Types and Exercise

By following your blood-type-specific diet program, maintaining your body in an anabolic state with the use of protein, and adding necessary nutrients to your daily program through supplementation, you can reach your genetic potential. But to reach your genetic potential and enjoy a healthy long life, you will also need to understand your body's genetics regarding your genetic structure and to follow a fitness plan to maximize the positives and minimize the negatives of your body type. I will provide a complete fitness plan for each body type in Section III of this book, but here is an overview of the three different body types.

THE PEAR BODY TYPE

The pear body type finds its weight distribution problems in the lower body—the hips, thighs, and buttocks. This body type is considered to be bottom heavy. The upper body is generally slender, with a shallow bustline and narrow shoulders.

The challenge for the pear body type is to redesign the body by filling out the chest/bust and adding width to the shoulders while isolating toning and firming exercises to the lower body area.

Characteristics of a pear:
- Narrow shoulders
- Straight waist
- Lower-body weight in hips, thighs, and buttocks
- Wide pelvic and hip structure
- Need to reduce lower body
- Need to build muscle mass in upper body

THE APPLE BODY TYPE

When the apple body type gains weight, the weight goes mostly to the upper body. It stores most of its body fat around the waist, upper back, and arms. The abdomen often protrudes or bulges forward. Apples usually have thin legs and buttocks, creating an out-of-balance symmetry with the upper body.

The challenge for the apple body type is to build the upper and lower leg muscles while shaping and toning the upper body. The apple will need to concentrate on the abdominal muscles also.

Characteristics of an apple:
- Upper body stores fat around waist, upper back, and arms.
- Lower body is undersized.
- Thin buttocks and legs
- Abdominal area out of proportion and protrudes
- Need to shape and tone upper body
- Need to build hips, thighs, and buttocks

THE BANANA BODY TYPE

Weight gain for the banana body type is distributed equally between the upper and lower body. The banana lacks shapeliness, tending to have a straight-line figure. Often the waist area for a banana is nearly as wide as the upper and lower body.

The challenge of redesigning the banana is to firm and tone

muscles to incorporate an hourglass shape. The banana should concentrate on the abdominal muscles and try to elongate the thighs and tone the buttocks.

Characteristics of a banana:
- Lacks pleasing lines and shapeliness
- Pelvic bone, ribs, and shoulders equal width
- Wide waist
- Need to firm and tone muscles
- Need to elongate thighs
- Need to tone buttocks

Positioned for Success

Your genetics have determined what you are and how your body responds, reacts, and performs. With the understanding of the principles I have outlined in this chapter, you are positioned for success—just as soon as you get started. By applying the information and strategies set forth in this book, you will discover how to eat foods compatible to your blood type and how to choose exercises compatible to your body type.

Genetically speaking, you and I have been given just so much clay to work with. Why not follow the right path and enjoy the journey reaching your genetic potential?

My desire is to help you reach a new level of improved health, physical appearance, and an energetic life as quickly as possible. But please remember, it is your *journey in life* that is most important. Your genetic predisposition is basic to your success. As you better understand the role your genetics play, you will better understand the science behind the dietary and exercise strategies through this book.

On your journey, take what you have learned, appropriate the experiences you have applied to your lifestyle, and pass them along for the good of others. That will add more worth to your life. *Roads were not built for destinations—they were built for the journey.*

Chapter 2

Bridging the Gap

After receiving my education in the field of naturopathy and spending many years as a health and fitness professional, I have found that my one-on-one relationship with my clients is the most productive part of my education. Whether consulting with a client in my office or taking a client through a workout in the gym, that one-on-one relationship is the most rewarding part of my profession. I derive great satisfaction as I watch a client accomplish what he or she set out to do with the help of my innate gifts of nurturing and tutoring. My greatest reward for pouring all my expertise and knowledge into them is experiencing their success—and knowing that I played a part in it.

Motivation and accountability are the two dynamics that make a one-on-one relationship so powerful and effective, whether they are applied to health and fitness, marriage and family relationships, or any other area of your life. Through the years I have seen many succeed because they dared to go the extra mile, and in the end, they have thanked me for their success because of my guidance and expertise, for which I am very blessed.

But let me also set the record straight—the one-on-one

relationship is a two-way street! As a result of the many years of working in one-on-one relationships with clients, I have greatly benefited as well. I have been fortunate to develop my innate abilities and sharpen my instincts for determining specific dietary requirements for clients by listening to them or reading the personal information they gave me. Their comments and answers to various questions have taught me how valuable the psychological and emotional areas of my clients are and the vital role they play in their overall health as well as in their potential to succeed. Through these insights, I have been able to see past their general reasons for wanting to get into shape and help them get in touch with their real reasons for doing so.

By observing their athletic abilities, their exercise performance, their body genetics, and how they responded to cues and directives, I have been able to make immediate adjustments to the exercise methodology that would better suit them. Yes, I have greatly benefited throughout all these years from the one-on-one relationships.

I took the time to share that with you so you and I can establish a one-on-one relationship also. Even though it will take place as we journey through this book, and not in person, you will be amazed at the progress you can make. How will it work? It will happen as you learn to trust me—and the information and guidelines I am providing for you in this book.

If you hired me as your personal trainer, you would have to trust me. So your dependency on my guidance in this book is not all that different. Knowing that what I am giving you comes in part from years and years of working in the trenches in those one-on-one relationships should give you a comfort zone. Ultimately those experiences provided me the expertise and ability to prescribe for you the specific dietary guidelines and exercise methodology for your genetics, just as if we were meeting one-on-one. The bottom line for you is to *trust* and then *apply* the information and strategies from this book that come closest to meeting your individual needs.

Perhaps you are afraid that you will never be able to accomplish your personal fitness and diet goals without the continual guidance of a personal fitness trainer. Should you doubt the possibility of succeeding without a personal trainer, please read Lynn's success story on page 307 in section four—"Real People, Real Results." Keep in mind that her extraordinary results did not come from training sessions in a gym with me as her personal trainer. Before we met, she had established the specific goals she wanted to accomplish. She was determined to do her best at attaining her goals. I didn't meet this woman personally—during the process of reaching her goals, she sought me out to help her develop individual prescriptions for diet and exercise. Obviously, her results speak for themselves. You can tell that by looking at her fabulous before and after photos.

No more time for wishing and hoping—now is the time to take action.

Fear Never Wins

It takes trust for you to be able to allow someone to take you by the hand and lead you to where you have never been before. Most people fail to reach their potential, never enjoying the benefits of the other side because they are afraid to take the first step. They become paralyzed by fear.

If you are fearful and untrusting, it may not be me in whom you are afraid to place your confidence. It may be the fear of failure that holds you back. Just remember that fear is an emotion. It breeds doubt, and doubt becomes an attitude issue that can slow down your progress and eventually lead to failure. To find out what kind of end results you are capable of, and to enjoy a healthier and more fulfilling life, you must be willing to leave the place where you are now—regardless of your present physical and mental condition. Stepping out of that place is the only way to experience a better lifestyle.

No more time for wishing and hoping—*now is the time to take action*. It is going to take a leap of faith to reach your full potential. If you are willing to step out and take that leap of faith, bridging the gap between wishful hoping and the joy of victory with the sweet smell of success, then take my hand and let's go, one-on-one.

The Gap

Years ago I made a business trip to Toronto, Canada. On the drive back to Buffalo, New York, my wife, Lori, my business agent Frank, and I decided to stop in Niagara Falls to eat lunch. If you have never been to Niagara Falls on the Canadian side, you must make plans to go sometime—it is totally awesome.

There are many restaurants in the Niagara Falls tour district. Five hundred twenty feet straight up the Skylon Tower there is a revolving restaurant, accessible only by an elevator that travels up the outside of the tower. That elevator ride in and of itself almost took my appetite away. Once we were seated, we were mesmerized by the sight of the falls and of the five-hundred-foot gorges below. You can see for miles and miles, both in America and Canada.

As I sat there, I thought of a story that took place in Niagara Falls many years ago when the Great Blondin walked across the falls on a tightrope while pushing a wheelbarrow. Obviously it was so unbelievable to watch. I could imagine the crowds of people who watched. As I thought about this incredible feat, I could see how it served as a prime example of how fear had paralyzed that crowd of onlookers from stepping out in faith to walk that tightrope also.

I could hardly imagine crossing that spectacular "gap" on a tightrope while pushing a wheelbarrow. Glancing down five hundred feet to the cataracts below, it seemed inconceivable that anyone would take such a step of faith. But the Great Blondin went across the falls and back on nothing more than a cable and a wheelbarrow that he pushed. When he returned to his starting point, the crowds cheered wildly, shouting out their approval of his fearless deed. "Do you think I could do it again?" he yelled to the crowd.

"Yes, we believe you can," they responded instantly. So off he went again, crossing the huge gap of dangerous whirlpools separating the United States and Canada. When he returned, the people cheered and applauded once more, amazed at his lack of fear.

Once more the acrobat asked the crowd, "Do you believe I could do it again?"

"Yes, yes, you can!" they called back in unison. Above the din of the crowd, one person yelled out, "I know you can!"

Hearing the voice, the Great Blondin yelled back these words: "If you know I can, then are you willing to get in the wheelbarrow and go across the falls with me?"

There was no answer—only silence.[1]

I wonder, *what happened to that person?*

Later during an interview, the acrobat was asked how he kept fear from interfering with his performance. How was he able to maintain his balance? He responded by saying that he overcame his fear as long as he stayed focused on the cable in front of him— instead of on the water below. By staying focused on the cable, he never saw anything else. Everything else was out of focus.

Has fear been preventing you from making a decision to seek a healthier, fitter lifestyle? What do you have to lose but excess body fat, a body that needs some redesigning, and the agony of digestive discomforts? Decide today to step out, focus on the goal, and go for it!

Decide today to step out, focus on the goal, and go for it!

Time for a Change

I am sure you have heard that familiar saying, "If a man can't change his mind, he can't change anything." Of course, this theory applies to women as well. So before you and I can go one-on-one, you have to make a commitment to being willing to change. In this book, I will cover all aspects of exercise and diet. You will be able to identify strategies that will work best for you. But you must consider first things first—and that is, *are you willing to change?*

We tend to be creatures of habit. Change comes very slowly and with reservation—if it comes at all. We tend to cling to our comfort zones and refuse challenges that will cause us to make changes. For example, you may have already, from past experience, found a particular diet plan that allowed you to lose weight. In your mind you think that anytime you need to lose a few pounds, all you have to do is follow that same diet plan again.

Stop for a moment and think that theory through from a different perspective. You will discover that the diet gave you temporary results at best. A plan that cannot keep you from gaining back the fat again obviously does not work. It gave only temporary results. It should be considered the last dietary path on this earth that you should want to travel.

At least I see it that clearly. So, are you willing to change your thinking? Assume that indeed what I am presenting to you in this book is a new, different dietary approach to eating that is more effective than your previous experience and one that can be adaptable for your lifetime. Would you be willing to change? Would it be worth the change?

Rather than returning to your former way of thinking by implementing your original diet plan, the one that only provided a temporary drop in weight, wouldn't it make good logical sense to make a change? Indeed, it does make good sense, particularly if this change can help you maintain your weight forever, avoid certain unnecessary health disorders, and give you a sense of mental victory because you were willing to stretch your boundaries to bridge the gap.

Consider that New Year's resolution where you joined with half of all America to start a jogging program—you remember, the one where you tried to get in shape all at one time, the one that nearly killed your knees. Why would you return to something that doesn't provide success as an end product? Worst yet, why would you think that what didn't work previously would eventually become profitable to you if you used it again? That's a sure way to go insane.

But if I can offer you an exercise program concept that is based on your body genetics and specifically designed for your body type, wouldn't it be worth the change to try an exercise program that can deliver the results you want?

On a separate sheet of paper, write down a list of reasons why you *should not* change. If your only reasons are staying out of shape, being tired all the time, aging faster than necessary, allowing the onset of unnecessary diseases and illnesses, plus not enjoying a lifestyle of vitality and high energy, then you might as well not bother with the list. My guess is that any valid reasons you could come up with would fit on the head of a pin!

I want you to be willing to open your mind to new things that can be helpful and beneficial. If you are willing to change, then there is hope. Not all changes can be achieved overnight. That's not even necessary. But change must begin for you to be successful.

The outward behavioral changes will take place naturally when you are ready and willing to change on the inside. Take a good look on the inside. Examine your deepest concerns about your health—or lack thereof.

Improving your health—or ignoring it—can affect the more

important areas of your life, such as family, relationships, career, or anything that means the most to you. On a separate sheet of paper, write down a list of positive values that will occur in the important areas of your life if you choose to embrace change. These may include not being tired and uncomfortable all the time, having the energy and stamina to do more with your family, having more energy for your career, or being able to engage in a sport that up to now has been impossible for you to do.

Now compile a list of fears or doubts that can prevent you from what you might accomplish with change. It may be the fear of failure that we talked about earlier. Or it may be the fear of making a commitment to something you have never tried before.

2-1

Reasons to Change— Positive Values

Family relationships—Being there for your loved ones: children, parents, wife, husband

Friends—Enjoying fellowship and socializing

Career/profession—Performance, appearance, image

Future—Preventative measures today for a solid tomorrow

Health—Getting rid of fatigue, excess weight, sickness and disease

Reasons Not to Change— Negative Fears

Fear of change—Lack of trust, doubts and fear of the unknown

Fear of commitment—Lack of discipline

Fear of failure—Past experiences

Laziness—Negative attitude, lack of motivation, shortsightedness

---

Compare your list of positive values to the list of your fears. Would you rather be paralyzed by fear from experiencing these positive values, or would you rather eliminate your fears so you can enjoy the values? This is a prudent and wise decision to make before you step out in faith, which is the first plan of action. The Holy Scriptures say, "For as he thinks within himself, so he is" (Prov. 23:7, NAS). Behavioral changes will be easier to make after you have reexamined your motives and fears.

Your list of positive values and of your fears may look something like Chart 2-1 on this page.

To make this transition in your thinking even easier, try focusing on the reasons to change—not on the changes themselves. Remember our tightrope walker—he was able to cross the huge gap between our country and Canada because he stayed focused on the rope, not on anything else. In actuality, the biggest gap he had to overcome was not the one that separated the United States and Canada—it was the gap between his fear of falling and the goal he wanted to achieve.

Goal Setting

As your one-on-one coach, I can give you all the information regarding the role your genetics play in your health and fitness plans. I can provide you with easy-to-follow dietary and exercise guidelines that are specific for your genetics and will provide the results you are looking for. I can even call you or e-mail you with words of encouragement. But if you are not equipped with goals, if you are not sure where you want to go on your journey, then it will be very difficult for you and me to get there. Establish your goals first. Set up a schedule for reaching each goal along the journey. Determine how you are going to reach each goal.

Include both short-range and long-range goals. Be sure that they are realistic enough that you can achieve them. When you see—and feel—the immediate results of short-term goals, they become golden nuggets of encouragement to help you continually press on to the long-range goals.

If you have set goals in the past and have not made much progress over the past few months or years, then reset your goals using a more realistic strategy. If this is the first time you are attempting to set fitness goals, making them realistic is vitally important to your success. Setting your goals is like deciding where you are going before you turn on the engine in your RV to begin a cross-country trip.

Before you begin your journey to a healthier lifestyle, decide where you are going—set those goals. Remember that your goals are your goals—and yours alone. Nobody can tell you what your goals should be. Your goals will become your personal destination stops along the path to a healthier lifestyle. Make them clear and distinct.

For example, if there is a particular dress size that you want to get down to, write that dress size down. If you want to get your blood pressure and cholesterol levels down, write down the normal levels you want to reach. If you are a man and want to build your chest and shoulder muscles, then write down the size you want to be.

Be specific. Don't just say you would like to weigh "somewhere around" 150 pounds. If your goal is to weigh 150 pounds, write down that amount. If you have a deadline for reaching a specific goal, perhaps a wedding or some other social event to attend, write down the date and set your goals. Your goals have to be clear as a bell, not fuzzy. They must be specific and exact.

When you are through mapping your destiny, then you are prepared to take the next step. The next step is to put a price tag on your goals. What is their value to you? Some might be more valuable than others,

> 2-2
>
> ## Setting Goals—Are You Making Progress?
>
> **Make clear, distinct goals**—not fuzzy goals.
>
> **Be specific**—list specifics like size, timeline, weight, outfit, or event.
>
> **Place a value on it**—how important to you is reaching this goal?
>
> **Verbalize it**—reinforce your positive thinking by repeating your goal.
>
> **Write it down**—place a list of your goals in a convenient location for review.

but affix a price to each. If you want to be healthier in order to save money that you have been spending on medications and trips to the doctor's office, figure the exact cost and write it beside your goal.

Maybe you are tired all the time, day in and day out, and you want more energy. Write down the exact value of more energy to you. There is a value to each and every goal you desire, so write down each goal and tag it with its value to you.

We are beginning to make progress, so let's recap. By now you have a better picture of where you are heading. You realize that first of all you have to be willing to make changes. Making a decision to change will give you the mental foundation to step out, progress, and see what lies ahead on the other side. Searching within and identifying your concerns and fears will enable you to make the behavioral changes that will become a part of your lifestyle. Soon all the doubts and fears that once held you hostage to failure and unhappiness will be stored in your trash bin, waiting to be deleted from your thinking. You have also written a map to follow—your specific, exact goals—and determined their values.

Now the next thing is a word of precaution. I want you to remember that once you have your goals in place and begin the journey, there will come possible roadblocks, detours, and holdups that can subtly blur your vision and interfere with your staying focused on your goals. As a necessary step of preparation, let's look at the importance of staying focused.

Staying Focused

When I was forty-eight years old, I was caught off guard by an experience I had while I was reading an article from a magazine. I realized I was really struggling to see the printed words. It was as if I had lost my vision overnight. I knew that sooner or later all of us begin to lose our nearsighted vision. But this was ridiculous. The day before I had been able to read the fine print easily. But on this day I could hardly see the lines on the pages.

I had to make one of two decisions. I could keep on trying to read, ignoring the aging signs and living with the aggravation and frustration of not being able to see up close. But that would only keep me from enjoying the pleasure of reading. I opted not to make that choice.

My other choice was to do something about it, and I did. I realized I needed some help if I were to continue reading—particularly anything up close. I humbly decided to visit the local pharmacy in my neighborhood and pick out a pair of glasses labeled 1.25 power. I put those idiotic-looking glasses on, and all of a sudden they weren't so idiotic-looking anymore. I was amazed at how clear the words were. I could actually read the fine print. So off I went with my first pair of glasses in forty-seven years.

A couple of years passed, and it was time to face reality again. I made an appointment with an optometrist for a thorough eye examination, something I hadn't done in twenty years.

At the doctor's office, he sat me down in a chair facing that familiar wall chart across the room. He directed me to cover first one eye, focus on the chart, and read the letters as far down the lines as I could. Then I repeated the procedure with the other eye. I was able to see as far as the bottom line with my left eye, but only halfway down with my right eye.

The optometrist swung that huge machine right up to my face so I could look through the various lenses. As he began making adjustments, he asked me to focus again on the chart and read the lines. We went through the entire eye exam, making adjustments with the lenses to determine what prescription I needed to correct my vision. After twenty minutes of making adjustments and corrections, he asked me to look through the lens on the machine one final time. As I did, I was able to see clearly and could read all the way down to the bottom line with both eyes. It was wonderful to see so clearly. Suddenly the letters didn't have fuzz growing on them!

Then he had me read the chart again, but without the lenses. That really blew me away! "That's how you were seeing things before you came in to see me," he reminded me. It was unbelievable how out of focus my vision had become over the years.

Now I have 20/20 vision—with my contacts. The fact that for more than twenty years I had been losing my vision hit me like a lead balloon. The change had been so subtle that I did not realize it until I no longer enjoyed reading and could no longer see my golf shots.

This same sort of subtle deterioration can happen to your goals if you are not prepared for the journey. You may start out all excited and ready to "knock 'em dead." You may have set your goals in place and have high expectations for reaching them. But don't forget the potential obstacles along the way that may interfere with your focus and try to cause you to fail to reach your goals.

The principle of focus is necessary to understand in order to conquer your goals in your fitness journey. You may start off with high expectations and calculate the course you plan to take. But you must also ignore all the doubters and skeptics who attempt to throw you off course. You must press on, refusing to allow anything to stop you. Nothing can be permitted into your life that could interfere with reaching your goals. Set your sights on your goals, and take off running.

> **Nothing can be permitted into your life that could interfere with reaching your goals. Set your sights on your goals, and take off running.**

Identify Your Food Triggers

If you haven't done this before, it's time to discover the hidden psychological motivations that literally trigger your reaction to food. Once you are aware of these inner drives, you can begin to make adjustments to build on your natural strengths while you avoid your weaknesses.

Food Triggers Grid

2-3

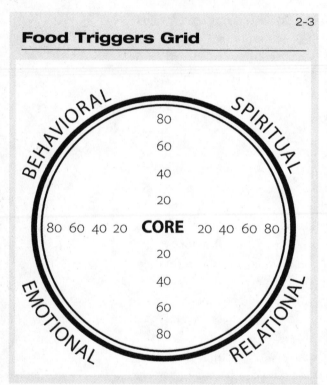

Before I go any further in explaining these triggers, here's a foundational principle to grasp: you must understand the powerful difference between the *physical* and the *psychological* drives that affect your eating patterns. *Hunger* is the physical need for food and can be measured medically when your blood sugar changes or when you hear your tummy growl as a result of powerful chemicals at work in your empty stomach. *Appetite* is quite different from hunger because it is based upon the psychological need to be satisfied on the inside.

Once you see the difference, you can take action to successfully manage your own food triggers. Learning how to identify your hidden food triggers speeds up the process of knowing how to manage these powerful inner drives instead of being controlled by your appetite or your impulsive desires for instant gratification.

The more you can honestly identify what your real motivations for eating are, the more power you will be able to access and redirect to have good health for the long term. I've created an evaluation tool to help guide you through this very important process. Please pause for a few minutes to complete the questionnaire in Appendix G of this book. Take the time to get serious and think about how to respond as honestly as possible to enable you to identify the real issues that may fuel your hidden struggles with food. After filling out the questionnaire, follow the directions in Appendix G for determining your score for each food trigger quadrant. Then return to this page and continue reading to evaluate your results.

Mark your score for each of the four quadrants on the grid on the previous page. Each quadrant can be understood in light of the following scores:

- 0–20   Not a major source of motivation to eat or food trigger
- 20–40   Mild source of motivation to eat or food trigger
- 40–60   Moderate source of motivation to eat and occasional food trigger
- 60–80   Major source of motivation to eat and likely food trigger

Each of these four quadrants (behavioral, relational, emotional, and spiritual) represents a major factor that can fuel your psychological appetite and stimulate your internal food triggers. These underlying dynamics can lead to overeating in order to stabilize an internal mood or motivation that has nothing to do with physical hunger. Every calorie taken in during the food-trigger process is eaten to satisfy a psychological craving, not an actual physical need for food.

Let's take a closer look at how these four food triggers could affect you and your ability to manage and control your own patterns of eating.

The top two quads are external and visible to everyone; the bottom two are more internal and harder to spot by others, especially if they don't know you. The left side is more about a personal view of situations, while the right side considers more the views or opinions of others.

In the exact middle of the four quadrants is the core. The core represents truth, and truth is the opposite of denial. This is where you should start when you begin looking at your scores. Although these evaluations can give you the honest awareness of your true motivations in dealing with food, they can't make you change inside.

They can guide you to change direction on the outside, leading you to a better place than you have been before—a place where you know what you need to do and you have some health-minded people around you to help you do the work to improve.

With this in mind, it's time to dig into more detail to understand each of the four quadrants that can trigger your cravings for food.

The Food Trigger Quadrants

BEHAVIORAL

This trigger deals with known areas of human behavior and personal lifestyle, the visible outward choices people make in terms of how they dress, talk, act, spend money, and react to others. If you score high in this category, you probably tend to use food to have control over something in your life, especially if you feel out of control in other parts of your life. Some common symptoms are stress; burnout; insomnia and chronic sleep problems; financial fears; fear of failure, job downsizing, or unemployment; feeling overwhelmed; tendency toward a lack of organization; a desire for instant relief, frequently at or near a meltdown in some area of life; always racing to try and avoid the next crisis; tendency to be so busy trying to manage life that you never have time to sit down and enjoy it. Yo-yo diets are most common in this quadrant.

RELATIONAL

This trigger has to do with the basic way you connect with or deal with others. If you scored high in this quadrant, relational factors can trigger the habitual need to use food to find connection with something in your life, especially if you are feeling disconnected with the people. It's also common for individuals with high relationship food triggers to prefer to eat with a stranger rather than sit and eat alone. People in this quadrant tend to see food as a connector (social eating can be very similar to social drinking). Frequent relational food triggers surround gatherings of family and friends. Common symptoms are misdirected love, loneliness, family of origin or generational factors, clingy or needy attachments, rescuing behavior, broken relationships, grief, loss, brokenness, rejection, hatred, bitter divorces, custody disputes, domestic violence, verbal or emotional abuse, fights with kids or extended family members, unresolved dysfunction or past family secrets such as abortion or adoption, and reactive disorders or attachment disorders from childhood. People with high relationship food triggers also tend to struggle with feelings of approval from others, which can lead to codependency.

EMOTIONAL

This trigger deals with how you use food to avoid feeling any negative experiences or emotions that might change your mood or motivations. People who fall into this category use food to find comfort during periods of pain or discomfort in their lives, commonly referred to as *self-medication*. Common symptoms are unrealistic expectations, continually seeking excitement, poor impulse control, major struggles with self-discipline or self-control, guilt, fear, depression, anxiety, isolation, phobias, panic disorder, grief, embarrassment, rage, moodiness, sadness, regrets, resentment, perfectionism, critical spirit, anger, trauma, PTSD (post-traumatic stress disorder), and a strong desire to appear emotionally "in control" of any situation. People with high emotional food triggers have a tendency to sit back and watch life through media images to avoid the fear of conflict in actually living.

SPIRITUAL

Let me start by explaining that when I discuss spiritual dynamics, I am not merely referring to your religious beliefs. Spirituality affects every decision you make every single day of your life. Spirituality flows from your core beliefs and strongest values. Religion tends to be more tied to our cultural and childhood experiences. Every person from every culture has a specific system of personal beliefs that can dramatically impact his or her life, but not everyone has taken time to really sit down to understand what this belief system means to them and, more importantly, what they can do about it to really evoke change. People who score high in the spiritual quadrant are people who, based on their core values, resolve to live a balanced life in harmony with their life's purpose and mission, and who tend to use food as a nutritional source to monitor and balance their bodies as a part of creating calm contentment and inner peace. Common symptoms include being driven toward selfless behavior, not being able to accept a compliment, afraid to indulge or enjoy simple pleasures, periods of extreme self-analysis, loneliness or emptiness if not feeling on task, always seeking a deeper meaning, lack of purpose, struggles with maintaining a lifestyle consistent with stated belief system, and always seeking to discover true self-worth from a spiritual connection with God's message of acceptance and forgiveness.

Renewing Your Mind

As I mentioned earlier, learning the difference between hunger and appetite is a good place to start when targeting your food triggers. Being honest with yourself is not always easy, but it might help to view the food trigger grid as a steering wheel, because your life can only go where you steer it. You have to make a choice to steer one way or the other. Which will it be? If you overcorrect or undercorrect, you end up off balance and slide to the left or right as your life ends up out of alignment (at best) or crashed (at worst). The more you keep your life focused on a straight path and headed in the direction you want to go, the quicker you'll get to where you want to be—a place of balanced inner strength with strong inner convictions about using food as fuel to power your body instead of using food as the solution for fear, insecurities, or frustration.

You might feel that the "no pain, no gain" saying fits here...except that this kind of pain isn't about working up a sweat. It's about doing some honest soul-searching to discover the keys to a better way of life. When you see the real issues inside you, it's like you are really seeing what matters most in your life for the very first time. Remember, once you see truth, you can never un-see it. Just live it out and enjoy the journey of self-discovery. And whatever you discover, it's vital that you keep a positive attitude. For more information, see my book *Never Go Back*, available at www.bodyredesigning.com.

Attitude

The right attitude will keep you right on course to reach your goals. Exercising the right attitude is the most important exercise you will ever do. I am certain you are *capable* of doing it, so I have all the confidence in the world that you *will* do it.

Because attitude is the single most important mental factor determining your success or failure, in order for attitude to have the greatest positive impact on the outcome of your plans it must remain positive. Whether your goals are to lose excess body fat, fill out your figure, or improve your overall state of well-being, it will be your attitude that makes the difference in succeeding or failing.

The success and productivity of your life evolve around two basic principles: the principle of wasting your time and the principle of investing your time. These principles can be applied to every aspect of body, soul, and spirit.

If your life has been at a standstill, and you have not made any progress for quite some time, now would be the perfect time to make a change. It is time to stop wasting your time and start investing your time. By reevaluating your attitude and making any necessary attitude adjustments with respect to your time, the results will be an investment in your life.

The truth of the matter is this: If you are wasting your time, then consequently you are wasting your life. Conversely, if you invest your time, then you are investing your life.

Regardless of whether you waste your time or invest your time, the results you experience are twofold—what you do with your time affects not only you but also the other people in your life. A man is not an island unto himself. Wasting time is never profitable. Wasting time has a negative connotation. People

---

2-4

Checklist of Pitfalls

Setting goals too high to reach—The greater the expectations, the greater the discouragement. Set plenty of short-range goals. As you obtain each one, you will gain continual motivation and tenacity.

Plateau effect—Progress comes in leaps and bounds. Establish a monthly timeline for checking with your progress.

Negative feedback—Consider the source. Make yourself accountable to someone who is positive and encouraging. Review your goals, repeat your goals, and mentally visualize them. Reject all negative words or comments.

Obsession—Stay balanced. Obsession is on the opposite end of neglect. Both are unhealthy. Keep focused, but enjoy the journey. Add humor to your lifestyle. Your balanced lifestyle is inspirational and appealing to others.

Negative thoughts—They come from the subconscious mind, which contains negative input. Choose to refute any and all such thoughts. Don't speak them, and remind yourself that you are an inspiration in transition.

around such a person are turned off by the negative attitude that accompanies a wasted life. A person who is wasting time—and therefore life—is a negative person and, consequently, more of a detriment than a value to the people around him.

On the other hand, if you invest your time, then great things happen. The results of investing are very positive. You accomplish more things in your life, you have the greatest potential for attaining your goals, and your life is fuller and worth living. Even your work becomes more enjoyable. The effect you have on people is very positive. People have a tendency to gravitate to people who have a positive attitude.

A positive attitude will carry you through dark times when doubt and discouragement arise in your soul. Others may jump ship when tough times come, running away as fast as they can. Consequently, their goals become nothing more than wishing and hoping. Don't do that. Let your positive attitude steer you to success.

Christopher Columbus faced continual resistance from the leaders of his country as he made plans to set out to discover a new land. His own peers and fellow seamen sneered at his wild ideas of discovering land on the other side of the ocean—that body of water so huge that it was frightening to imagine crossing it. He had never journeyed across the ocean—and neither had anyone else. There wasn't even any certainty that his belief that the earth was round was true. The possibility of falling off the earth threatened to intimidate his attitude.

There were rumors of sea monsters large enough to destroy a sea vessel, devouring him and his crew. Disease and plagues of deadly illnesses could possibly claim his life and those of his shipmates. Everybody and everything seemed to oppose his goals and plans. But they all misjudged one primary element that Columbus possessed—his positive attitude! His tenacity made all the difference—it brought success to him in his endeavor, and it will do the same for you and me.

Today we enjoy the freedom and lifestyles of living in America because Christopher Columbus set his mind in stone. He had his plans in place. He mapped the course, kept his focus on reaching

America, and did not allow anyone or anything to come against him or discourage him from reaching his goal.

What if Columbus had allowed the threat of possible negatives to affect his attitude? Where would we be today?

How about it? Are you ready for an attitude adjustment? Remember, people who invest their time are investing in their own lives as well as in the lives of others. They are in it for more than what they get for themselves. They are not takers but givers. They understand that they can be a positive influence on others who, like themselves, have struggled with differing issues but learned how to overcome.

Let me share a story with you that will illustrate the point I am making. A beggar lived in a run-down, dilapidated hut on the outskirts of a small village. Every day he journeyed into the village to beg for handouts from the village people.

After begging all day long, each evening he left the village and returned to his hut. There he emptied out his bag to see what he had received that day. He did this every day, month after month, year after year.

The village people were very proud of their village. They all worked hard to keep their village clean and neat. They made it a safe place for their children to play and for the old folks to walk at night. They were wonderful people who cared for one another, and they loved their king.

The king was a generous man. He adored the village people for their giving and caring spirits. Once a year the king visited the village, bringing gifts for everyone. This was the biggest event of the year for the people in the village. On the day the king was scheduled to arrive, the people made sure all the streets were spotless. Every limb on every tree was trimmed with colorful ribbons, and the whole village was prepared for the king's arrival. The streets were lined with the families and friends from the village as they anxiously awaited his entry.

This year was a big day for the beggar also. He actually managed to be the first in line this time. He stood with his bag outstretched, waiting for the king's carriage to stop so he could get a gift. As the carriage pulled up before the beggar, instead of giving the beggar

Nothing can stop the man with the right mental attitude from achieving his goal; nothing on the earth can help the man with the wrong mental attitude.
—Thomas Jefferson

a gift, the king spoke to the beggar, asking, "What do you have to give to the king?"

The beggar frantically searched through his bag to find something insignificant to give the king from the things he had received from the village people that day. Finally he pulled out a small token and handed it to the king. Then the king reached out his hand and placed something in the beggar's bag, moving on to the next person.

Needless to say, the beggar was so excited—he had received something from the *king*! His gift came from the king, not just the ordinary people of the village. Quickly he ran back to his hut to see what he had received from the king. He emptied his collections for the day, spreading the goods out on the bare floor in the room. Excitedly he examined everything he had received. Suddenly he saw a tiny, shiny speck of gold. The king had given him gold!

But suddenly he became very saddened. As he looked at that speck of gold, a terrifying thought came to his mind: "If this speck of gold is what I received from the king for giving him the least of my possessions, what would I have received if I gave my whole bag to the king?"[2]

What if you gave your all to accomplishing your fitness goals? Your fitness journey will not end when you reach your own personal goals. You will go on to impact others. You will be an encouragement and inspiration to others who, like you, would like to feel healthier, have more energy, and enjoy a strong, healthy body. They are watching you to see how you will do. Some will not make a move to begin their own fitness journey until you have succeeded at yours. So remember, you can pass the torch to others by pouring your best efforts into your life and by maintaining a positive attitude.

Bloodtypes Bodytypes and YOU

Section II

Thermogenic Weight-Loss Program—Instinctive Eating According to Your Blood Type

Chapter 3

Your Colon: Good Health From the Inside Out

It's time to discuss colon function. This is where good health starts. Before we discuss any more about your blood type, the foods you eat, and the outcome, you need to understand the correlation between colon function and optimum health.

Colon health is all about functionality, and the function of your colon is directly related to proper elimination, or bowel movements. I know this is a dirty topic, but if you desire optimum performance and optimum results where your body is concerned, then this topic needs to be addressed. You see, good health starts on the inside and works out. Improving your health and ridding your body of poisonous toxins that contribute to poor health, disease, and sluggish metabolism all starts with what I call your "INvironment."

I get a lot of e-mails and letters from people saying, "Dr. Joe, I want to make some changes to my health. I want to get in good shape. I want to be healthy for my family. Where do I start?" Well, addressing colon function is the starting point. Why? Because it's directly related to the outcome of your health. There is a direct correlation between the colon and just about every illness and disease known to mankind. The condition of your colon will determine your health.

To understand this, you have to first understand what the colon is. The colon is a muscular tube that measures about five feet long and has an average diameter of approximately two and a half inches. It starts on the lower right of the abdomen and ascends to the level of the liver, where it bends to the left and crosses the abdomen. At the level of the spleen it descends down the left side of the abdomen to the pelvis and empties into the rectum. Its major functions are to absorb water and nutrients from partially digested food that enters from the small intestine and to send waste out of the body. I often describe it as a garbage bag that holds all the waste products of the foods that we've consumed, cellular debris, and so forth. These things need to be dumped out of our bodies, and the colon acts like a trash can that temporarily holds all of the garbage until it's time to take out the trash for good.

The colon works through involuntary muscle movement called *peristalsis*. This muscular action moves the digested food through the colon, as well as toxic fecal matter, and expels it from the body.

I call the time it takes your food to travel through your digestive system *transit time*. The total transit time from the time you eat a meal until you eliminate the waste products should be sixteen to twenty-four hours with a properly functioning colon. And a person with a healthy colon should have three bowel movements every day, shortly after every meal is eaten. That's the natural process.

Think of a newborn baby. What does it do? The baby cries, you feed him, and shortly after, the baby poops. The elimination process is very efficient! It's 100 percent functional! But as we grow and our lifestyle habits and food choices change, we start to see the correlation between our dietary choices and the development of digestive problems.

The Malfunctioning Colon

Think about the average American diet—refined white flour, sugar, fast foods, processed foods, sodas. It's no surprise that studies have shown that the average American's transit time is ninety-six hours![1] That's right—ninety-six hours. I have clients who have told me that they only have one bowel movement in a week's time. That's one bowel movement in seven days!

Most people who come to me for help with this problem ask me how the elimination process in their bodies got so bogged down. The answer is simple: we pollute our digestive system. How? Remember in grade school when you would mix white flour and water together to make paste for papier-mâché? When we ingest foods that are refined white flour products, the very same thing starts to happen. A pasty mucus forms in our digestive tract. This gooey mucus builds up in the colon.

You see, the colon is very porous. It's designed that way so that it can absorb nutrients that will benefit the body. Now imagine the colon wall getting plastered just as the walls of the rooms in your home get plastered. If you eat refined white flour products for twenty years, and I'm sure you probably have, you've been "plastering the walls" of your colon. This interrupts the function of your colon. Now its ability to absorb nutrients that your body needs has been greatly impeded.

As your colon gets more and more "plastered," the diameter of the colon starts to narrow, just like the process that occurs during hardening of the arteries. The inside of the colon becomes narrower and narrower because of all of the buildup on the walls of the colon. Then bowel movements become difficult.

Sugary foods and fried foods also pollute our colons and bodies in the same way. I know we love some of these foods, but when we eat them on a regular basis, what we're doing is actually sabotaging the function of our bodies that keeps us healthy.

You see, when the digestive process of the colon is slowed down too much because of the refined sugar and flour that are plastering the walls of the colon and narrowing the passage, the fecal matter and mucus can become impacted. The fecal matter itself is now impacting all of that toxic waste into the colon. Instead of helping your body eliminate those toxins, your colon is actually storing them.

In some autopsy cases it has been recorded that impacted fecal matter found in the cadaver's colon has weighed forty or more pounds. Can you imagine that? According to his autopsy, John Wayne had forty pounds of impacted fecal matter in his body at death. Elvis Presley reportedly had sixty pounds.[2]

Your colon can be highly polluted with impacted fecal matter, infested with parasites, or functioning extremely abnormally for long periods of time before any symptoms appear.

I've worked with clients who had a little pouch or bulge developing below the naval and they think it's fat. But this little bulge is often the result of the colon getting so impacted with fecal matter that it's getting larger and larger. And if those toxins do nothing but sit in there month after month over a period of time, putrefaction occurs, which directly impacts your entire body. After a period of time your colon may start to leak. This condition is called leaky gut syndrome and causes toxins to be absorbed into your bloodstream and circulate throughout your body.

If you are experiencing the following symptoms, it may be a sign that you have a malfunctioning colon:

- Headaches
- Skin problems
- Foul breath
- Lack of energy
- Stomach pain
- Constipation

Possible results of a malfunctioning colon include:

- Colon disorders (irritable bowel syndrome, celiac sprue, acid reflux, diverticulitis, constipation, etc.)
- Colon cancer
- Hypercholesterolemia
- Parasitic infestation

Did you see the last item on the list above? Not only do you need to be aware of all of the poor health symptoms and conditions that a malfunctioning colon can produce, but you also need to realize that it can also set the stage for parasite infestation. Parasites love to get into your digestive system. First, they work their way into your colon and then eat. And they get first dibs, by the way, and you get their leftovers.

Second, they not only eat your food, but they also eliminate in your colon. They have great elimination systems, and so all of that waste from the parasites is traveling through your body and your blood system and poisoning you.

Thirdly, those parasites want to have families. So they build colonies inside you, and you don't even know this is going on. You just feel like you have the blahs, but you don't know why. It all starts with an improperly functioning colon.

Now, if you keep the colon functioning properly, these little critters never have a chance to build their little colonies inside you because it takes about thirty-six hours for them to incubate. You can have the upper hand if you are taking proper care of your colon.

Medications

Let's say you are practicing all the healthy lifestyle principles you learned thus far, but for some unknown reason, you start experiencing a bad case of the blahs. You're feeling bad day in and day out, and it becomes a chronic condition, so you go to the doctor. You tell the doctor what is ailing you, and what does the doctor do? Not being able to pinpoint the culprit or root problem, your doctor determines some plan of attack to go after the symptoms you've described. You are given a handful of prescription medications—or "symptom stoppers," as I call them—with hopes of fixing the problem. As time passes, you still experience the original problems, but now they have become more intense. Remember transit time? Remember that anything that slows down normal colon function can be directly related to poor health conditions. Well, the medications that were prescribed to "mask the symptoms" can't cure the root problem and are now contributing to your constipation, which in turn slows down the elimination process or normal colon function and worsens your painful condition.

Your colon can be highly polluted with impacted fecal matter, infested with parasites, or functioning extremely abnormally for long periods of time before any symptoms appear. One main reason is that the nerve endings that signal your brain about pain, discomfort, or disruption are few and far between in your intestines. So by the time you see the doctor because the pain has you nearly bent over, you have well surpassed the need to cleanse and detoxify your colon. In fact, until you cleanse and detox the colon, you probably can't eradicate the root problem to your discomfort, pain, and potential poor health. Unfortunately, the polluted colon is often overlooked as a possible root problem by many medical doctors.

Two Principles of Colon Health

There are two things that you can do to help your body recover optimum colon health.

1. Stop polluting
2. Cleanse

How do you stop polluting? Your lifestyle practices need to line up with your goals to be healthier, maintain your ideal weight, and live a more vibrant and disease-free life. By taking a bird's-eye view of what is going into your body from time to time, you will have better control of your future health.

I want you to use the space I'm providing here to conduct a three-day dietary analysis. Write down everything you eat for breakfast, lunch, dinner, and snacks. Include what you drink and any medications you take. Note how many bowel movements you have each day as well.

Day 1

_____

_____

_____

Day 2

_____

_____

_____

Day 3

_____

_____

_____

All foods, beverages, and even medications influence your colon's function and health. Certain foods and beverages disrupt normal colon function and may contribute to a myriad of health disorders that can easily be avoided. By now you know that refined sugars and flours are really poor food choices for your body because they clog the porous lining of the colon wall. Another example of foods that can play havoc with colon function are foods that are not compatible with your blood type, such as dairy and wheat products, both of which have shown to be problematic for blood type A and O individuals. Minimal intake of wheat products may not disturb colon function for blood type As. I will be giving you in-depth guidance on foods to avoid for your blood type later in this book, but for now, suffice it to say that becoming aware of the foods you eat and the direct effect they have on your health is the place to start.

After reviewing the foods and beverages you have consumed for three days, you now have a better idea of exactly what you have ingested. To benefit from the three-day dietary analysis, review your list of foods and beverages and circle any that are known to disrupt normal colon function. Examples include refined sugar and white flour products, fried foods, processed foods, and sodas.

Now that you are aware of the foods and beverages you have consumed that are interfering with your colon health, the next step is to start to eliminate (or at least minimize) the foods from your diet that have contributed to disrupting your normal colon function. Replace them with healthy foods and beverages such as high-fiber foods and alkaline water.

High-fiber food sources such as vegetables, fruits, and some cereals like bran will contribute to better colon health from a dietary perspective. Hydration is vitally important to good colon health in order to assist the transit time or elimination. I prefer to drink restructured alkaline water that is ionized or electrically charged because it provides more hydration to the cells of the tissue. When the intra and extra cellular environments are alkaline, it creates an environment that is not conducive to cancer. Doing your best to chill out or reduce the stress in your life is a good practice for a healthy colon. If you can't reduce your stress due to circumstances beyond your control, then you need to counter the stress with a de-stressor like regular exercise. Regular exercise assists the colon in the elimination process by causing increased blood circulation to the colon area.

We'll get into a more extensive discussion of exercise later on in this book. However, even if you eat healthily, manage your stress

> **High-fiber food sources such as vegetables, fruits, and some cereals like bran will contribute to better colon health from a dietary perspective.**

as much as possible, and exercise regularly, you still need to cleanse and detoxify your colon. I do a colon cleanse at least twice a year. I refer to it as spring and fall cleaning.

If you're not having three healthy bowel movements a day, you are considered to be clinically constipated. I should pause for a moment to define a healthy bowel movement for you. Elimination should be easy, not strained. The stool should be solid, light brown in color, long and large in diameter, and should break apart upon toilet flushing. (I told you this was going to be a dirty topic, didn't I? It might not be fun to think about, but determining whether your colon is functioning properly is vital to improving your overall health!)

So, if you're not having three healthy bowel movements a day, if you've never done a colon cleanse before, or if every time you have a bowel movement you hear *plop, plop*, then I strongly encourage you to engage in a colon cleanse and detoxification program rather than just popping an over-the-counter laxative. The laxative softens the hardened stool, making it easier to pass through and be eliminated from your body. In an emergency situation a laxative can do the job. (I recommend Body Genetics Cape Aloe.) I strongly encourage you to take laxatives that come in natural herbal formulas that will cleanse and detoxify your colon rather than laxatives that come as over-the-counter medications, but again, only if needed for an emergency situation. A laxative should only serve as a temporary patch job. What you need to understand is that the longer you remain constipated or holding impacted fecal matter in the colon, the narrower the passageway or the thicker the walls of the colon become. If you continue in this condition, it may lead to having a portion of your colon removed—a procedure that can likely be avoided if you change your habits today and start to maintain normal colon function. So laxatives, whether natural or over-the-counter drugs, are not a long-term solution to healing your colon and preventing future problems.

If you want a complete and thorough colon cleansing experience, I strongly recommend that you purchase my INNER OUT fourteen-day colon cleansing and detoxifying system that has three phases. The first is a preparation phase to destroy parasites and break up impacted fecal matter and mucous buildup. The second phase is a minimal four-day juice fast phase where you avoid solid foods for proper removal of parasites, impacted fecal matter, and mucus. The third phase is a return to normal eating using a natural supplement that includes probiotics (good bacteria; *pro* = for, and *biotics* = life) in order to restore and fortify your colon.

On a related note, remember that every time you or your children take antibiotics (*anti* = against, and *biotics* = life), you are not only taking a mediation that causes a diminishing effect of good bacteria that the colon needs for health and function, but you are also building an immunity to good bacteria that your body may need for protection and good health. So colon cleansing should be a systematic approach that supports normal colon function, detoxification, and restoration.

When you start cleansing and detoxifying, you will be amazed and possibly a little disgusted at the sight of what you've eliminated. I have had some clients with some pretty amazing stories, and I'll refrain from giving you the details! Suffice it to say, you will be glad all of that toxic buildup is no longer inside of you polluting your system, and ultimately, your life!

Dr. Joe's Healthy Colon Tips

You need to get your digestive system working properly or you won't be able to absorb the nutrients from all of the foods and supplements you'll be learning about in the rest of this book. In summary, here are my recommendations for repairing and maintaining optimum colon function:

1. Keep a dietary record.
2. Avoid refined sugar, white flour, and fried foods. Choose food selections that are compatible with your blood type.
3. Eat 30 grams of fiber each day from natural sources such as bran, psyllium, flaxseed, oatmeal, and fruit.
4. Drink alkaline water daily (half your body weight in ounces).
5. Minimize stress as much as possible in your life.
6. Exercise three to five times weekly.

7. Conduct a colon cleanse and detoxification program a minimum of two times a year, or when needed.

Talking about the colon may be a dirty topic, but we all deal with it. By addressing it and taking it on one-on-one, we're making sure that you're going to be able to maximize the rest of the valuable information in this book. All of the information you're about to learn about your genetics and what to eat and what to avoid is important, but it will be disrupted if your body's colon isn't functioning properly. Now that we've addressed colon health, we have set the stage for the rest of the journey so that we can enjoy all of the full benefits of good health.

Chapter 4

The Blood-Type Weight-Loss Program (Thermogenic Weight-Loss Program)

In the next chapter, I will be addressing the issue of how you can become an "instinctive eater" as it applies to the blood-type-diet theory. I will teach you the basics of why and what to eat for the rest of your life to improve your health and illness profile, and specifically how instinctive eating is the basis for reaching your ideal weight for life. Before I take you there, however, I want to focus on your goals for losing weight. You will notice as you read this chapter that I make reference to the thermogenic weight-loss program instead of the blood-type weight-loss diet. The reason is simply because of how my fat-burning meal replacements, when working in concert with the blood-type-diet concept, create a thermogenic or fat-burning effect in the body—the perfect combination for jump-starting your metabolism. But when your expectations for losing weight and keeping it off for life are high, the anticipation of that reality can be devastating if you do not reach your goals, particularly if you are stuck in the old mentality of "dieting" your weight off. From this point forward, you will see that there is a much more effective and simpler approach to this weight-loss issue than you ever thought.

Keeping Weight Loss Simple

My approach to weight loss and keeping it off for life is based on your body mechanics and bodily functions as the key elements for losing weight successfully. It is simple to be successful at losing weight and keeping it off for life if you remember to apply these two basic principles:

1. Jump-start your metabolism; then feed it to keep it in motion.
2. Eat food compatible to your blood type, and don't diet.

When you begin to understand the vital role that bodily functions (metabolism) play in losing weight, you will soon discover that all the efforts you have used through sheer willpower to "hang in there" with diets have become a thing of the past. My approach for losing weight will minimize your effort and maximize the results by allowing your body to be the "natural" calorie burner it was designed to be.

EXPECTATIONS

Achieving your body's ideal weight for life will involve personal considerations for each person because every person is different. As I mentioned previously in the book, to be successful, one must first be willing to *change*, which starts with a change in mental attitude. Though this attitude change is one of the toughest exercises we face, it is fundamental for success.

As you think about the various areas in your life that can interfere with your ability to lose weight or maintain proper weight afterward, you will agree that a *change of attitude* plays an absolutely huge part in your success or failure. The way you think about your lifestyle directly affects your weight problem.

For example, many people find themselves suffering from being overweight because of poor eating habits such as eating on the run, late-night snacking, or improper food selections. They need to change the way they think about eating. Nearly every client I have had has said that they lack the time to eat proper meals—especially breakfast—because of hectic schedules. Many people say they do not have time for exercise. The lack of regular exercise contributes to failure for losing weight, so if a person needs to lose weight, he or she needs to think differently about making exercise a part of their lifestyle.

Others struggle with eating disorders, which are sometimes caused by the way they think about themselves. And some don't know what to think about their weight problem, so they just try various protocols hoping something good will happen. Those who take medications with side effects that prohibit weight loss or cause weight gain will need to refocus their attention on eradicating the root problem so they can in turn reduce or eliminate the use of medications (if applicable).

In the end, your success for losing weight and keeping it off for life will depend to a large extent on your willingness to make necessary changes such as those mentioned above. It will also involve your analyzing your current state of health, your lifestyle, and your level of determination and desire to win the battle.

KEY TO YOUR METABOLISM

Having said that, however, there is still the issue of your body's mechanics or bodily functions that are key to successful weight loss and keeping it off for life. This key unlocks the secret of your *metabolism*. Before you can expect to lose your first pound, you have to learn to ignite or stimulate your metabolism and then keep it in perpetual motion. Once you get your metabolism in motion, the weight-loss process begins automatically because you are in the process of improving your BMR (basal metabolic rate).

The BMR, which reflects your body's ability to burn calories while you are resting, is the key to understanding your body as a calorie-burning machine. Regardless of how much weight you need to lose or how quickly you want to lose it, improving your body's basal metabolic rate is the key to your success.

Think for a moment about how many hours a day you are *inactive*—sitting, lying down, sleeping—versus the hours you are *active*, and you begin to understand your need to rev up that BMR. Therefore, your primary focus point for weight loss must be on ways to stimulate your metabolism. This focus will keep your mind thinking correctly and will help to deter it from rethinking former thoughts related to "dieting." Results from the calorie-burning effect that come from stimulating your metabolism are far greater and longer lasting than you could ever expect from "dieting it off." The two most effective methods for stimulating your metabolism are *eating* and *exercising*. For now, we will focus on eating.

The "Fire" in Your Fireplace

Let me give you a simple picture story or analogy to help you get a handle on weight loss for life. The story draws a parallel between your body's ability to burn calories and the way a fire in your fireplace warms your family room. The fire is symbolic of your metabolism; the kindling or wood that is burned by the fire is symbolic of food calories your metabolism burns. The end result, a warm family room from the blazing fire in your fireplace, is symbolic of you reaching your weight-loss goals for life by keeping your metabolism in perpetual motion.

Since I am originally from Buffalo, New York, where the winter weather is extremely cold, I can easily relate to the pleasure and enjoyment (not to mention the necessity) of a blazing fire in the fireplace. Try to imagine that you are living in Buffalo, New York, in the middle of winter—high temperatures do not climb above 20 degrees, and the frigid lows plummet to below zero.

If you plan to survive such a winter by warming the family room where you spend most of your time indoors, then knowing how to make a fire in the fireplace that will burn continually is vitally important. Your goal is to keep the family room warm day and night. To achieve your goal, you will need to know first how to ignite the fire and, second, how to *sustain* it indefinitely to maintain its heating capacity.

IGNITING THE FIRE

You will need special combustible materials like kindling to ignite a fire in your family room fireplace. By igniting the kindling you create a flame, which is capable of burning more kindling. It is also important to choose dry kindling to readily ignite a fire and avoid excessive smoke. Obviously, the flame created by kindling is not powerful enough to warm the family room, but it is a start. To get the blazing fire you need for warmth, all you need to do is add more kindling—regularly—along with larger-sized logs. As the fire blazes, it burns the kindling easily, which ignites the logs, and your expectation of having a warm family room becomes a reality.

SUSTAINING THE FIRE

Since a warm family room is dependent on the warmth generated by the fire, the second step to insure that warmth is to keep the fire burning. Maintaining the fire is easier than igniting the fire because all you have to do to keep the family room warm is to continue to *feed the fire*. It is important to realize that should you stop feeding the fire, it will go out, and the room will grow cold again. If that happens, you will have to start the entire process over again by igniting the kindling.

APPLYING THE "FIRE" ANALOGY

The parallel between the blazing fire in the family room, which easily burns the kindling, is the manner in which your metabolism will burn calories if it remains *stimulated*. Using the right kind of kindling is important for igniting the fire, and adding logs keeps the fire blazing for comfortable warmth. In that same way, foods you eat that are compatible to your blood type are necessary to keeping your metabolism "burning" more efficiently. The faster the metabolic rate, the easier it is for your body to burn calories. And the longer you eat this way for sustaining your metabolism, the easier it will be to reach and maintain your ideal weight for life.

Thermogenesis: Igniting Your Body's Fire

To get from our analogy of igniting and sustaining the fire in the fireplace to the specifics of achieving your weight-loss goals, we need to consider two parallel steps: *thermogenesis* and *metabolic momentum*.

The first step to take before you can expect to lose weight is to "ignite" or *stimulate* your metabolism. Just like igniting the fire in the fireplace, you must ignite your metabolism through a process called thermogenesis. Thermogenesis allows the body to burn fat to create energy.

For thermogenesis to occur, you must create a thermodynamic effect in the body by stimulating specific fat cell receptors, which will then elicit a breakdown of fat. This process for breaking down stored fat is known as *lipolysis*. Lipolysis causes the body to use stored fat as fuel for energy. Simultaneously, this stimulation causes an increase in your metabolic rate and is the precursor for creating *metabolic momentum*. By increasing your metabolic rate, your body becomes that "natural" fat burner it was designed to be, and you begin losing weight.

METABOLIC MOMENTUM

Just as you feed more logs to the blazing fire in your fireplace throughout the day, you can create metabolic momentum by feeding your body, which stimulates your metabolism. Metabolic momentum, like thermodynamics, creates a perpetual state of internal energy production or calorie burning, which is imperative for weight loss. If kept up long enough, maintaining your metabolic momentum will cause you to reach your ideal weight and maintain it for life. Imagine! The most natural and sensible way to keep your metabolism in perpetual motion is by *eating*—not by depriving yourself of food through dieting! And making the right food selections compatible to your blood type is extremely effective for igniting your metabolic momentum, much like selecting dry kindling to ignite a clean fire readily.

WHY EAT FOOD(S) COMPATIBLE TO YOUR BLOOD TYPE?

Have you ever tried to ignite a fire with wet twigs? It is difficult and results in more acrid smoke than actual flame. Eating foods that are not compatible to your blood type is like trying to ignite a fire with wet twigs. As you make food selections (kindling) that are compatible to your blood type, your body will burn calories more efficiently because the protein molecules (lectins) found in these foods do not interfere with proper digestion and assimilation of calories.

In fact, eating compatible food for your blood type assists the body in losing weight by eliminating excess toxins that are stored in the fat cells, which in turn shrinks the size of your fat cells. Selecting food that is compatible to your blood type also serves as a medicine for healing and repairing bodily functions, which is absolutely necessary for calorie expenditure.

WHY AVOID INCOMPATIBLE FOODS?

Foods that are incompatible for your blood type will slow down your metabolic rate, making it difficult to lose weight and possibly even causing weight gain. Dietary lectins are found in most foods. These lectins work either on behalf of an individual or against her, depending on whether the food is compatible with her particular blood type. When a food with a dietary lectin is beneficial for the individual, it is because the lectins function as scavengers that remove debris and toxins from various systems in the body—liver, blood, intestines, and so forth.

Foods with dietary lectins that work *against* the normal bodily functions of the individual are considered "avoid" foods (not junk foods) and should be avoided. Let's use wheat as an example of an "avoid" food since it is very common. Wheat—whether whole wheat or refined wheat—has wheat gluten agglutinin lectin (found in the kernel), which makes it incompatible for most people. As the wheat product is digested, the lectins attach or glue themselves to the red blood cells in the gut wall, creating a clumping of cells, known as agglutination. This clumping effect breaks down the function of that particular system and, in this case, interferes with proper digestion. Since the body is sensitive and very responsive, it sends out signals or symptoms such as gas, bloating, or worse— such as IBS or colon inflammation—indicating that something is wrong. Until that particular food is avoided, that system cannot heal or return to normal function, regardless of ways we choose to medicate the symptom(s).

Agglutination occurs in any system in the body. For example, if the insulin cell receptors are affected by a particular food that is not compatible, it will slow down the metabolic process and cause the body to store calories—the opposite of what you want to happen. So by avoiding foods with dietary lectins that work against the bodily systems for certain blood types, the body can return to normal function and induce optimum health and metabolic function.

A maximum metabolic rate can be produced by eating food that is compatible to your blood type and avoiding food that is not.

By increasing your metabolic rate, your body becomes that "natural" fat burner it was designed to be, and you begin losing weight.

It's the biochemical response to food compatible with your blood type that promotes ideal weight for life.

It's the biochemical response to food compatible with your blood type that promotes ideal weight for life. As your body responds favorably by eating according to your blood type, the results are improved bodily and systemic function. As I mentioned earlier, my approach to losing weight has everything to do with our bodily functions or mechanics. For our purpose, selecting foods that are compatible for your blood type (red blood cells) improves the body's digestive and metabolic systems, which means a faster metabolism (blazing fire), better nutrient assimilation, and digestion.

Everyone must eat to survive, so why not eat the foods best suited for us?

RECAP

Losing weight and reaching your ideal weight for life has never been so easy yet so misunderstood—until now! Simply remember:

1. *Thermogenesis* is the igniting and stimulating effect on your metabolism and is responsible for starting the calorie-burning process. Thermogenesis also serves as a precursor for creating metabolic momentum.

2. *Metabolic momentum* is keeping your metabolism in perpetual motion.

3. *Eating* is one of the most efficient methods for maintaining metabolic momentum—not food deprivation through dieting.

4. Eating food that is *compatible to your blood type* is an individualized method of eating for obtaining maximum health, reducing illness, losing weight, and maintaining your ideal weight for life.

The Program

It is a proven fact that it takes a minimum of twenty-one days to adapt a new behaviorism and make it a part of your lifestyle. By following my weight-loss program for at least twenty-one days, not only will you improve your mental adaptation powers and increase the likelihood of success, but you will also be well on your way to improving your BMR (basal metabolic rate), which represents your body's ability to burn calories while you are resting.

PROGRAM OVERVIEW

This weight-loss program has a timeline of twelve weeks, which is intended to serve as a springboard to launch you into a lifetime of good health, high energy, and the ability to maintain your ideal weight for life. For the sake of simplicity, variety, and convenience, I have prepared seven varieties of breakfast, lunch, and dinner, plus in-between-meal snacks, to choose from that are compatible for ALL blood types. By virtue of eating foods that are compatible to your blood type over the next several weeks, your BMR will increase and begin functioning at a more efficient level. The result—weight loss.

Highly recommended for the program is my temporary meal-replacement system designed to speed up the weight-loss process. The meal-replacement snacks in the system are formulated to supercharge your metabolism so you can lose weight more efficiently. I highly recommend these meal-replacement snacks if you are in a hurry to lose weight. Some people, due to poor health, need to drop excess weight rapidly, while others are in a hurry because of some special event they have to attend.

I also recommend my meal-replacement snacks for those who are too busy to prepare a meal because of their hectic schedule, which makes regular meal preparation impossible. I would prefer that you have a meal-replacement snack rather than skip a meal. I have formulated these meal-replacement snacks not only to be tasty and nutritious but also with special natural ingredients that make them a *true* fat-burner, causing your body to release stored body fat for energy. My meal-replacement snacks have been tested and proven to be effective by the weight-loss focus group I conducted in September 2002. (See pages 72–86.) More current inspirational testimonials and results can be found in section four, "Real People, Real Results."

Over the twelve-week program, your body will develop a greater fat-burning capacity, which creates metabolic momentum. Should you choose to include the meal-replacement system, you will eventually convert over to eating regular meals and less meal

Eating food compatible to your blood type and including meal replacements are intended to work in concert with your body's chemistry for losing weight and reaching your ideal weight for life—a winning combination!

replacements. Because the menus I have included are compatible to all blood types, you can involve the entire family without guess-work for meal planning. Remember, eating correctly for your blood type innately enhances caloric metabolism, improves food digest-ibility, and enables a healthy digestive system—the way you were designed to function. All this contributes to a speedy (BMR) basal metabolic rate.

MEAL-REPLACEMENT SYSTEM

The meal-replacement system is a temporary tool designed to help jump-start your weight-loss process. You are more likely to succeed at losing weight if the program remains easy and conve-nient, especially when it comes to planning and preparing meals. By substituting any meal from the seven varieties of break-fast, lunch, and dinner found in my Thermogenic Weight-Loss Program with any combination of meal-replacement snacks that best fits your enjoyment and schedule, success with the program is greatly increased.

The meal-replacement system has three basic components: chocolate bars, strawberry-filled cookies, and fat-burning tablets. See Chart 4-1 for a sample day using these products.

MEAL-REPLACEMENT SNACKS

There are many bars, cookies, or snacks on the market that are considered meal replacements because they contain less calories than are found in a normal meal. But when you read the labels care-fully, you will discover that they still contain plenty of processed ingredients with names that you cannot pronounce. And the most common ingredient in abundance is refined sugar. (A trace of sugar taken as a condiment is compatible for all blood types.)

It is true that when a person takes in fewer calories than they burn, they will lose weight. I have found that the downside to this process is that most people will go hours without eating (skipping meals), which causes their metabolism to slow down and become sluggish (the fire going out).

FAT-BURNING BARS AND COOKIES

Please don't misunderstand. Remember, using meal replacements is intended for a temporary period and to jump-start your metabolism, so when I suggest that you use meal replacements in place of eating meals, it is to contribute to the fat-burning process. It is not because that is an ideal plan. I believe it is best when you prepare all your meals and snacks from whole foods, compatible to your blood type. But in the real world, most people don't have the time. Preferring that you do not skip meals, and thus avoiding the detrimental slowing down of your metabolism, I have formulated these fat-burning meal replacements with their unique, healthy formula.

As I mentioned earlier, a speedy metabolism is absolutely necessary for losing weight and keeping it off. That's why I have added fat-burning ingredients in the meal-replacement bars and cookies. This way you get the best of both worlds—a more efficient metabolism via a convenient meal-replacement snack with natural fat-burning ingredients.

FAT-BURNING TABLETS

As a dietary supplement, the fat burner in tablet form has become the king amongst those who want to lose weight. The tablets are easy and convenient to take, and they work very well when the diet is correct and the individual is exercising. Most fat burners have *ma huang* (a Chinese herb) or *ephedrine* (American version), both of which promote weight loss but, unfortunately, are also associated with inducing health problems like elevated blood pressure and heart palpitations. My tablets are ephedrine-free, with all-natural ingredients that induce the fat-burning process without the negative side effects.

It is important to note that eating according to your blood type allows your body to digest food properly by not interrupting the proper function of your saliva, digestive enzymes, and hormones. Supplementing your meals with meal replacements and supplements

4-1

HOW TO USE MEAL-REPLACEMENT PRODUCTS

Breakfast: Take one fat-burning tablet and eat a strawberry-filled cookie and a protein shake (Body Genetics).

Lunch: Take one fat-burning tablet and eat a chocolate meal-replacement bar with 8 to 10 ounces of water.

Dinner: Eat a full meal from suggested menus.

Note: Try a variety of meal replacements to see which work best with your schedule, for your energy level, and for taste.

is intended to work in concert together until you have reached a weight that is ideal for you. Exercise, which produces lean muscle mass and stimulates your BMR, also contributes to a positive body composition, which serves as a tremendous indicator and component to the success of losing weight and keeping it off!

The key for starting the weight-loss process is to initially rev up your BMR—rate of metabolism while resting.

WHERE TO START

Your immediate goal is to rev your metabolism and ignite the fat-burning process. The combination of the meals from the menus listed for the weight-loss program on pages 89–95 and my BMR meal-replacement snacks will ignite the metabolic fire, creating metabolic momentum. Each meal is compatible for all blood types, which removes your concern of not knowing your blood type.

These meals will naturally cause your body to digest and burn calories more efficiently. To help speed up the weight-loss process and get maximum results, I am suggesting that you implement my meal replacements as directed. As you progress through the program, you will gradually convert to eating more food and utilizing the meal replacements less often.

Also as you progress through the program, you will notice that you have increased energy, less digestive disorders, better sleep at night, and a healthier appearance. You will also notice changes in the way your clothes fit. Once you have reached the weight that is ideal for you, simply maintain it by eating foods that are compatible to your blood type—not by dieting!

Twelve-Week Protocol

My focus group results proved this program to be successful and showed that the participants who substituted two meals per day lost the most weight. (Total meal substitution per day may vary according to individual's preference.)

FIRST MONTH

Ignite the fat-burning process by substituting any two meals with your choice of fat-burning meal-replacement bars or cookies for twenty-eight days.

Select your meals from the list of seven delicious varieties of breakfast, lunch, and dinner choices that are compatible to all blood types. These meal selections provide a balance of nutritional values plus variety. Include a midmorning and midafternoon snack when needed. These snacks will enhance your metabolic momentum.

SECOND MONTH

Continue the fat-burning process you have ignited in the first month by substituting any two meals with your choice of fat-burning meal-replacement cookies or bars for the next twenty-eight days. Select your meals from the list of seven delicious varieties of breakfast, lunch, and dinner choices that are compatible to all blood types. Remember that these meal selections provide a balance of nutritional values plus variety. Include a midmorning and midafternoon snack. These snacks will enhance your metabolic momentum.

THIRD MONTH

This is the final month of the twelve-week program. After using my fat-burning meal replacements for the first seven days, they may be eliminated (optional). For the remaining twenty-one days, enjoy eating three full meals, along with snacks, daily.

By now you should have lost inches and weight as well as lowered dress and pant sizes because your body has a more efficient BMR, which has shifted your body into a continual fat-burning mode. You should also be experiencing more energy and an improved wellness profile. You will reach your ideal weight and maintain it by continuing to eat foods that are compatible to your blood type—not by dieting.

SUMMARY

The fat-burning process will continue as long as you stay the course. For the final twenty-one days of the program, enjoy eating from any of the seven varieties of breakfast, lunch, and dinner in the program. Remember, these final twenty-one days represent the minimal period of time for improving your adaptation powers to make a new behaviorism a part of your lifestyle—forever. This twenty-one-day period also promotes the correct mentality for eating, and not dieting, while it produces a more efficient BMR. Include a midmorning and midafternoon snack when necessary. These snacks enhance metabolic momentum.

The program starts with the use of temporary meal replacements but ultimately encourages eating food compatible to your blood type to maintain your ideal weight for life.

4-2

TWELVE-WEEK PROTOCOL AT A GLANCE

FIRST MONTH

Days 1–28   Two meal replacements; enjoy one full meal and morning and afternoon snacks.

SECOND MONTH

Days 1–28   Two meal replacements; enjoy one full meal and morning and afternoon snacks.

THIRD MONTH

Days 1–7   Two meal replacements; enjoy one full meal and morning and afternoon snacks.

Days 8–28   No meal replacements; enjoy three full meals and morning and afternoon snacks.

Author's note: You may or may not have reached your ideal weight at the end of the twelve-week program. Continue eating foods that are compatible to your blood type. Chapters 7 through 10 will provide you with additional varieties of meals, snacks, and recipes for your specific blood type. Should you feel the need to continue with my meal replacements, then do so.

Weight-Loss Focus Group Analysis

In September 2002, I conducted a weight-loss focus group that lasted twelve weeks, ending in December 2002 (Christmas week). The "theory" for my weight-loss program was thoroughly tested by the participants with exciting, calculable results. I have included a few of the participants' success stories to encourage you to take the challenge of choosing a proven protocol.

CRITERIA

The following criteria served as safe parameters for successfully completing this twelve-week protocol:

1. To follow their individual blood-type-diet concept as the baseline for making food selections

2. To implement my fat-burning meal replacements (in conjunction with eating) as a means for preventing meal skipping and as a proven method for stimulating their BMR or basal metabolic rate

3. To follow specific exercises based on their body type for increasing lean muscle mass and improving their figures

My primary goal for conducting the focus group was to prove that the aforementioned criteria could create a thermodynamic (fat-burning) foundation for the development of a positive body composition, which would be reflected by their fat-to-muscle ratio within the twelve-week period.

A positive body composition (PBC) is produced by a reduction in the percentage of body fat and an increase in lean muscle mass. This positive body composition is exactly the physical body condition that every individual who wants to lose weight must acquire, both for immediate (short-term) results and for eventually reaching and maintaining an ideal weight for life (long-term goal). As the positive body composition improves, the fat-to-muscle ratio improves. As the fat-to-muscle ratio improves, your body's ability to burn fat improves—the perfect condition for your body to do all the work.

This physical condition is exactly what every competitive bodybuilder seeks to achieve. Their goal is to develop maximum muscle mass through an extreme methodology of competitive training while producing definition (muscle clarity) in the process. The muscle clarity is produced by a reduction in the percentage of body fat they carry, which, of course, is very, very low by extreme dieting methods.

Of course, their goal is very extreme in comparison to the goals of the participants in the focus group, and probably compared with your goals too, but this positive body composition is necessary for all of us to be successful. For bodybuilders, the *bottom line* or foundation for accomplishing their competitive physiques is the same as your bottom line to achieve ideal weight—creating a positive body composition. The difference is that you are not going to the extremes of competitive training and severe dieting. However, as long as you maintain a positive body composition, reaching your ideal weight for life is possible.

Another goal I had for the focus group was to determine the significance of implementing my fat-burning meal-replacement system to their food menus to assist in the weight-loss process, testing the validity of their unique fat-burning properties. I also wanted to measure

Keep your fire blazing because YOU are an *inspiration* in *transition*!

their impact on preventing meal skipping because of everyday life-style schedules and the convenience of using them as replacements.

In addition, I wanted to prove the necessity of including an exercise program along with their weight-loss program. Because many of the participants were not exercising on a regular basis or not at all, I insisted that they start with a progressive daily walking program, including as well a program of resistance training three times a week. The participants received an exercise program that was tailored to their body type so they could develop lean muscle mass; the exercise program would also target their problem areas for the individual body type. I knew that their increase in muscle mass would take away the total pounds lost recorded at their month-to-month weigh-ins. But it was important because it would contribute to producing a positive body composition, which leads to more weight loss later.

To document their progress, each participant was required to report to our on-site nurse each month for measuring, weighing, and body fat percent calculations. Each participant was assigned to one of three groups—A, B, or C—and each group was given specific instructions as to how many meals they should replace per day for each month of the twelve-week program.

The total amount of weight loss measured on the scales may appear to be less dramatic because the participant has gained muscle mass while losing body fat. The secret for weight-loss success is found in the quality of the body weight (determined by the ratio between lean muscle mass and body fat), not the weight itself. For example, a person may look great or terrible at 150 pounds, depending on their body composition.

GROUP INSTRUCTIONS

I divided the groups into different plans so I could compare results based on their meal-replacement regimen. That would let my clients know what to expect depending on how they approach the program. The following criteria were set for the three groups:

- Group A substituted two meal replacements per day for the first month, one meal replacement per day for the second month, and one meal replacement per day for the third month.

- Group B substituted two meal replacements per day for all three months.

- Group C substituted one meal replacement per day for the first month and two meal replacements per day for the second month. For the third month, this group substituted two meal replacements for the first two weeks of the third month and one meal replacement per day for the last two weeks of the third month.

Success is all about attitude!

RESULTS

When the twelve-week program concluded, the results were very exciting. Group A produced significant results, but not as significant as groups B and C. Group B produced the best results of all three groups. Of course, the individual results varied among the participants, just as they will in any program. However, every participant who completed the program experienced weight loss, loss of inches, and reduction in body fat percent. In addition, they all reported increased energy, improved mental alertness, and dramatic relief from previous digestive disorders such as gas, bloating, cramping, heartburn, GERD, constipation, and difficulties with sleep.

Unfortunately, it is commonplace to have individuals drop out of any focus or testing group for various reasons. After ruling out legitimate reasons for participants to leave the program, I have concluded that the most important element for continuing the program is having the proper attitude. That's why I am an advocate of maintaining a constant level of commitment to be successful, because success is all about attitude!

The following is a percentage breakdown of participants who dropped out of the twelve-week program for various reasons (the third month put all the participants in the middle of the holiday season):

- First month—5 percent
- Second month—15 percent
- Third month—21 percent

It is a very good statistic, but one to consider as you decide to begin this weight-loss protocol, that 59 percent of the participants who began the program actually finished it. Your level of commitment will determine your ability to enjoy the lasting results of the participants who completed the protocol.

INDIVIDUAL SUCCESS

The charts on pages 79–84 show the physical statistics of several of the participants who completed the program. In order to understand the significance of their personal statistics, it will help you to know the ideal fat-to-muscle ratio for women and men.

4-3

FAT-TO-MUSCLE RATIO AND LEAN MUSCLE RATING

WOMEN

Ideal: 22 percent body fat/78 percent lean muscle

Competitive sports: 20 percent body fat or less

Competitive bodybuilding (without drugs): 12 percent

(For women, 30 percent or more body fat is considered clinically obese.)

MEN

Ideal: 18 percent body fat/82 percent lean muscle

Competitive sports: 15 percent or less

Competitive bodybuilding (without drugs): 10 percent

(For men, 25 percent or more body fat is considered clinically obese.)

PARTICIPANTS' STATISTICS AS A FOCUS GROUP

The composite characteristics of this focus group that tested my protocol are interesting. Their ages varied from twenty-nine to sixty. The average body fat for the group at the start of the program was 41.5 percent, nearly 50 percent over ideal range. At the conclusion of the program, that group average dropped to 32.4 percent, over a 21 percent reduction. Their average weight was 177.3 pounds, and their average height was 5 feet 4 inches.

I found a couple of interesting links with the participants and their blood types. The majority of the participants (76 percent) were the combination of blood types O and A. Blood type O represented 42 percent, and blood type A represented 34 percent. The blood type B and AB participants equally split the remaining 24 percent.

This group showed a higher than average ratio of certain blood types, particularly the B and AB participants. According to my studies of the world population of blood types, blood type Os represent 50 percent; blood type As, 40 percent; blood type Bs, 8 percent; and blood type ABs, 2 percent.

The ratio in my focus group seemed a bit unusual in comparison to the world population blood types, until I considered my studies of blood types and their link with vocations and professions. The study showed that most blood type B and AB individuals gravitate to professions that involve business management, business decision-making, business organization, money management, and so on, as their personalities would dictate. Some were associated with being entrepreneurs as well as successful millionaires. Of course, blood type O and A individuals would be found in that mix, but not as predominately as Bs and ABs.

As it turned out, many of my participants came from corporate America and had positions in corporate management at various management levels, including some business decision-makers. Their vocations accounted for the higher-than-normal ratio of blood type B and AB participants.

As you study the statistics of the various participants' results, keep in mind that their results represent their willingness to adhere to eating according to their blood type, adding the meal-replacement system, and exercising according to their body type. Their statistics are not the end of their conquest for losing weight, but in fact they represent the beginning of reaching their ideal weight for life.

Weight-Loss Focus Group Summary

After reviewing the results for each participant, I needed to determine if the criteria for the focus group participants produced the results for which I had designed it. Remember, my primary goal was to prove that the program could positively impact the participants in creating a *positive body composition.*

The most critical feedback I was looking for pertaining to successful results was the *reduction* in body fat percent and *an increase* in muscle mass, not necessarily the *total* weight loss. Successful weight loss is never determined by the total amount of weight lost alone, as many people believe (although it does make for great infomercials).

While total weight loss is the main criterion for measuring the success of most weight-loss programs, this weight-loss total represents an unhealthy loss of muscle tissue, water loss, and then body fat, in that order. This total weight loss may look better, but the health and body composition of the person probably does not. As I have stated, successful and healthy weight loss is measured by the proper correlation of body fat versus lean muscle mass or body composition.

A negative body composition (NBC) induces body fat by prohibiting a healthy functioning BMR (basal metabolism rate). This condition is always related to the sedentary lifestyle where the body readily stores calories instead of burning them. The danger of a weight-loss diet low in calories and insufficient nutrition is that it can cause a negative body composition.

A positive body composition (PBC) can only happen when the diet plan (including exercise) is muscle sparing and prevents the body from cannibalizing its own muscle tissue, which is a common casualty with nearly all crash weight-loss diets. When there is specificity in nutrition and exercise according to an individual's needs, he or she will develop lean muscle mass, reduce body fat percentage, and increase BMR because of positive body composition.

The results of my focus group weight-loss program proved extremely positive. The majority of participants had elevated body fat ranges above 30 percent, which typically represents the average female. A small percent of participants reached a healthy body fat-range in twelve weeks because they started the program with a below average body fat measurement, which is the exception and not the rule (unfortunately). Yet all the participants showed significant improvement in reducing body fat and increasing lean muscle mass. Everyone who completed the program made strides toward developing a positive body composition and an improved fat-to-muscle ratio.

After compiling the data, I concluded that the criteria for my weight-loss program were extremely successful, producing a positive body composition in each participant. The prognosis is also good: if the participants maintain a positive body composition, they will eventually reach their ideal weight for life—the ultimate long-range goal.

4-4

Group A

Participant #1	Age: 35	Blood type: O	Height: 5 feet

	PRE-PROGRAM	POST-PROGRAM	RESULTS
Weight	133 lbs.	123 lbs.	-10 lbs.
Chest	38½"	35¼"	-3¼"
Waist	31¼"	27"	-4¼"
Hips	37¼"	33¾"	-3½"
Thigh/r	21½"	20¼"	-1¼"
Thigh/l	22"	20½"	-1½"
Body fat %	28%	19¾%	-8¼%

TOTAL LOSS: 10 pounds; 13¾"; 8¼% fat
Fat-to-Muscle Ratio and Lean Muscle Rating:
> From: 28% body fat/72% lean muscle
> To: 19¾% body fat/80¼% lean muscle

This participant did not have much weight to lose but needed to reduce, redesign, and firm her shape. In addition to eating for her blood type, she followed my body-type workout program specifically for the apple shape. Her results produced a more balanced figure, but more importantly, a lower body fat percent. As she continued to lower her body fat percent, she demonstrated a tremendous example of having a positive body composition. Her goal was to look great for her wedding day—I'd say she made it!

Group A

| Participant #2 | Age: 56 | Blood Type: AB | Height: 5'3" |

	PRE-PROGRAM	POST-PROGRAM	RESULTS
Weight	149 lbs.	139 lbs.	-10 lbs.
Chest	41¼"	39"	-2¼"
Waist	33"	30"	-3"
Hips	39"	36½"	-2½"
Thigh/r	22¾"	22"	-¾"
Thigh/l	22½"	21½"	-1"
Body fat %	30%	24%	-6%

TOTAL LOSS: 10 pounds; 9½"; 6% body fat
Fat-to-Muscle Ratio and Lean Muscle Rating:
From: 30% body fat/70% lean muscle
To: 24% body fat/76% lean muscle

This participant also needed only a minimal reduction in body fat, and through the program she put herself into a very healthy range. More significant is the fact that at 56 years of age and a blood type AB, her efforts will greatly help to prevent the onset of cardiovascular disease and enhance her long-term health profile. Continuing her pear-shape workout program and eating for her blood type, she has started her body transformation into a satisfying hourglass shape.

4-6

Group B

| Participant #1 | Age: 50 | Blood Type: O | Height: 5'3" |

	PRE-PROGRAM	POST-PROGRAM	RESULTS
Weight	169 lbs.	141 lbs.	-28 lbs.
Chest	44"	38¾"	-5¼"
Waist	38¾"	32"	-6¾"
Hips	45"	39½"	-5½"
Thigh/r	23"	21"	-2"
Thigh/l	23"	21¼"	-1¾"
Body fat %	44%	30%	-14%

TOTAL LOSS: 28 pounds; 21¼"; 14% body fat
Fat-to-Muscle Ratio and Lean Muscle Rating:
      From: 44% body fat/56% lean muscle
      To: 30% body fat/70% lean muscle

This participant made incredible progress. Her body type is a classic apple shape; she carries most of her weight in the upper body, particularly in the hip and abdomen. She followed my apple-shape workout program for her body type along with eating for her blood type. As she turned fifty years old during the program term, she also turned around the potential for unnecessary health problems by lowering her body fat percentage a whopping 14%.

Her goals were to build her self-confidence by improving her figure and to fit into a new outfit for the Christmas holidays. She was so successful that she had to return the new outfit she had purchased; it was too large! Her new statistics represent a reduction of over five dress sizes.

Group B

Participant #2	Age: 39	Blood Type: O	Height: 5'5"

	PRE-PROGRAM	POST-PROGRAM	RESULTS
Weight	224 lbs.	207 lbs.	-17 lbs.
Chest	45¾"	43"	-2¾"
Waist	41¼"	39"	-2¼"
Hips	49¼"	44"	-5¼"
Thigh/r	30"	28½"	-1½"
Thigh/l	29¾"	28¼"	-1½"
Body fat %	54%	40%	-14%

TOTAL LOSS: 17 pounds; 13¼"; 14% body fat
Fat-to-Muscle Ratio and Lean Muscle Rating:
    From: 54% body fat/46% lean muscle
    To: 40% body fat/60% lean muscle

Because this participant was carrying a dangerously high percent of body fat, creating metabolic momentum was first priority. As I have mentioned, women who carry 30 percent of body fat are considered to be clinically obese. The combination of eating for her blood type and exercising for her body type was directly responsible for reducing her body fat and preventing premature health problems. Her pear-shape exercise program contributed to increasing lean muscle mass and, in concert with her blood type diet, contributed to making great improvements.

4-8

Group C

| Participant #1 | Age: 47 | Blood Type: AB | Height: 5'5" |

	PRE-PROGRAM	POST-PROGRAM	RESULTS
Weight	182 lbs.	160 lbs.	-22 lbs.
Chest	41"	38"	-3"
Waist	40¼"	35½"	-4¾"
Hips	45"	41¼"	-3¾"
Thigh/r	24¾"	23¼"	-1½"
Thigh/l	24¾"	22¾"	-2"
Body fat %	44%	35%	-9%

TOTAL LOSS: 22 pounds; 15"; 9% body fat
Fat-to-Muscle Ratio and Lean Muscle Rating:
From: 44% body fat/56% lean muscle
To: 35% body fat/65% lean muscle

Her pear-shape figure required exercises specifically for reshaping her body type into the desirable hourglass she achieved as shown in her new statistics. As a blood type AB individual, making new dietary changes in following the blood type diet (without skipping meals) in addition to her exercise program has proven my approach for losing weight to be the "dynamic duo" for excellent results in a short time. Her goal was to feel good about herself by looking better and also to be an example to her children by changing her lifestyle habits. She achieved both goals during this three-month period.

Group C

| Participant #2 | Age: 47 | Blood Type: O | Height: 5'5" |

	PRE-PROGRAM	POST-PROGRAM	RESULTS
Weight	173 lbs.	159 lbs.	-14 lbs.
Chest	43"	40¾"	-2¼"
Waist	38½"	36¼"	-2¼"
Hips	42"	40"	-2"
Thigh/r	23½"	22¼"	-1¼"
Thigh/l	23½"	22"	-1½"
Body fat %	36%	31%	-5%

TOTAL LOSS: 14 pounds; 9¼"; 5% body fat
Fat-to-Muscle Ratio and Lean Muscle Rating:
From: 36% body fat/64% lean muscle
To: 31% body fat/69% lean muscle

For this participant, lowering her body fat to just one point above the clinically obese is a great accomplishment in a short period of time. Following the banana-shape workout program in concert with her blood-type diet plan, she dropped almost three dress sizes and is closer to reaching her ideal weight. Also, she reported that once she started eating for her blood type, her sleep pattern improved and she was able to get a good night's rest. She also found relief from previous stomach disorders and a nasal condition.

Health Benefits

Some of the most important, tangible health benefits received from this twelve-week protocol include the following:

1. The reduction in body fat provides a form of detoxification and cleansing, since most toxins are stored in fatty tissue cells.

2. Lower body fat assists in the prevention of coronary heart disease and various cancers.

3. Increase in lean muscle mass promotes weight loss and maintenance, improved bodily functions, and stronger joints.

4. Body-type exercise programs that target problem areas promote symmetry by using a circuit-training tempo, which improves circulation, strengthens the heart muscle and immune system, regulates blood sugar, and promotes fat loss and muscle mass increase. It improves mental alertness and contributes to better sleeping patterns as well. And it helps rid the body of stored toxins through perspiration, besides firming, toning, and strengthening the entire body.

5. Eating food compatible to one's blood type contributes to improving likely illness profiles, promotes weight loss, contributes to longevity, and helps eliminate common diseases and disorders.

6. Meal replacements assist in stimulating the basal metabolic rate (BMR), providing additional nutrition when substituting full meals, which contributes to jump-starting the fat-burning process. And they are convenient in helping you avoid the bad habit of skipping meals.

This participant in my focus group is enjoying the obvious results of the program—a loss of five dress sizes in twelve weeks.

Menus

Supplementing your diet is vitally important. Because of nutrient-deficient soils and polluted water and air, nearly all vegetation growing in our world today is lacking in the God-given minerals and elements originally planned to help supply humans with the nutrition needed to sustain life. So even with your best effort to eat healthfully, you will most likely be deficient in minerals and vitamins. When you add regular exercise to your lifestyle, it is also important that you increase your supplements and protein intake due to the extra demands placed on your body. There are also specific supplements you can take when you are planning to lose weight. Then, consider the toll stress takes on your body, and you can see how easy your body can become depleted of needed nutrients. For all these reasons, I strongly recommend that you take daily supplements. Please go to Appendix A, "Nutrition Support Ideas," for recommendations. (See page 316.)

Things to Remember Before You Start

I'm sure you have heard about the high-protein, high-fat, no-carbohydrate diet concept for losing weight by now. That is an ancient concept that has worked for decades and has been a staple diet strategy, particularly among every bodybuilder who ever walked on a posing platform.

Only recently has it become more popular and more mainstream because of the work and marketing efforts of the late Dr. Atkins. Though I agree with eating a high-protein diet, especially for weight-loss purposes, I don't go along with high protein, high fat, and no carbohydrates exclusively. Your body requires a *balance* of nutrition from food and nutritional supplements. Then when there is an emphasis placed on protein in your meals, you will get a fat-burning effect.

In the following pages you will find seven varieties of breakfast, lunch, and dinner menus that I incorporated into your weight-loss program, all of which lean toward being high in protein, but not exclusively. There are also fruits, vegetables, some cereals, and some breads that provide carbohydrates and starches, but which, in ratio to the protein content of each menu, are minimal. You will notice that my meal replacements are moderate in protein as well, closer to a 40-30-20 ratio of carbohydrates, proteins, and fats (unless you combine them with a protein

4-10

INSIDERS' TIPS FOR LOSING WEIGHT

1. Start each morning with a 10-ounce glass of water with freshly squeezed lemon.

2. Drink ionized (alkaline) water for neutralizing the acid buildup from proteins and exercise.

3. Drink up to 50 percent of your body weight in fluid ounces (water) throughout each day.

4. Do not eat two to three hours before retiring at night.

5. Smell your food before eating, chew slowly, and don't drink while eating—for best digestion.

6. Take nutritional supplements regularly and include a digestive enzyme with your meals.

7. Avoid juices, table salt, and carbohydrates at night.

8. Exercise daily.

9. Think thin, think outside the box, and believe your success is waiting for you.

10. Stay the course! Stay focused!

shake for a higher protein content). Because the ingredients include fat-burning herbs, they will still create the fat-burning effect you require.

These menus are also compatible for all blood types, which is purposely done for the sake of convenience and with the hope of including the entire family, if appropriate. You will discover that some foods may be neutral for your blood type as well as beneficial, and a few may even be found in your avoid food list. But keep this in mind: when a food, condiment, juice, spice, or herb is in your avoid food list but is found in near trace amounts, it may be consumed without any concern of interfering with your health or progress.

Thermogenic Weight-Loss Program Breakfast Menus for All Blood Types

SCRAMBLED EGGS 1

Upon rising, 8–10 oz. water with ½ squeezed lemon

- 2 or 3 scrambled eggs with crumpled feta cheese
- 1 slice toasted spelt or Ezekiel raisin bread with whole-fruit jam
- 1 cup green tea (coffee for blood type A, AB)

OR

- 1 meal replacement

Midmorning snack (if hungry)
- 10–12 oz. water
- ¼ cup almonds and carob chips

OR

- Body Genetics Protein Shake or Thin Tastic Protein Bar

SCRAMBLED OR POACHED EGGS 2

Upon rising, 8–10 oz. water with ½ squeezed lemon

- 1 or 2 scrambled or poached eggs
- 1 or 2 slices turkey bacon (not pork)
- 1 slice millet bread with butter
- 1 cup green tea with honey (coffee for blood type A, AB)

OR

- 1 meal replacement

Midmorning snack (if hungry)
- 10–12 oz. water
- 1 slice fat-free mozzarella cheese with apple

OR

- Body Genetics Protein Shake or Thin Tastic Protein Bar

CEREAL 3

Upon rising, 8–10 oz. water with ½ squeezed lemon

- 1 bowl Cream of Rice with soy milk (skim milk for blood type B, AB)
- 1 slice toasted millet or Ezekiel bread with almond butter

OR

- 1 meal replacement

Midmorning snack (if hungry)
- 10–12 oz. water
- ¼ cup macadamia nuts and pineapple chunks

OR

- Body Genetics Protein Shake or Thin Tastic Protein Bar

CEREAL 4

Upon rising, 8–10 oz. water with ½ squeezed lemon

- 1 bowl granola cereal with soy milk (low-fat milk for blood type B, AB)
- ½ grapefruit
- 2 slices toasted Ezekiel or millet bread with butter and blackberry jam

OR

- 1 meal replacement

Midmorning snack (if hungry)
- 10–12 oz. water
- 1 apple, pear, or peach

OR

- Body Genetics Protein Shake or Thin Tastic Protein Bar

CEREAL   5

Upon rising, 8–10 oz. water with ½ squeezed lemon

- 1 bowl oat bran, oatmeal, or spelt cereal with soy milk (skim milk for blood type B, AB)—add almond slivers and raisins
- 1 slice gluten-free toast with butter or nut butter
- 1 cup coffee (peppermint tea for blood type O, B)

OR

- 1 meal replacement

Midmorning snack (if hungry)
- 10–12 oz. water
- ¼ cup walnuts with pitted prunes

OR

- Body Genetics Protein Shake or Thin Tastic Protein Bar

CHEESE OMELET   6

Upon rising, 8–10 oz. water with ½ squeezed lemon

- 2-egg cheese omelet with low-fat mozzarella cheese and scallions
- 1 slice toasted brown rice bread with whole-fruit jam
- 1 cup ginseng tea

OR

- 1 meal replacement

Midmorning snack (if hungry)
- 10–12 oz. water
- 2 large brown rice cakes with almond butter

OR

- Body Genetics Protein Shake or Thin Tastic Protein Bar

POACHED EGGS   7

Upon rising, 8–10 oz. water with ½ squeezed lemon

- 2 or 3 poached eggs
- 1 slice mozzarella cheese
- 2 slices turkey bacon (not pork)
- 1 slice toasted Ezekiel or millet bread with butter
- 1 cup green or peppermint tea

OR

- 1 meal replacement

Midmorning snack (if hungry)
- 10–12 oz. water
- ¼ cup almonds, walnuts, and raisins

OR

- Body Genetics Protein Shake or Thin Tastic Protein Bar

Thermogenic Weight-Loss Program Lunch Menus for All Blood Types

MEAT AND SALAD 1

- 1 6-oz. serving meat (beef—O, A; chicken—A, O; lamb—O, B, AB; veal—O, B; turkey—all blood types)
- Salad with romaine lettuce, feta cheese, scallions, broccoli, and dressing from list on page 95
- 1 cup green beans
- ½ cup pineapple chunks
- 10–12 oz. water (drink after meal)

OR

- 1 meal replacement

Midafternoon snack (if hungry)
- 10–12 oz. water
- Body Genetics Protein Shake or Thin Tastic Protein Bar

PATTIES AND SALAD 2

- 6-oz. turkey or veggie patty (beef for blood type O, B)
- 1 slice fat-free mozzarella cheese, mayonnaise or mustard
- Carrots and celery sticks
- Green salad (not iceberg) with walnuts, red onions, avocado, and dressing from list on page 95
- ½ cup sliced apples
- 10–12 oz. water (drink after meal)

OR

- 1 meal replacement

Midafternoon snack (if hungry)
- 10–12 oz. water
- Handful of almonds and a piece of fruit

OR

- Body Genetics Protein Shake or Thin Tastic Protein Bar

CHEF'S SALAD WITH TURKEY 3

- Chef's salad with romaine lettuce, dressing from list on page 95, 1 hard-boiled egg, 3–4 oz. sliced turkey, 1 oz. feta cheese, scallions, carrots, and celery
- 1 cup grapes
- 10–12 oz. water (drink after meal)

OR

- 1 meal replacement

Midafternoon snack (if hungry)
- 10–12 oz. water
- Handful of macadamia nuts, almonds, or walnuts with apple and pitted prunes

OR

- Body Genetics Protein Shake or Thin Tastic Protein Bar

TURKEY SALAD SANDWICH 4

- 6 oz. white turkey meat cubed, mixed with chopped onions, celery, water chestnuts, and low-fat mayonnaise
- Romaine lettuce
- 2 slices Ezekiel bread (toasted, if desired)
- Carrots and celery sticks
- ½ cup raisins and almonds
- 10–12 oz. water (drink after meal)

OR

- 1 meal replacement

Midafternoon snack (if hungry)
- 10–12 oz. water
- 1 strawberry-filled cookie

OR

- Body Genetics Protein Shake or Thin Tastic Protein Bar

TUNA SANDWICH   5

- 4–6 oz. albacore tuna with low-fat mayonnaise
- 2 slices wheat-free, Ezekiel, or millet bread
- 1 cup steamed broccoli, carrots, and red onions
- ½ cup diced pineapple
- 10–12 oz. water (drink after meal)
OR
- 1 meal replacement

Midafternoon snack (if hungry)
- 10–12 oz. water
- 1 cup of mixed fruit
OR
- Body Genetics Protein Shake or Thin Tastic Protein Bar

SOUP AND SANDWICH   6

- 1 cup carrot or vegetable soup
- 4–6 oz. sliced turkey breast
- 1 slice low-fat mozzarella cheese
- 1 slice Ezekiel or gluten-free bread
- Mustard or low-fat mayonnaise
- ½ cup mixed raisins, chocolate chips, and almonds
- 10–12 oz. water (drink after meal)
OR
- 1 meal replacement

Midafternoon snack (if hungry)
- 10–12 oz. water
- 1 slice low-fat mozzarella cheese with apple
OR
- Body Genetics Protein Shake or Thin Tastic Protein Bar

GRILLED CHEESE SANDWICH   7

- 2 slices Ezekiel or millet bread brushed with olive oil
- 2 slices low-fat mozzarella cheese
- 1 cup steamed carrots, green beans, or broccoli
- 1 large apple
- 10–12 oz. water (drink after meal)
OR
- 1 meal replacement

Midafternoon snack (if hungry)
- 10–12 oz. water
- 1 strawberry-filled cookie
OR
- Body Genetics Protein Shake or Thin Tastic Protein Bar

Thermogenic Weight-Loss Program Dinner Menus for All Blood Types

FISH 1

- 6–8 oz. broiled ocean salmon or tuna steak in lemon with white wine and tarragon
- 1 cup steamed broccoli and zucchini
- 1 cup brown rice
- Salad with romaine lettuce and dressing from list on page 95
- Scallions and walnuts
- 10–12 oz. water (drink after meal)

OR

- 1 meal replacement

Evening snack (two or more hours before bedtime)
- 8–10 oz. water
- Body Genetics Protein Shake or Thin Tastic Protein Bar

BURGER 2

- 6-oz. turkey burger with red onions (beef for blood type O, B)
- Salad with romaine lettuce or kale, feta cheese, almond slivers, and scallions
- Oregano Feta Dressing (page 95)
- 1 cup string beans with chopped garlic and olive oil
- 1 cup mixed raisins and carob chips
- 10–12 oz. water (drink after meal)

OR

- 1 meal replacement

Evening snack (two or more hours before bedtime)
- 8–10 oz. water
- Body Genetics Protein Shake or Thin Tastic Protein Bar

OPEN SANDWICH 3

- 1 can (4–6 oz.) albacore tuna mixed with diced celery, scallions, and low-fat mayonnaise
- 1 slice Ezekiel or gluten-free bread
- Mixed greens salad with goat or feta cheese, mashed garlic, chopped broccoli, and olive oil and lemon juice dressing
- 1 cup peas (green, snow, or pod)
- Fruit bowl: 1 cup grapes, pineapple slices, walnuts, and carob chips
- 10–12 oz. water (drink after meal)

OR

- 1 meal replacement

Evening snack (two or more hours before bedtime)
- 8–10 oz. water
- Body Genetics Protein Shake or Thin Tastic Protein Bar

FISH AND CHIPS 4

- 8 oz. baked or broiled filet of cod, red snapper, or tilapia with lemon juice
- 5–6 oz. sweet potato chips
- 1 cup broccoli
- Carrots and celery sticks
- Fruit bowl: 1 cup grapes, strawberries, and semisweet chocolate chips
- 10–12 oz. water (drink after meal)

OR

- 1 meal replacement

Evening snack (two or more hours before bedtime)
- 8–10 oz. water
- Body Genetics Protein Shake or Thin Tastic Protein Bar

MEAT 5

- 1 (6–8 oz.) meat serving (red meat—O; chicken—O, A; lamb—O, B, AB; Cornish hen—O, A; veal—O, B; turkey—all blood types)
- Mixed greens salad sprinkled with goat, feta, or low-fat mozzarella cheese; scallions; grated carrots; and dressing from list on page 95
- 1 cup brussels sprouts
- Fruit bowl: 1 cup diced pineapple, grapes, strawberries, and walnuts
- 6–8 oz. green tea
- 10–12 oz. water (drink after meal)
OR
- 1 meal replacement

Evening snack (two or more hours before bedtime)
- 8–10 oz. water
- Body Genetics Protein Shake or Thin Tastic Protein Bar

TUNA AND PASTA 6

- 4–6 oz. spelt pasta combined with 4 oz. albacore tuna mixed with low-fat mayonnaise, scallions, red onions, garlic, olive oil, and lemon juice
- 1 cup steamed broccoli
- Fruit bowl: 1 cup grapes, strawberries, pineapple chunks, and cherries
- 10–12 oz. water (drink after meal)
OR
- 1 meal replacement

Evening snack (two or more hours before bedtime)
- 8–10 oz. water
- Body Genetics Protein Shake or Thin Tastic Protein Bar

JUMBO SALAD 7

- 1 head romaine lettuce mixed with 4–5 oz. turkey slices
- 2 hard-boiled eggs (remove yolks if desired)
- 1 cup grated low-fat mozzarella cheese
- 1 cup carrot slices, scallions, and chopped broccoli
- 1 slice of toasted Ezekiel bread brushed with olive oil (cut in small cubes for croutons)
- Vinegarless Dressing (page 95)
- Fruit bowl: 1 cup slivered almonds, black currants, cherries, and carob chips
- 10–12 oz. water (drink after meal)
OR
- 1 meal replacement

Evening snack (two or more hours before bedtime)
- 8–10 oz. water
- Body Genetics Protein Shake or Thin Tastic Protein Bar

Selected Dressing List

VINEGARLESS DRESSING

½ cup fresh lemon juice (3–4 lemons)
¼ cup Braggs Amino
1 tsp. garlic powder
1 cup cold-pressed olive oil
1 cup black currant oil
1 tsp. minced onions
½ tsp. curry or turmeric

Place all ingredients in quart-sized container with lid and pouring feature. Mix ingredients well. Add water if too thick, or use less oil. Can store in refrigerator for 3–4 weeks. *Makes 2¾ cups.*

RED ONION DRESSING

½ cup fresh lemon juice (3–4 lemons)
¼ cup Braggs Liquid Amino
1 cup cold-pressed olive oil
1–2 Tbsp. finely chopped red onions
½ tsp. dried mustard
½ tsp. dried oregano or parsley
½ tsp. dried thyme, minced or pressed

Combine all ingredients in jar or plastic container. Shake vigorously to blend. Let set at room temperature for one hour before using to allow flavors to blend. Can store in refrigerator for 3–4 weeks. *Makes 1½ cups.*

OREGANO FETA DRESSING

2 oz. crumbled feta cheese
2 Tbsp. fresh lemon juice
1 Tbsp. olive oil
1 clove crushed garlic
½ tsp. dried crushed oregano

Put all ingredients in food processor and pulse until mixed. Can store in refrigerator for 3–4 weeks. *Makes 1 cup.*

Chapter 5

How to Become an Instinctive Eater

Throughout the years, there have been too many different diet plans to even try to list them all. Each one promises to be your "knight in shining armor"...your "pot of gold at the end of the rainbow"...your "holy grail" to health. My goal in this book is not to help you pick a diet plan that will bring you success. We have been there, done that.

Neither do I intend to poke holes in the various diet plans, both popular and unpopular, that are available to you. Why not? The answer is simple: I am most interested in helping you to understand better the concept of instinctive eating. Then I will leave the rest up to you.

Instinctive eating is uniquely different from the typical diet plan. Instinctive eating requires that you grasp hold of your genetic or cellular profile, using that knowledge as the baseline or fundamental foundation for the way you eat.

You will understand the difference between diet plans and instinctive eating as you read the following pages. But more important than what you read—*you will experience the difference once you give it your best shot*. My intention here is to help you see what instinctive eating is and why it makes good sense to implement it

If you are a dieter, have tried dieting to some degree, or would like to take your first healthy step in the right direction, then get ready for some fascinating and life-changing information that you can try for yourself.

as a part of your lifestyle. So if you are a dieter, have tried dieting to some degree, or would like to take your first healthy step in the right direction, then get ready for some fascinating and life-changing information that you can try for yourself.

My experience throughout the years has taught me that the greatest majority of people who have searched for a diet plan wanted one that would help them to reach a goal of permanent weight loss. Yet seldom—if ever—have they found a plan that could succeed at that! For one reason or another, the plan they chose did not work—at least not for permanent weight loss. No doubt the main reason was that it was just too difficult to adapt to that diet plan as a lifestyle change.

Most people would love to find the answer to their fatigue, weight, and health problems so they could feel better and enjoy their lives more. That's a normal human desire. But sometimes it takes a wake-up call to get a person's attention—something like a heart attack, stomach disorder, or chronic illness that steals your money and, more importantly, your life.

The desire to better ourselves and to live longer lies within each of us. It's part of our natural, innate mechanism for survival. My main objectives are to get you on the path to instinctive eating and to keep you from the frustrating and unnecessary physical and emotional roller-coaster rides so often associated with diets.

In my book *Seven Pillars of Health*, I explain the perils of dieting by taking you on a cruise to Diet Island.[1] I think once you read it, you will absolutely identify with it.

If you have sought long-term results by following a diet plan that focuses strictly on end results, now would be a great time to take your first step by changing your thinking. Just the thought of going on a diet causes words to surface—words like *sacrifice*, *deprivation*, *going without*, and *struggling to stay on a diet*.

Who said that making healthier food selections was a matter of pure sacrifice? Who said you could never deviate from the letter of the law? Certainly not me! That kind of behavioral response has caused thousands of people like yourself to end up thinking that making healthy food selections is nothing more than a punishment/

reward system of eating. Consequently, this mind-set will prohibit lifestyle adaptation.

The problem with this diet mentality is this: the focus is on the end results. It disregards the essentials—improving your health, becoming disease free, and living a longer, healthier life with more energy. These essentials require a lifestyle adaptation.

You may have been victimized by the commercial slants placing all the emphasis on cosmetic results—not lifestyle. If you are wondering if marketing the "body beautiful" is a powerful tool, just ask any marketing genius from one of the huge weight-loss companies. I am sure they will tell you that it is much harder to sell good health than it is to sell the promise of beauty. Understand what I am saying here. While each one of us will have motivational influences that initially engage us to make dietary changes, in order to be successful over the long haul we must focus on the journey—not the destination.

Focus on the Journey

The road you travel, the path you choose to enjoy the journey of your life, needs to become your focus point, not merely the destination. When the focus is placed on the wrong thing, failure is inevitable. That is why the majority of the diet plans you have tried before never lasted.

As you analyze your dieting experiences in retrospect, you will probably agree that they were more of a "suck-it-up-and-give-it-all-the-willpower-you-can-muster-for-as-long-as-you-can" kind of experience—definitely not a journey.

Focusing on the journey offers many more rewards along the way than focusing only on the end results. The journey experience allows you to enjoy the many benefits available by making

---

5-1

Benefits of the Journey Experience

- Continual awareness of your body's reactions to certain foods
- Realization of the positive or negative side effects from certain foods
- A constant increase in energy
- Better cholesterol readings
- Less need for medications
- Less down time caused by sickness and ill health

adaptable dietary changes for a lifetime. These benefits come in many packages. (See Chart 5-1.)

Focusing on the journey will help you to enjoy life by spending more time with your family and friends and less time visiting hospitals and doctors. The path or road you decide to travel determines the lifestyle with which you will live.

Are you ready to make your choice? Are you ready to begin the journey?

Instinctive Eating

In the previous chapter I gave you a complete weight-loss program to follow if losing weight was your goal. I also mentioned that the primary purpose for the weight-loss program is to help jump-start your metabolism so you can lose weight. And ultimately, this plan will teach you that *eating* instead of *dieting* is the healthy and natural way to be successful with your weight and health for life. So in this section of the book you will learn how to become an instinctive eater. You may be asking the question: What is an instinctive eater? Instinctive eating is best understood by observing the creatures in the animal kingdom.

Let's look at the lioness as one example. This cool cat has never taken a course in Nutrition 101 or purchased the latest weight-loss diet plan on the market. She was never influenced by medical and scientific documentation teaching her that all food is OK to eat as long as she ate it in moderation. This feline has never been formally educated.

But how fascinating it is to note that the lioness possesses something far superior to what has—or has not been—scientifically proven. She has a dietary mechanism for survival, which is *instinctive eating*. When it comes to eating, there are no guidelines for her to follow. There are no daily menus to follow. But when dinnertime rolls around, she absolutely knows what she should eat. The lioness will always order meat for dinner. She would not be caught dead climbing a banana tree to eat bananas.

Her eating habits are not accidental. Nor are they coincidental. Animals eat instinctively because their inherent, natural dietary mechanism for survival determines what they eat.

Consider the horse for a moment. A horse is a horse, of course. But when was the last time you saw a farmer strap a feed bag filled with chopped beef onto a horse? Try going to your local 4-H club to ask if chopped beef is OK for your horse. You would be laughed out of the barn. A horse's feed bag is always filled with oats.

Put a horse out to pasture, and it will naturally eat grass. Did you ever see a horse run through a pasture chasing squirrels or rabbits for a midafternoon snack?

You would be intrigued by what you can learn about animals. For example, did you know that most animals of the same species generally live to be the same age? Their dietary mechanism for survival allows them to live to the potential life span of that species. A very few may die of cancer or other rare diseases or get killed by a predator, but most animals die of old age.

Not so for us humanoids; we are different. We generally die at a young age from a variety of different diseases, many of which are associated with our diets. Or we live out our last years in a less-than-desirable physical condition. I have always said that when it is my turn to go to heaven, I want to check out of Dodge City doing 180 miles per hour—not spending the last twenty years of life using a walker because I was negligent with my health.

The very thought of living to be one hundred years of age is, for most humans, quite a stretch. Up until now we did not have a clue about how to eat instinctively. Most people eat for reasons that fall far short of supplying our bodies with sound nutrition, good health, and longevity. We all come from a huge dietary mixing bowl that swings like a pendulum. Some people or groups insist that everybody should be a vegetarian, while others refuse to give up their meats. Others will support the high-carbohydrate, zero-protein-and-fat diet, while others support a high-protein, high-fat, and no-carbohydrate diet. Throw in our taste buds, ethnic traditions, religious beliefs, social settings, and the dilemma of the emotional, bulimic, or anorexic eater, and it is easy to see why we have a lot to learn from the dietary instincts of our "inferior" animal counterparts.

Unless you have lived with gorillas for many years and learned all about instinctive eating as Anthony Hopkins did in the movie

Your first step in becoming an instinctive eater will be knowing your blood type. Are you a type A, B, AB, or O?

Instinct, how could you experience benefits from instinctive eating? How could you become an instinctive eater if at first you didn't have some guidelines or dietary strategies from which to learn? Remember, we have never been enlightened to know how to eat instinctively. We must first learn.

The dietary guidelines in this book are based on your blood type. Your first step in becoming an instinctive eater will be knowing your blood type. Are you a type A, B, AB, or O? (See page 107 to find out how to determine your blood type.)

I believe personally that I am communicating to you an approach to eating that is the most effective, individual, and accurate method of making food selections that can become an adaptable lifestyle change. Because this method is genetically based, it will prove itself by the many ways your body responds to certain foods.

I do not expect you to take my word for it without some basic understanding and ultimately testing its validity for yourself. This is especially true when it comes to making dietary changes. The dietary changes must not impose restrictions so unrealistic that you find it impossible to reach your goals or so unattainable that the changes cannot become part of your lifestyle.

On the other hand, you must remember that anything worth doing is worth doing right. My desire is to help you live a healthy, more energetic, and sickness-free life for as long as possible. What I am recommending is doable. If it wasn't realistic enough to live with, we would both be wasting our time. I want you to become a "believer" like me, the people in this book who share their experiences, and thousands of others who have put this dietary approach to the test.

Genetic Baseline

One of the primary reasons why different blood types respond differently to certain foods is due to the effect dietary lectins have on the host's body. Dietary lectins are protein molecules found in food. If a food is not compatible to your blood type, these lectins can create havoc in your body systems. These negative responses occur due to a chemical phenomenon referred to as *agglutination*. The lectins will bond themselves randomly to blood cells in an organ or bodily system and begin to interfere with the natural and normal function of that particular system or organ.

Typically, blood cells have a slippery surface and are unaffected by dietary lectins as long as the host consumes foods that are compatible. But dietary lectins present in foods that are incompatible with your blood type wreak havoc by attaching themselves to the blood cell.

Think for a moment about what would happen if you tried to roll a tennis ball over a strip of Velcro. The tennis ball would stick to that Velcro strip just like glue and be impossible to roll. This is what happens when you ingest foods that are not compatible to your blood type. Instead of the dietary lectins rolling over the blood cells in that system, they will stick like glue to the surface of the blood cells.

Let's take your digestive system for example. Suppose you consume some food that is not compatible to your blood type. The dietary lectins begin to attach themselves to the blood cells on the wall of your intestines. As this process continues, a clumping of blood cells takes place that begins to interfere with the normal function of that digestive system. Now your problems have just begun.

You may not be aware this is taking place, but your digestive system knows. It just took a hit, and it is beginning its downward spiral. Your body knows that it has just been poisoned, and it tries to let you know by sending you signals or warning signs. Sometimes these warnings or signals are subtle and less dangerous, giving you symptoms like gas, bloating, or indigestion—things we normally just ignore.

But ignoring these symptoms is a dangerous thing to do. They often indicate a serious problem or disease that needs an immediate solution if we want to maintain good health.

If these symptoms persist, the next order of business is usually to medicate. Medicating a symptom is a behavioral reaction that most people do when they discover that part of their normal bodily function is malfunctioning. They respond this way because of their immediate need for satisfaction and relief. Often they are also unaware of good prevention and cure techniques.

Instead of addressing the root problem that is causing your body to send out these helpful warnings to you, you end up experiencing the possible loss of function of that system by medicating the symptoms. The time finally comes when these warnings can no longer be ignored or sufficiently medicated. You become nearly incapacitated by cramping, abdominal pain, continual fatigue, and the lack of energy.

Instinctive eating can help you to pick up immediately on the signals your body is sending.

Soon you find yourself dealing with chronic digestive disorders like diverticulitis, irritable bowel syndrome (IBS), celiac sprue disease, and possibly the eventuality of cancer of the colon. At this point, your quality of life has taken a major dive.

How unfortunate it would be if your house were on fire and the firemen came and squirted water only on the smoke. With that kind of negligent approach, it would not be very long before there was nothing left of your home. This is exactly what happens to your health and quality of life when you ignore the warning signs that your body is sending out.

Instinctive eating can help you to pick up immediately on the signals your body is sending. You will quickly become aware of the negative responses your body warns you about when you eat incompatible foods.

The things that I just described about your digestive system do not have to happen to your health. You can avoid them by learning to become an instinctive eater. You only have one body to carry you throughout life; why wouldn't you want to take care of it?

One day as I was mailing books at the local post office, one of the clerks asked me what the book was all about. After explaining the concept to her, I asked her why she had asked.

She told me that she had constant stomach pain and was taking medication for it. She was overweight and tired all the time. I gave her a book and told her to follow the dietary guidelines and menus for at least three weeks. I advised her to do her best to avoid the "Avoid" foods listed for her blood type.

As we talked, I asked her if she was a blood type B, which she said she was. I told her it would be imperative to avoid eating chicken. She was flabbergasted, because chicken was her staple. She ate it almost daily.

About three weeks later I went back to the post office, and out from behind the counter this woman jumped. "What do you think?" she asked. (Keep in mind that I didn't know her.) Before I could say anything, she said that she had dropped sixteen pounds. She had no more stomach pain, was off her medications, and felt great. Plus, she had tons of energy.

She confessed that one day her daughter brought over some fried chicken, but she ate only one piece. Twenty-four hours after she ate it, she had an upset stomach. The taste of the chicken had actually been totally unappealing to her. "I never would have believed it if I didn't try it," she said to me. "It was the easiest thing I ever did!"

Learning to be an instinctive eater may not be the easiest thing you will ever learn to do—but it will be one of the healthiest things you ever do for yourself. The next section will help you to get started by showing you how to complete a simple four-week test for instinctive eating. It's one test you will be glad you took.

Once you complete the test period, your body has experienced a thorough cleansing and overhaul.

Your Four-Week Test Plan

Now that you have had this informal crash course in Instinctive Eating 101, you have a better understanding about the connection that exists between your specific blood type and the food you eat. By now you should be motivated to test this concept and prove it for yourself.

This four-week test period is what I refer to as your window of opportunity. If you will take this opportunity, believing that your good health is worth this investment of time, I believe you will discover for yourself that what I have told you will work for you.

This information can become your ticket to great health. By following the dietary and exercise guidelines in this book, you can turn your health around, control your weight, increase your energy, stabilize your blood sugar, lower your cholesterol and blood pressure, and possibly get off prescription medications once and for all.

God did not make any mistakes when He made you and me. He created us to live long, healthy lives, and He placed on this earth all the necessary food sources for us to do just that. Just because we may not understand something new or unfamiliar does not mean we should discard it as useless to us.

The world of science is making continual biological advancements. Science is decoding and breaking down the understanding of DNA codes at a surprising rate. An entirely new world of health possibilities is right around the corner. Daily we are learning to better understand our bodies and how to keep them in optimal health.

Something as simple as adapting to a better dietary lifestyle by making behavior changes in advance of the onset of disease instead of after disease invades our body can increase our potential for living longer and healthier.

Learning how to more accurately appropriate these new discoveries and biological findings may one day show us how to prevent diseases before they occur, simply by addressing the root issues. Something as simple as adapting to a better dietary lifestyle by making behavior changes in advance of the onset of disease instead of after disease invades our body can increase our potential for living longer and healthier.

This simple four-week test will give you the opportunity to experience for yourself, without any outside influences, that what I am telling you is real—and that it works. It will answer many of your questions about whether there truly is a connection or link between your blood type and diet, health, disease, energy, weight loss, low blood sugar, sugar cravings, and longevity. Keep in mind that individual results will vary because we are all different, even those of the same blood type. Each person is still uniquely made. Because none of us share the same physical conditions, medical history, or body genetics, it is imperative for you to let your body be your only teacher. You can do that as you learn to become an instinctive eater.

Beginning Your Four-Week Test

Before you begin your four-week test, you will want to know your blood type. Chart 5-2 can help you to determine your specific blood type.

After you have determined your blood type, it is time to prepare for your four-week test. First, check with your physician before following these dietary guidelines. This four-week test is not to be misconstrued as a substitute for medical recommendations.

For the next four weeks, you will be monitoring the foods you eat. You will choose from the food groupings given in this book. However, the important thing to remember will be to choose from the appropriate food groupings for you. There are approximately sixteen food groups given for each blood type, which include all the various foods we eat as well as condiments, spices, and juices. These food groups will give you a wonderful array of food to choose from, with many varieties in each group.

Each blood type has three categories for each food group—beneficial foods, neutral foods, and avoid foods:

1. Beneficial foods—foods that your body, according to your blood type, treats as medicine for healing systems and improving bodily function and performance

2. Neutral foods—foods that your body, according to your blood type, treats as compatible sources of energy

3. Avoid foods—foods that your body, according to your blood type, treats as poisons and toxins. (These are not necessarily junk food. It may be your favorite food, one that all this time you thought was good for you.)

Determining Your Blood Type

5-2

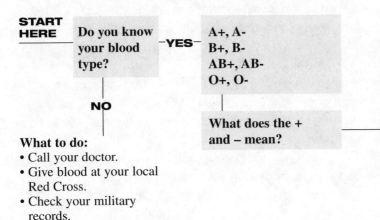

START HERE — Do you know your blood type? —**YES**— A+, A- B+, B- AB+, AB- O+, O-

NO

What to do:
- Call your doctor.
- Give blood at your local Red Cross.
- Check your military records.
- Purchase a Home Blood Testing Kit.

What does the + and – mean?

The + and – are a separate blood grouping called the Rhesus, or Rh, system. It does not factor into diet or disease, but it is significant for childbearing (women who are Rh-), in organ transplants, and in blood donations.

Blood type O— universal donor

Blood type AB— universal receiver

Blood type A— can only receive blood from another blood type A

Blood type B— can only receive blood from another blood type B

Window of Opportunity

The four-week test can be your window of opportunity. To get the most accurate results, follow the guidelines given below.

AVOID THE AVOID FOODS

During the next four weeks, do your best to avoid eating the avoid foods listed for your blood type. No one will be 100 percent successful at doing this, but give it your best attempt. Look for continued progress—not perfection. Avoid foods are foods that are not compatible with your specific blood type; therefore, they should be avoided.

During this test period your body will undergo a detoxification process. Much of the detoxifying will take place within your digestive system, which is greatly influenced by the association of your blood type and dietary lectins from the food you eat. You will begin experiencing some wonderful changes. Some of the symptoms that you may have been experiencing prior to this test, such as gas, bloating, irritable bowel syndrome, and gastroesophageal reflux disorder (GERD), have been known to disappear during this test period. In most cases, these symptoms disappear in just a few days.

Within weeks, you may also experience a considerable drop in your elevated cholesterol and blood pressure levels—without the use of medications. If you struggle with hypoglycemia, or low blood sugar, your blood sugar levels will stabilize.

Within several days, you could discover that you have more than enough energy to last all day long instead of feeling your energy drop off in the middle of the day, as I did while struggling with hypoglycemia for fifteen long, unbearable years. Thank God, I haven't had low blood sugar problems since.

Along with the foods you avoid, avoid also the diet mentality that focuses on the end results only. Do not become trapped by thoughts of what you cannot eat. That's the old way of diet thinking. The avoidance of the avoid foods is not a form of punishment, nor is it a form of imprisonment. You can eat anything you want! But by adhering to these guidelines for this test period, you will have the opportunity to experience a cleansing and relief from some of the digestive disorders your body has been dealing with.

Keep in mind that the avoid foods play havoc with blood lipids and the proper function of your digestive system, immune system, liver, and kidneys. The more you adhere to the guidelines for the test period, the greater the opportunity for your body to rid itself of damaging dietary lectins. Eliminating these dietary lectins found in the avoid foods will give you positive results now—and long term. You will accumulate the knowledge you need to truly become an instinctive eater.

Avoiding the avoid foods for your blood type will bring another benefit—weight loss! The toxins that have been stored up in the fat cells of your body as a result of eating the wrong foods will be eliminated, and the fat cells will begin to shrink as part of the detoxification process. Your digestive system and your metabolism will start to function properly and more efficiently as you eliminate dietary lectins, like wheat gluten, that slow down metabolism and digestive system functions. The results will be a healthy colon, a speedy metabolism, and loss in body fat—all without going on a diet! I refer to the loss of body fat as a by-product of instinctive eating—not the by-product of dieting. I think you will agree.

> **Along with the foods you avoid, avoid also the diet mentality that focuses on the end results only. Do not become trapped by thoughts of what you cannot eat.**

CONCENTRATE ON THE BENEFICIAL FOODS

You may be wondering, "If I avoid the avoid foods, what can I find to eat?" You will have a delectable array of good nutritious foods from which to choose. Simply make your food selections from the fourteen-day menus or pick and choose your favorite food selections from the beneficial foods category for your blood type.

As you consider your food choices, you will discover that there are more food selections in the beneficial foods and neutral foods than you found on the avoid foods list, so don't despair. Do not even bother trying to count calories during the four-week test period—just eat. A good rule to follow is this: eat when you are hungry, but stop when you are comfortably satisfied.

In some of the food groupings, you will see that there are no beneficial foods from which to choose. Your first choice should be to forgo that particular food group, but if you must make a selection, do so from the neutral foods. Remember, the more correctly you eat for your blood type, the better the results, and your beneficial foods will promote the best results.

Once you complete the test period, your body has experienced a thorough cleansing and overhaul. You should have some wonderful experiences to share. Many people have called, e-mailed, or written my office to share their positive experiences during their four-week test. I would love to hear from you too. (See page 317 for contact information.)

Once you complete the test period, your body has experienced a thorough cleansing and overhaul.

MONITOR YOUR PROGRESS

It will be important to monitor your responses during this four-week period. Here are four important steps in the monitoring process:

1. If possible, have blood work done to know your current cholesterol readings before you start.
2. If possible, have your blood pressure taken before you start.
3. Record medication dosages, which medications, and for what condition you are taking them.
4. Record your progress by comparing the changes from your current condition list to the test results list.

Use Chart 5-3 to monitor your progress.

As you learn to eat correctly for your blood type, your body will function more properly, your metabolism will stay revved up, and your digestive system will operate more efficiently. You will be able to control your weight without dieting and live longer with less to no incapacitating illnesses. More importantly, you will be able to enjoy your life to its fullest.

Eventually, your journey will allow you to be like the lioness that didn't need a menu to follow or a course in Nutrition 101 to eat instinctively. The lioness didn't need to be told that her way of eating was or was not scientifically proven because her response to and innate desire for meats made her food selections an evidence-based concept. She was an innate instinctive eater—and you will have learned to be an innate instinctive eater also.

For determining your blood type, go to www.bodyredesigning .com and order a Home Blood Typing Kit.

5-3

Monitor Your Progress

Body Signpost	Current Condition	End of Four Weeks	Test Results
1. Cholesterol level	/	/	
2. Blood pressure	/	/	
3. Low blood sugar or hypoglycemia (yes/no)			
4. Body weight	lbs.	lbs.	Lost _____ lbs.
5. Body fat percentage	%	%	
6. Energy level (high/low)			
7. Allergies: Hay fever, sinus, headaches, etc.			
8. Digestive symptoms: Gas, bloating, diarrhea, constipation, IBS, GERD, stomach pain, arthritic-like pain, etc.			
9. List any medications you are taking for the allergies or digestive symptoms described.			

Chapter 6

Diet and Nutrition

In this chapter I will discuss the benefits of eating for your blood type; the importance of whole, unprocessed foods; and how to make this ideal a reality in your life. I have designed this section to help coach you along in your process. You *can* do it! You have already taken the first step just by reading this book!

The most important thing to remember when following any food plan is to make the food you eat interesting and delicious. If you are not enjoying what you put in your mouth, it really doesn't matter how healthy the food is. You won't eat it again. I know I wouldn't! An entire section has been created full of delicious recipes specific to each blood type. There is careful cross-referencing in the master index of the recipe section to insure those families with mixed blood types can peacefully coexist. Also, each recipe is marked with the blood types that it was meant for. You might actually find a variation of your favorite dish in there modified to suit your blood type. I promise you that you will not have to eat dull, bland, or boring foods in order to implement this program in your life.

Eating healthily does not have to be boring. In fact, on your journey to good health you will no doubt find many new and interesting foods that you otherwise would never have experienced. The key to healthy eating is really to be a bit daring and try new things. The key is to *try*. The basic guidelines for this program of eating are simple:

- Eat more protein than carbohydrates to keep your body in an anabolic state and your glycemic index as low as possible.

- Complex carbohydrates should be preferred over simple carbohydrates.

- All foods you choose should be compatible with your blood type.

- Decrease saturated fats. Use blood-type-appropriate monounsaturated and polyunsaturated fats instead.

- Drink plenty of water (alkaline).

- Eat a minimum of one large serving of dark leafy vegetables (such as kale, chard, collard greens, mustard greens, dandelion greens, or arugula) each day. The variety will depend upon your blood type requirements.

- Eat unprocessed foods whenever possible. Choose fresh foods.

- Eat organic foods whenever possible.

Protein, the Anabolic State, and the Glycemic Index

Every time you eat protein, the body produces glucagon and enters an anabolic state. This is the same state that happens when we abstain from excessive carbohydrates. Glucagon shifts the body into a burning mode. Proteins are converted to ketones, which are utilized for energy. Fat is released from the cells to be used as energy. The kidneys release excess water. Weight loss is the result.

Conversely, a catabolic state is when carbohydrates are converted to sugar in your body. The pancreas secretes insulin to keep the sugar levels in balance. The excess insulin places your body into a catabolic state. Catabolic state simply means that the insulin converts the protein into fats. These fats then are stored, resulting in excess weight. Another by-product of excess insulin production is the increase of cholesterol. The kidneys retain excess fluids, and glucose (sugar) is used as energy instead of fat. If our bodies are in a continual catabolic state, we subject ourselves to the risk of heart disease, high blood pressure, high cholesterol, and many other health problems.

There is a definite difference in which types of carbohydrates cause a catabolic state. Simple carbohydrates such as white bread, wheat bread, and rice cakes enter the bloodstream at a rapid rate. Foods such as these have a high glycemic index rating. Other complex carbohydrates such as cherries, apples, peanuts, soybeans, peaches, and rye bread enter the bloodstream much more slowly, thus resulting in a lower glycemic index rating. The slower the introduction into the bloodstream, the better. Please refer to the glycemic index chart to gain a better understanding of this principle.[1]

Bear in mind that when we talk about protein, we are referring to lean, good-quality animal protein, fish, tofu, tempeh, and some legumes. Whenever possible it is advisable to consume

Glycemic Index of Common Foods

6-1

Cereals	100+
Puffed rice, rice cakes, puffed wheat	133
Maltose	110
Glucose	100
White bread, whole-wheat bread	100
Carrots	92
Oat bran, rolled oats	88
Honey	87
White rice, brown rice, corn, bananas	82
All Bran, kidney beans	72
Raisins, macaroni, beets	64
Pinto beans, sucrose	59
Peas, potato chips, yams	51
Sweet potatoes, sponge cake	46
Oranges, navy beans, grapes, 100% rye bread	40
Nonfat yogurt	39
Tomato soup	38
Apples, chickpeas, ice cream, yogurt, milk	35
Lentils, peaches	29
Cherries, grapefruit, plums	25
Soybeans	15
Peanuts	12
Juice ratings:	
Peach, plum, cherry, grapefruit	Low
Pear, orange, apple, grape	Moderate
Banana	High

"organic" or "free-range" animal products. These animal products are free from antibiotics, bovine growth hormones, steroids, and other sundry chemical residues. While these products may cost slightly more, it is important to remember that the quality of the food you put into your body is just as important as the specific types. It is not my intention to endorse high-fat protein sources, which will cause untold troubles for all readers. Refer to your food lists for the specific protein sources of each blood type.

To purchase protein powder compatible with your blood type, or for more information on Body Genetics Protein Shake, the blood type–compatible protein drink mentioned throughout this book, see Appendix A.

Blood Typing

Your blood type can tell a lot about you. It is a great place to begin when you are trying to choose what to eat. There are a lot of diets on the market. However, none are specifically tailored to an individual's needs. Most are very generic. How many times have you had a friend who could eat certain foods and have no ill effects, but when you ate the same foods, you experienced bloating, weight gain, and other discomforts? We are not all alike. Knowing your blood type and the associated beneficial foods is one further step in being able to personalize a plan of eating.

The following food lists are intended to provide you with the benefits of prior research that indicates which foods tend to be best suited for each blood type. While these lists are not written in stone, they do provide the foundation for a blueprint of foods best suited for each blood type. However, because all individuals vary to some degree in body chemistry, your reaction to each food may vary. Only trial and error will tell you which foods are best for you.

It is important to take notice of adverse reactions to specific foods. Some ABs may not tolerate grape juice or sour cherries, which are very beneficial. Because of their body chemistry, these foods are too rich or are not tolerated well. Some may not tolerate tofu and wine at the same sitting. It may be necessary for some time to pass before they have a glass of wine.

Listen to your body. If what you are eating does not agree with you, *stop.* Your body has an instinctive mechanism and knows what its needs are and what it can tolerate. Remove any foods that you are having difficulty digesting immediately. There is no need to force your body to accept food that it instinctively rejects.

These food lists also do not account for the consumption of protein, fat, and carbohydrates as they relate to the body's secretion of glucagon and insulin. For that reason, the menus provided will help you with the balance to insure an anabolic state.

As you review the food lists, keep in mind that the beneficial foods tend to metabolize faster and easier because of blood enzymes. Conversely, avoid foods that do not digest or metabolize well and thus disrupt normal metabolism. It is for this reason I suggest that when you start this regimen you eat as many foods from the beneficial foods as possible, slowly adding neutral foods as you gravitate to your specific goal.[2]

Also, since you may be eating more protein than you are used to, you need to drink plenty of water. Water is the universal solvent that aids in digestion and waste removal. As a rule of thumb, divide your body weight by 2; then convert the pounds into ounces of water. This will give you the amount of water you should be drinking each day. Example: 150 pounds ÷ 2 = 75 ounces of water a day.[3]

BLOOD TYPE A

The foods most harmful to As in the long run are meat and dairy. The elimination of these two food groups will allow type A individuals the greatest potential to avoid heart disease and cancer. Tofu, soy products, unsalted redskin peanuts, red wine, and green tea are especially good for type As because they help fight cancer.[4] Type As typically have lost the ability to make pepsin, a protein-digesting enzyme. Therefore, a more vegetarian diet or one of less-dense protein products such as chicken, turkey, and Cornish hens is more easily digestible for As. Whole grains such as quinoa, millet, brown rice, and wild rice are preferable over wheat products due to an oversensitivity to such products.[5]

> Listen to your body. If what you are eating does not agree with you, *stop.*

BLOOD TYPE B

I encourage type B individuals to eliminate all wheat, corn, tomatoes, peanuts, and especially chicken from their diets. Chicken contains a dangerous lectin that may agglutinate the blood and can also lead to heart disease, cancer, diverticulitis, irritable bowel syndrome, spastic colon, and intestinal tract illnesses.[6] Blood type Bs share the diet of both types A and O, which means they can eat and happily digest a wide range of foods. Type Bs can tolerate dairy products in moderation. Fermented dairy products like yogurt, kefir, and cottage cheese would be the best for type Bs. Moderation is the key word for type Bs, who can handle a little bit of everything but should not go overboard on any single food.[7]

BLOOD TYPE AB

As the rarest blood type, AB is considered the modern blood type. ABs are very rare, making up less than 4 percent of the American population.[8] The single worst food for ABs is chicken. Chicken contains a dangerous lectin that may agglutinate (clot) the blood and may also lead to heart disease, cancer, and/or a host of other digestive and intestinal tract illnesses. Tofu, soy products, salted redskin peanuts, red wine, and green tea are especially good for type AB because they help fight cancer and heart disease.[9] Most dairy products can be tolerated in moderation.

BLOOD TYPE O

Type O appears to be the oldest blood type. Both dairy and grains should be eaten sparingly.[10] Many Os are lactose intolerant. Soy milk and soy cheeses are the easiest and most tasty ways of replacing those much-loved dairy products. Type Os have a greater predisposition to celiac/sprue disease, which is the inability to digest gluten. Therefore, try to stay away from the predominantly gluten-rich grains—wheat, rye, oats, and barley.[11] I also recommend that they eliminate most dairy, nuts, and grains, with the exceptions listed in the beneficial and neutral food lists. Type Os that eliminate the avoid dairy and grain products and stick to lean protein tend to have very low cholesterol levels and stay quite healthy.[12]

The Fat Issue

Saturated fats are primarily derived from animal sources and rarely from plants. One characteristic of animal saturated fats is that when stored at room temperature, they solidify. Examples would be meat, butter, and cheeses. The common store-bought plant saturated fats you might recognize are coconut oil, peanut oil, cottonseed oil, and palm kernel oil. There is a close association of cholesterol-related health issues with these types of fats, including potential obstruction of arteries, which could cause heart failure. Studies suggest that excessive saturated fat consumption is also linked to some forms of cancer.

Olive oil is the highest in mono-unsaturated fats available.

Monounsaturated and polyunsaturated oils do not promote the accumulation of cholesterol in the arteries as do the highly saturated fats. One of the best examples of these less destructive oils can be found in olive oil. Olive oil is the highest in monounsaturated fats available. In our "fat-crazed" society we tend to forget to differentiate saturated fats from monounsaturated and polyunsaturated fats. So enjoy that dressing you made with heart-friendly olive oil!

Green Leafy Vegetables

Dark leafy green vegetables such as kale, chard, collard greens, mustard greens, dandelion greens, and arugula are especially important to mention. These vegetables have a host of benefits for everyone. They improve digestion of fats and proteins and improve circulation. Mustard greens in particular aid in dissolving stagnant or congealed blood. Dark leafy greens are considered the "blood cleaners" of the vegetable kingdom. They provide much-needed chlorophyll, which inhibits viruses and colds. Vitamin A, vitamin C, and calcium are also part of the benefits. Some are rich in fiber as well. Women who are concerned about getting enough calcium should try eating an extra serving of these healthy greens.

Unprocessed, Fresh, and Organic Foods

Eating healthily can sometimes be daunting given the current advertising environment in this country. There are plenty of people touting that this product or that product is the best. But in the end, most fall short of being healthy or nutritious at all. We as Americans consume vast quantities of processed foods laden with sugar, fats, and highly processed wheat. Items touted as "fat-free" should be a warning signal to each of us. In order for a product to be tasty yet fat free, the manufacturer will boost the sugar content. Sucrose, which is the standard white table sugar, contributes to diabetes, hypoglycemia, and many other ailments. However, the point here is that there is nothing in these foods you really need. Products that are "fortified" or "enriched" are merely attempts to put back into the food that which has been processed out.

In my humble opinion, it's best to wipe the slate completely clean when it comes to processed foods.

In my humble opinion, it's best to wipe the slate completely clean when it comes to processed foods. All the vitamins, minerals, and nutrients you need can be found in the simplest, fresh produce. Again, the important factor is that you are making an investment in yourself. *You* are your most valuable asset. So the quality of what you put into your body is vitally important.

We covered organic and free-range animal products earlier. There are also organic vegetables, fruits, and virtually every other kind of produce you can imagine. For something to be organic, it has to be free of toxic chemical insecticides, fungicides, pesticides, and herbicides. There is a tremendous difference in taste between an organic carrot and one harvested by traditional methods. Just try it! But more important than the taste is the basic principle of not putting anything laden with chemicals into your body.

If organic products are not available in your area or are undesirable to you, the next best thing would be to buy from local farmers. Most cities host some phenomenal fresh markets. If you are unsure of where to find a fresh market, contact your local Department of Agriculture. Farmers boast both traditional and organic produce. By buying from the farmers direct, you are insuring that you are getting the freshest produce possible, thereby giving you the maximum amount of vitamins and minerals. Also, you are avoiding the extra chemicals and waxing that is used to preserve the produce in transit to large grocery stores.

If you prefer the convenience of ordering online, you can visit the following sites. They can provide you with a variety of dried goods from grains, pastas, and legumes to condiments.

- www.organicfruitsandnuts.com
- www.edenfoods.com
- www.kalustyans.com

You can also e-mail the following for information:

- rosebock@flex.net
- magedson@unicomp.net
- slanker@neto.com
- jmoseley@webwide.net

For chemical-free meat and grains, contact the following organizations: Organic Meats—Coleman Natural Products, Inc., 1767 Denver West Blvd., Suite 200m Golden, CO 80401, (800) 442-8666; Specialty Meat and Poultry—D'Artagnan, 280 Wilson Ave., Newark, NJ 07105, (800) 327-8246; Spelt Flour and Pastas—Purity Foods, 2871 W. Jolly Rd., Okemos, MI 48864, (517) 351-9231.

The 80/20 Approach

A few hard-core disciplined individuals may be able to handle a night-and-day dietary change. But the majority of people will find chipping away at the mountain of dietary change a better option to go by. This group of people may make six steps forward, but two steps backward every so often. They will reach the goal, but it won't be a perfect journey. So before you decide to make a 180-degree turn, trying to make all your dietary changes at one time, you might want to consider my 80/20 approach. It will allow you to enjoy the journey more.

Making dietary changes can be very difficult. All of us have made emotional associations with our food choices. We may have established an elaborate reward-and-punishment system: *If I'm good for three days, I can reward myself with that.* Or, *If I cheat once, I can't have that for a whole month or more.* Or you may be an emotional eater—not necessarily eating out of hunger but more as a coping skill for handling your emotions.

Physiological factors like sugar addiction may make it difficult for you. This is common and due to a constant overresponse of insulin, which robs the blood of its sugar, causing low blood sugar and promoting a craving for sweets. Generally, sugar addiction occurs from eating too many carbohydrates, particularly an overabundance of simple sugars that are not compatible to one's blood type.

Keep working until you can successfully choose and eat foods compatible to your blood type 80 percent of the time.

Sometimes making dietary changes is difficult simply because of poor eating habits—like late-night eating, skipping breakfast, or eating fast foods.

Whatever the reasons, there is a greater likelihood that you will be successful if you work your way up the path methodically. Keep working until you can successfully choose and eat foods compatible to your blood type 80 percent of the time. Choose the remaining 20 percent of your food selections for taste. Of course, I would prefer that all of us could make proper food choices 100 percent of the time, but we cannot do that—so relax.

Give yourself the benefit of the doubt. Don't place undue stress on yourself and potentially risk your long-term success. That is why I am suggesting my 80/20 approach to instinctive eating. It allows for a gradual adjustment and will feel more realistic. In this way you will make instinctive eating more adaptable to your permanent lifestyle. If you will follow this plan, before long you will find that the 20 percent has shrunk to 15 percent or less.

Putting It Into Action

We have gotten past all the "technical" information. So how do we put all this information to work? It's simple. I have tried to make this foolproof and easy. Just follow the steps below.

MEAL PLANNER

Make copies of the Meal Planner Chart located on page 132. The structure of your food plan is outlined below:

- Breakfast
- Snack
- Lunch
- Afternoon snack
- Dinner
- Evening snack
- Before bedtime—Body Genetics Protein Shake (See Appendix A.)

This may seem like a lot of food. However, eating good, healthy food at several sittings during the day helps to keep your metabolism revving at its maximum. Conversely, if you ate six times a day, consuming sugary, high-carbohydrate foods, you would no doubt gain weight and feel extremely sluggish.

BLOOD TYPE

Identify your blood type. (See Determining Your Blood Type on page 107.) Then go to the chapter pertaining to that type. There you will find the following information:

- Beneficial Foods Grocery List
- Neutral Foods Grocery List
- Avoid Foods List
- Sample meal plans for fourteen days

Note: All the breakfasts are listed together, as are all the lunches, dinners, and snacks.

BENEFICIAL AND NEUTRAL LISTS

Highlight all the foods you like or are familiar with from the beneficial and neutral lists. Seeing so many foods highlighted should give you the confidence that you can do this!

FILL IN PLANNER

Fill in your Meal Planner Chart with the meals that appeal to you in the menu section. You can mix and match the meals. The meals are not listed in any particular order. Breakfast #3 can peacefully coexist with lunch #13. Or you can create your own meals.

Since I am blood type O, I will show you an example of what my day's selection might look like. Some meals are picked from the meal outline section, and others are my own creation. Remember, you are not confined to the meals that we have suggested.

Give yourself the benefit of the doubt. Don't place undue stress on yourself and potentially risk your long-term success.

Sample Pick-a-Meal Daily Plan #1

6-2

DAY	Breakfast	Lunch	Dinner	Daily Record
1	**#9** Tex-Mex Omelet	**#5** Grilled Beef Cheeseburger	**#12** Roasted Pheasant	☑Body Type Exercises ☑Cardiovascular Training ☑Nutritional Supplements ☑Protein Drink
	Snack #1 Apple and Almond Butter	**Snack #5** Rice Cake	**Snack #11** Almond Bomb Smoothie	

If you skim through the menu section for each specific blood type, you will find several menus that closely resemble menus for other blood types. Perhaps only the fruit or the cheese components have been revised. Also, there are several meals that can be consumed by several of the blood types without any changes. This will aid you in your process of planning for your family.

Sample Pick-a-Meal Daily Plan #2

6-3

DAY	Breakfast	Lunch	Dinner	Daily Record
12	2 eggs 1 pc. Ezekiel bread	**#1** Chef's Salad #1	**#5** Steak Onions and Mushrooms Steamed Kale	☑Body Type Exercises ☑Cardiovascular Training ☑Nutritional Supplements ☑Protein Drink
	Snack #1 Apple and Almond Butter	**Snack #8** Trail Mix	**Snack #14** Very Berry Smoothie	

Tips for Making It Work

1. *Remove avoid foods.* I suggest removing the foods you love that may be on the avoid list from the household immediately. Donate them to charity or to a neighbor. They will be thankful for them.

2. *Plan ahead.* Try to fill in a week's worth of meal planning at first. From your meal plans you can create your shopping lists.

3. *Try something new.* Each week try to incorporate one or two new foods into your meal plans. For As, ABs, or Os, if you have never tried tofu or tempeh, give it a whirl. Or try a new dish from our recipe section. You might discover that you really enjoy foods that previously you would not have tried.

4. *Cook your own meals.* This will cut down on the frustration of having your food prepared with spices, condiments, or preservatives that may be undesirable for your blood type. Food you prepare yourself tastes better.

5. *Use healthy cooking methods.* Choose your preparation methods carefully to avoid excess saturated fats and undesirable ingredients. Desirable cooking methods include boiled, broiled, baked, steamed, sautéed (light on the oil), grilled, or poached. Undesirable cooking methods include fried, pan-seared, or BBQ (too much sauce).

6. *Rotate foods.* If you eat the same food every day, you are bound to get bored. I would suggest giving yourself a three- to five-day rotation of foods. For example, if you eat amaranth flakes for breakfast on Monday, try not to eat these same flakes until Thursday. There are a variety of other cereals or menu possibilities for you to choose from in the interim. Your taste buds will be happy, and so will your metabolism. If you eat the same foods over and over, your metabolism is not challenged; therefore, it slows down. By giving your body many different varieties of fuel (food), it constantly remains challenged and working hard for you.

7. *Exercise.* Discover your body type, and then follow the guidelines given in this book.

8. *Find a buddy.* Support is always helpful. You can coach each other through the program. You don't have to be the same blood type.

9. *Drink plenty of water.* Oftentimes we mistake our bodies' need for more water for hunger pains. Try drinking a small glass of water when you think you're hungry.

10. *Chew...chew...chew.* Eat slowly and chew your food very well. This will aid the digestion process.

11. *Put your fork down.* Put your fork down between bites. This will slow down your meal consumption time and enable you to actually allow your body to feel full.

12. *Remember that this program is a "lifestyle change."* It is not a diet. Diets are temporary. Lifestyle changes are a lifelong practice.

13. *Take it easy.* Be patient with yourself. Any new regimen will take some getting used to.

14. *Take time for yourself.* Do something you enjoy at least ONCE a week. Doing something good for yourself helps you to remember that you are alive and worth the investment of having better health, a fuller life, and a deeper commitment to yourself.

Dining Out Tips

1. *Have a game plan.* First and foremost know what the structure of your meal will look like *before* you go into a restaurant. We all have a tendency to glaze over when we see the glossy menus the waiter hands to us. For example, the components of your dinner should look like this:

   • Lean protein the size of your palm
   • 1 serving dark leafy green vegetables
   • 1 serving other vegetable
   • 1 serving carbohydrate (optional)

I usually will go to a restaurant that serves fish or steak. A meal out for me might consist of a tuna or beef steak, sautéed spinach, a side salad, or a side order of O-appropriate vegetables and wild rice.

2. *Ask questions; special requests are OK.* Ask your waiter what is in the dish you are considering if you are unsure. Most waiters are happy to provide such information. If you would like a change to the dish, within reason, do not hesitate to ask. Most establishments are used to accommodating their customers' special dietary needs.

3. *Remove bread from the table.* There is no need to tempt yourself.

4. *Place a glass of water in front of you.* Drink after you eat. It may seem difficult, but if you chew thoroughly, it will be a snap.

5. *Choose desserts carefully.* If your dessert craving kicks in, try to pick a fruit-based dessert. It is usually the safest. Poached pears or peaches are delicious. Otherwise, forgo the dessert in the restaurant and have something you have prepared yourself when you get home. This may be a good time to use the 80/20 rule.

6. *Enjoy your dinner companions.* Focus on the people you are with rather than the food. After all, part of a good meal out is the company.

The Assault on Body Fat

If one of your goals is to lose weight, then let me take this time to help you fully understand the difference between losing weight and losing body fat. When clients explain to me that one of their goals is to lose weight, I know exactly what they mean, or rather what they need. Since talking about losing body fat is sometimes too embarrassing or too revealing to most, it is easier just to say "weight" instead. If that makes you feel better, then fine, but don't miss what I am saying here. All of us, myself included, when talking about losing weight are actually referring to losing body fat, and that's a fact. So unless you or I have to weigh a certain weight on the scale, our weight means virtually nothing significant. It is the ratio between our body fat percentage and lean muscle weight that matters most. It always has been and always will be our body composition. So now that we have that hurdle behind us, let's move on.

The ratio between our body fat percentage and lean muscle weight matters most.

Excess body fat has to go for all the health reasons associated with carrying too much fat as well as for cosmetic reasons. As you begin experiencing the benefits from eating food compatible to your blood type, you will experience how they affect your bodily functions, performance, and health, plus influence your body composition. So rest assured that this approach to eating that is based on your blood type is accurate, individualized, balanced, and healthy. Now what I want to do is give you some insights into losing body fat so you can reach your potential sooner.

Your furnace for burning body fat is muscle tissue, so you want to be very certain that you do not lose muscle. The less muscle tissue you carry as part of your body composition, or the more muscle tissue you lose from dieting, the more difficult it will be to lose body fat. In fact, less muscle tissue diminishes your body's ability to burn or utilize fat by severely slowing down your metabolism or your body's ability to burn fat calories, creating a negative body composition. Since fat is burned inside your muscle and improper dieting can cause your body to lose muscle, then what you have done is sabotaged your fat-burning furnace by dieting. Your metabolism is key when it comes to burning calories, and yes, you must stimulate your metabolism so your body becomes a calorie burner, but let's look at a couple internal systems that must be considered or factored into the fat-burning formula also. The two systems I'm referring to that are necessary for consideration but are usually ignored are the endocrine (hormone) system and the digestive system.

For example, in the endocrine system the stimulation of IGF-1 (insulin growth factor), growth hormone, and glucagon allows your body to burn body fat at an alarming rate. These hormones cause your body's metabolism to go into an "anabolic state," or fat-burning mode. They recruit dietary fats (fats you eat) along with stored body fat to go to your muscle tissue to be converted for energy. You might want to consider these hormones as fat-burning hormones. Of course, they serve the body in other ways, but for our purpose they are key for "releasing the grease." Furthermore, by stimulating these hormones, your body will use fat for energy instead of its preferred source of fuel—carbohydrates. Without concerning yourself with every detail of how the endocrine system functions, let's concentrate on glucagon.

LEAN MUSCLE—YOUR BEST WEAPON

The way I suggest for you to wage war against that stubborn body fat is to create metabolic momentum. Metabolic momentum is simply getting your metabolism revved up and blazing like a fire in your fireplace. Your metabolism will become a blazing fire that will burn fat calories for energy, just as using wood as kindling in your fireplace causes the fire to blaze. Your body now becomes a calorie burner instead of a body that stores calories. To make this happen, there are two primary factors you must include in your strategy.

First, in order to stimulate the fat-burning process and elevate your metabolic rate, you must build muscle tissue—there's no getting around it. You have to exercise! Your program provided in this book is designed for your specific body type, and it will also provide the necessary stimulation for building lean muscle tissue. (Ladies, don't be afraid to gain muscle weight.) I'm not talking about bulging muscles but lean weight. Your program will promote an increase in your lean weight, which is where the furnace for burning body fat is located. When your body composition is such that you show an increase in muscle mass (see Chart 15-1, page 283), your body must utilize more calories. That means twenty-four hours a day. That means even when you are sleeping, sitting at your desk at work, or just driving your car. Because you have more muscle mass, your body will burn more calories more efficiently and constantly while you are inactive. Of course, as you increase your activity level, you burn more calories as well, so building lean muscle will give you the best of both worlds.

Second, by making dietary changes or adjustments in which you increase your protein intake, you cause a glucagon (fat-burning hormone) response. This again is referred to as an *anabolic state.* By placing more emphasis on protein and reducing your carbohydrates or sugar intake, you reduce the sugar, or glycogen storage, which then allows your "fire to rage." This fire takes place in the mitochondria, or power plant in the muscle tissue. The mitochondria is the fat-burning furnace in your muscles and is where fat is converted to energy for your body to use. If your intake of carbohydrates exceeds your protein intake, then the body creates an insulin response that suppresses your metabolism over time, the very thing you are trying to stimulate. Increasing your protein intake always influences your body to naturally increase glucagon production. This increase in glucagon production also influences other fat-burning hormones that contribute to burning fat. Therefore, eating meals and snacks that have a greater percent of protein are considered anabolic meals or snacks, and they will contribute to a leaner, healthier body. If you are physically active, your body requires more protein to meet its demands. If your goal is to lose those extra fat calories that are stored up in your body, then I suggest you make it a point to eat more protein.

Add a Protein Shake

As you make your meal and snack selections for your blood type, you should consider adding a protein shake or protein powder to your meals and snacks, or substitute a meal or snack with a protein shake or smoothie.

6-4

Protein and Exercise

Your body needs up to 5 percent more protein when you start to exercise regularly.

Recommended daily protein intake

Weight	Moderate exercise	Light exercise
110 lb.	60 grams	43 grams
135 lb.	72 grams	51 grams
154 lb.	84 grams	60 grams
176 lb.	96 grams	68 grams
198 lb.	108 grams	77 grams

Protein sources:
(Protein per 100 g serving)
- Roasted peanuts
  26 grams
- Tuna
  26 grams
- Beef (lean)
  24 grams

Muscles use proteins to grow and to repair damage

Smoothies are a great way to add variety and color to your meals. Add protein powder to your smoothies, and they can be used as part of your breakfast, a snack, or dessert. The only real preparation for smoothies is to keep freezer bags full of your favorite fruits on hand.

It is very important to have enough protein in your diet. Protein helps promote muscle tissue repair and strength, strengthens your immune system and heart, keeps blood sugar level (combats low blood sugar and hypoglycemia), creates protein synthesis, and stimulates a glucagon (fat-burning hormone) response, which you now know aids your body to burn fat calories more efficiently. Ultimately, your diet with ample protein will contribute to a leaner, healthier, fat-burning body. (See Chart 6-4 for information about how much protein you need.)

> Your diet with ample protein will contribute to a leaner, healthier, fat-burning body.

Add Nutritional Supplements

Your body is your superstructure, and the better condition you keep it in, the greater quality of life you will enjoy. When you eat correctly for blood type, your body will return to its naturally designed way of functioning. It will show improvements in performance and strengthen itself against disease and illness. By exercising regularly in concert with your diet, your body will undergo an increase in muscle and strength, improved circulation, and improved body composition. But sometimes our best intentions are hindered by our schedules and everyday demands, not allowing us the proper time for eating and exercising though we should do our best to prioritize. This is why it is important to supplement your body with nutrients that will help safeguard your health whether you are in the gym or not. But supplementing your body with blood-type specific nutrition is key. By simply including my Body Genetics A.M./P.M. daily multiple vitamin and mineral nutritional supplements and my Body Genetics Protein Shakes, you are ensuring your body of a very sound nutritional base. (See Appendix A, "Nutrition Support Ideas.")

Now you are ready to select your blood type options and begin. The next four chapters contain these specific eating plans.

Pick-a-Meal Planner

BLOOD TYPE: _____   **BODY TYPE:** _____

DAY	Breakfast	Lunch	Dinner	Daily Record
1				☐ Body Type Exercises ☐ Cardiovascular Training ☐ Nutritional Supplements
	Snack	Snack	Snack	☐ Protein Drink
2				☐ Body Type Exercises ☐ Cardiovascular Training ☐ Nutritional Supplements
	Snack	Snack	Snack	☐ Protein Drink
3				☐ Body Type Exercises ☐ Cardiovascular Training ☐ Nutritional Supplements
	Snack	Snack	Snack	☐ Protein Drink
4				☐ Body Type Exercises ☐ Cardiovascular Training ☐ Nutritional Supplements
	Snack	Snack	Snack	☐ Protein Drink
5				☐ Body Type Exercises ☐ Cardiovascular Training ☐ Nutritional Supplements
	Snack	Snack	Snack	☐ Protein Drink
6				☐ Body Type Exercises ☐ Cardiovascular Training ☐ Nutritional Supplements
	Snack	Snack	Snack	☐ Protein Drink
7				☐ Body Type Exercises ☐ Cardiovascular Training ☐ Nutritional Supplements
	Snack	Snack	Snack	☐ Protein Drink

NOTE: Add your chosen option number to the small boxes above for ready reference.
Write the name of each option in the space provided.

Chapter 7

Blood Type A

Blood Type A
Grocery List of Beneficial Foods

Meats—
All Anabolic
- [ ] None

Seafood— All
Anabolic
- [ ] Carp
- [ ] Cod
- [ ] Grouper
- [ ] Mackerel
- [ ] Monkfish
- [ ] Ocean salmon
- [ ] Pickerel
- [ ] Rainbow trout
- [ ] Snapper
- [ ] Sardine
- [ ] Sea trout
- [ ] Silver perch
- [ ] Snail
- [ ] Tilapia
- [ ] Whitefish
- [ ] Yellow perch

Beans/
Legumes
- [ ] Adzuki
- [ ] Black
- [ ] Black-eyed peas
- [ ] Green
- [ ] Lentils,
  domestic,
  green, red
- [ ] Pinto
- [ ] Soy, black, brown,
  green edamame*

Eggs/Dairy
- [ ] Soy cheese*
- [ ] Soy milk
- [ ] Body Genetics
  Protein Shake*

Nuts/Seeds
- [ ] Flaxseeds
- [ ] Organic peanut
  butter
- [ ] Pumpkin seeds
- [ ] Redskin peanuts,
  unsalted

Oils
- [ ] Linseed (flaxseed)
- [ ] Olive

Cereals
- [ ] Amaranth
- [ ] Kasha

Breads
- [ ] Millet bread
- [ ] Ezekiel bread
- [ ] Flour, rice,
  oat, rye
- [ ] Rice cakes
- [ ] Sprouted wheat

Pastas/
Grains
- [ ] Artichoke pasta
- [ ] Kasha
- [ ] Oat flour
- [ ] Rice flour
- [ ] Rice pasta
- [ ] Soba noodles
- [ ] Spelt noodles

Vegetables
- [ ] Alfalfa sprouts
- [ ] Artichokes
- [ ] Beet leaves
- [ ] Broccoli
- [ ] Broccoli sprouts
- [ ] Carrots
- [ ] Chicory
- [ ] Collard greens

- [ ] Dandelion greens
- [ ] Escarole
- [ ] Garlic
- [ ] Horseradish
- [ ] Kohlrabi
- [ ] Leek
- [ ] Okra
- [ ] Onions, red,
  Spanish, yellow
- [ ] Parsley
- [ ] Parsnips
- [ ] Pumpkin
- [ ] Romaine
  lettuce
- [ ] Spinach
- [ ] Swiss chard
- [ ] Tempeh*
- [ ] Tofu*
- [ ] Turnips

Fruit
- [ ] Apricot
- [ ] Blackberries
- [ ] Blueberries
- [ ] Boysenberries
- [ ] Cherries
- [ ] Cranberries
- [ ] Figs, dried, fresh
- [ ] Grapefruit
- [ ] Lemons
- [ ] Pineapple
- [ ] Plums, dark green,
  red
- [ ] Prunes
- [ ] Raisins

Juice
- [ ] Apricot
- [ ] Black cherry
- [ ] Carrot
- [ ] Celery
- [ ] Grapefruit
- [ ] Pineapple
- [ ] Prune

Spices/
Condiments
- [ ] Barley malt
- [ ] Blackstrap molas-
  ses
- [ ] Garlic
- [ ] Ginger
- [ ] Miso
- [ ] Mustard
- [ ] Shoyu
- [ ] Soy sauce
- [ ] Tamari

Beverages
- [ ] Coffee, regular,
  decaf
- [ ] Green tea
- [ ] Red wine
- [ ] Water, alkaline
- [ ] Water and lemon

Herbal Teas
- [ ] Alfalfa
- [ ] Aloe
- [ ] Burdock
- [ ] Chamomile
- [ ] Echinacea
- [ ] Fenugreek
- [ ] Ginger
- [ ] Ginseng
- [ ] Hawthorn
- [ ] Milk thistle
- [ ] Rose hips
- [ ] St. John's wort
- [ ] Slippery elm
- [ ] Strawberry leaf
- [ ] Valerian

*Anabolic (higher
in protein than
carbohydrates)*

Blood Type A
Grocery List of Neutral Foods

**Meats—
All Anabolic**
- [ ] Chicken
- [ ] Cornish hens
- [ ] Turkey

**Seafood—
All Anabolic**
- [ ] Abalone
- [ ] Mahimahi
- [ ] Ocean perch
- [ ] Pike
- [ ] Porgy
- [ ] Sailfish
- [ ] Sea bass
- [ ] Shark
- [ ] Smelt
- [ ] Sturgeon
- [ ] Swordfish
- [ ] Tuna, albacore
- [ ] Weakfish
- [ ] White perch
- [ ] Yellowtail

**Beans/
Legumes**
- [ ] Broad
- [ ] Cannellini
- [ ] Fava
- [ ] Jicama
- [ ] Peas, green, pod, snow
- [ ] Snap
- [ ] String
- [ ] White

Eggs/Dairy
- [ ] Eggs*
- [ ] Farmer's cheese*
- [ ] Feta cheese*
- [ ] Frozen yogurt, low fat
- [ ] Goat cheese*

- [ ] Mozzarella, low fat*
- [ ] Ricotta, low fat*
- [ ] String cheese*
- [ ] Goat milk
- [ ] Kefir
- [ ] Yogurt, low fat

Nuts/Seeds
- [ ] Almond butter*
- [ ] Chestnuts
- [ ] Filberts*
- [ ] Hickory*
- [ ] Litchi
- [ ] Pecans
- [ ] Pine (pignoli)
- [ ] Poppy seeds
- [ ] Sesame seeds
- [ ] Sunflower butter
- [ ] Sunflower seeds
- [ ] Tahini (sesame butter)
- [ ] Walnuts*

Oils
- [ ] Canola
- [ ] Cod liver

Cereals
- [ ] Barley
- [ ] Buckwheat
- [ ] Corn flakes
- [ ] Cream of Rice
- [ ] Kamut
- [ ] Oat bran
- [ ] Oatmeal
- [ ] Puffed millet
- [ ] Puffed rice
- [ ] Rice bran
- [ ] Spelt

Breads
- [ ] Brown rice
- [ ] Corn muffins
- [ ] Fin crisp
- [ ] Gluten-free bread
- [ ] Oat-bran muffins
- [ ] Oatmeal
- [ ] Rye bread, 100 percent
- [ ] Rye Crisps
- [ ] Rye Vita
- [ ] Spelt bread
- [ ] Wheat bagels

**Pastas/
Grains**
- [ ] Corn meal
- [ ] Flour, barley, bulgur, wheat, graham, spelt, sprouted wheat
- [ ] Quinoa
- [ ] Rice, basmati, brown, white, wild
- [ ] Spelt pasta

Vegetables
- [ ] Arugula
- [ ] Asparagus
- [ ] Avocado, Florida
- [ ] Bamboo shoots
- [ ] Beets
- [ ] Bok choy
- [ ] Brussels sprouts
- [ ] Caraway
- [ ] Cauliflower
- [ ] Celery
- [ ] Chervil
- [ ] Coriander (cilantro)
- [ ] Corn, white, yellow
- [ ] Cucumber
- [ ] Daikon
- [ ] Endive

- [ ] Fennel
- [ ] Ferns
- [ ] Green olives
- [ ] Green onions
- [ ] Kale
- [ ] Lettuce, Bibb, iceberg, mesculen
- [ ] Mushrooms, abalone, enoki, portobello, tree oyster, shiitake
- [ ] Mustard greens
- [ ] Raddichio
- [ ] Radishes
- [ ] Rappini
- [ ] Rutabaga
- [ ] Scallion
- [ ] Seaweed
- [ ] Shallots
- [ ] Sprouts, mung, radish
- [ ] Squash, all types
- [ ] Water chestnuts
- [ ] Watercress
- [ ] Zucchini

Fruits
- [ ] Apples
- [ ] Black currants
- [ ] Dates
- [ ] Elderberries
- [ ] Gooseberries
- [ ] Grapes, black, concord, green, red
- [ ] Guava
- [ ] Kiwifruit
- [ ] Kumquat
- [ ] Limes
- [ ] Loganberries
- [ ] Melon, casaba, canang, Christmas, crenshaw, musk, Spanish

- [ ] Nectarines
- [ ] Peaches
- [ ] Pears
- [ ] Persimmons
- [ ] Pomegranates
- [ ] Prickly pears
- [ ] Raspberries
- [ ] Starfruit
- [ ] Strawberries
- [ ] Watermelon

Juices
- [ ] Apple
- [ ] Apple cider
- [ ] Cranberry
- [ ] Cucumber
- [ ] Grape
- [ ] Vegetable

Blood Type

A

Blood Type A
Grocery List of Neutral Foods (cont'd.)

Beverages
- [ ] White wine

Herbal Teas
- [ ] Chickweed
- [ ] Colts foot
- [ ] Dandelion
- [ ] Dong quai
- [ ] Elder
- [ ] Gentian
- [ ] Goldenseal
- [ ] Hops
- [ ] Horehound
- [ ] Licorice root
- [ ] Linden
- [ ] Mulberry
- [ ] Mullein
- [ ] Parsley
- [ ] Peppermint
- [ ] Raspberry
- [ ] Raspberry leaf
- [ ] Sage
- [ ] Sarsaparilla
- [ ] Senna
- [ ] Shepherd's purse
- [ ] Skullcap
- [ ] Spearmint
- [ ] Strawberry leaf
- [ ] Thyme
- [ ] Vervain
- [ ] White birch
- [ ] White oak bark
- [ ] Yarrow

Spices/ Condiments
- [ ] Agar
- [ ] Allspice
- [ ] Almond extract
- [ ] Anise
- [ ] Arrowroot
- [ ] Basil
- [ ] Bay leaf
- [ ] Bergamot

- [ ] Brown rice syrup
- [ ] Brown sugar
- [ ] Cardamom
- [ ] Carob
- [ ] Chervil
- [ ] Chives
- [ ] Chocolate
- [ ] Cinnamon
- [ ] Clove
- [ ] Coriander (cilantro)
- [ ] Corn syrup
- [ ] Cornstarch
- [ ] Cream of tartar
- [ ] Cumin
- [ ] Curry
- [ ] Dill
- [ ] Dulse
- [ ] Honey
- [ ] Horseradish
- [ ] Jams/jelly, from appropriate fruit
- [ ] Kelp
- [ ] Maple syrup, pure
- [ ] Mint
- [ ] Mustard, dry
- [ ] Nutmeg
- [ ] Oregano
- [ ] Paprika
- [ ] Parsley
- [ ] Peppermint
- [ ] Pimiento
- [ ] Rice syrup
- [ ] Rosemary
- [ ] Saffron
- [ ] Sage
- [ ] Salt
- [ ] Savory
- [ ] Spearmint
- [ ] Stevia**
- [ ] Sucanat**
- [ ] Tamarind
- [ ] Tapioca
- [ ] Tarragon

- [ ] Thyme
- [ ] Turmeric
- [ ] Vanilla
- [ ] White sugar

* Anabolic (higher in protein than carbohydrate)
** Natural herbal sweetener

Beneficial, Neutral, and Avoid Foods lists have been adapted and expanded from the following sources: Peter J. D'Adamo, *Eat Right for Your Type* (New York: Putnam Publ. Group, 1997). Steven M. Weissberg and Joseph Christiano, *The Answer is in Your Bloodtype* (Lake Mary, FL: Personal Nutrition USA, 1999).

Blood Type A
List of Foods to Avoid

Meats
- Beef
- Buffalo
- Duck
- Goose
- Heart
- Lamb
- Liver
- Mutton
- Partridge
- Pheasant
- Pork, all
- Rabbit
- Veal
- Venison
- Quail

Seafood
- Anchovy
- Barracuda
- Bass, sea
- Beluga
- Bluefish
- Bluegill
- Catfish
- Caviar
- Clams
- Conch
- Crab
- Crayfish
- Eel
- Flounder
- Frog
- Gray sole
- Haddock
- Hake
- Halibut
- Herring, fresh, pickled
- Lobster
- Lox (smoked salmon)
- Mussels
- Octopus
- Oysters
- Scallops
- Shad
- Shrimp
- Sole
- Squid (calamari)
- Striped bass
- Tilefish
- Turtle

Beans/ Legumes
- Copper
- Garbanzo (chickpeas)
- Kidney
- Lima
- Navy
- Red
- Tamarind

Eggs/Dairy
- American cheese
- Blue cheese
- Brie
- Buttermilk
- Camembert
- Casein
- Cheddar
- Colby
- Cottage cheese
- Cream cheese
- Edam
- Emmenthal
- Gouda
- Gruyère
- Ice cream
- Jarlsberg
- Milk, skim, 2 percent, whole
- Monterey Jack
- Muenster
- Neufchâtel
- Parmesan
- Provolone
- Sherbet
- Sour cream, nonfat
- Swiss cheese
- Whey

Nuts/Seeds
- Brazil
- Cashews
- Pistachio

Oils
- Corn
- Cottonseed
- Peanut
- Safflower
- Sesame

Vegetables
- Cabbage, red, white, Chinese
- Eggplant
- Mushrooms, domestic
- Olives, black, Greek
- Peppers, red, yellow, green, jalapeño
- Potatoes, red, white, sweet
- Tomatoes
- Yams

Fruit
- Bananas
- Coconuts
- Mangoes
- Melons, cantaloupe, honeydew
- Oranges
- Papaya
- Plantains
- Rhubarb
- Tangerines

Cereals
- Cream of Wheat
- Familia
- Farina
- Granola
- Grape Nuts
- Wheat germ
- Shredded wheat
- Wheat bran

Breads
- Seven grain
- English muffins
- High-protein bread
- Pumpernickel
- Wheat-bran muffins
- Wheat matzos
- Whole-wheat bread

Pastas/ Grains
- Semolina pasta
- Spinach pasta
- White flour
- Whole-wheat flour

Spices/ Condiments
- Capers
- Gelatin
- Ketchup
- Mayonnaise
- Pepper, black, peppercorn, white, red pepper flakes
- Pickles, all kinds
- Relish, all kinds
- Tabasco sauce
- Vinegar, apple cider, balsamic, red, white
- Wintergreen
- Worcestershire sauce

Juice
- Orange
- Papaya
- Tomato

Beverages
- Beer
- Liquor
- Seltzer water
- Sodas

Herbal Teas
- Black tea, regular, decaf

Blood Type

Blood Type A
14-Day Pick-a-Meal Breakfast Options

HOT CEREAL*   1
- 4 oz. vegetable juice
- Medium bowl of oatmeal with soy milk
- ¼ chopped apple and raisins
- 4–5 chopped walnuts
- 1 piece brown rice bread with whole-fruit jam
- 10–12 oz. coffee or strawberry leaf tea

HOT CEREAL*   2
- 3 oz. black cherry juice
- Medium bowl of oatmeal made with soy milk
- Blackberries, blueberries, or raspberries
- 4–5 chopped filberts
- 1 piece Ezekiel bread with whole-fruit jam
- 10–12 oz. coffee or strawberry leaf tea

HOT CEREAL*   3
- 3 oz. prune juice
- Medium bowl of Kasha (hot) with soy milk
- 4–5 walnuts
- ½ chopped pear
- 1 piece sprouted wheat bread with almond butter
- 10–12 oz. coffee or green tea

PANCAKES*   4
- 2 medium spelt and walnut pancakes
- Blueberries, blackberries, or strawberries
- Pure maple syrup
- Side of ricotta cheese
- 10–12 oz. coffee or green tea

DRY CEREAL*   5
- 4 oz. pineapple chunks
- Medium bowl spelt flakes with soy milk
- 1 piece 100 percent rye bread with almond butter
- 10–12 oz. coffee or strawberry leaf tea

NUT BUTTER*   6
- ½ grapefruit or 4 oz. grapefruit juice
- 1 Ezekiel bagel
- Organic peanut butter and whole-fruit jam
- 10–12 oz. coffee or green tea

SMOOTHIE*   7
- Almond Bomb Smoothie (page 210)
- 1 piece Ezekiel or millet bread with whole-fruit jam
- 2 plums
- 10–12 oz. green tea or peppermint tea

SMOOTHIE*   8
- Vanilla Cherry Smoothie (page 211)
- 1 piece 100 percent rye or millet bread with whole-fruit jam
- 10–12 oz. coffee or green tea

EGGS*   9
- ½ grapefruit
- 2 poached eggs
- Steamed asparagus
- 1 piece rye toast with whole-fruit jam
- 10–12 oz. coffee or green tea

EGGS*   10
- 4 oz. vegetable juice
- *Cheese Omelet*
    2 scrambled eggs with scallions
    Soy cheese or goat cheese
- Corn muffin with whole-fruit jam
- 10–12 oz. coffee or green tea

* Anabolic (higher in protein than carbohydrates)

EGGS*   11

- *Salmon Scrambled Eggs*
    2 scrambled eggs
    Crumpled salmon pieces
    Alfalfa sprouts
- 2 sliced kiwifruit
- 1 piece Ezekiel or millet bread with
  whole-fruit jam
- 10–12 oz. green tea or chamomile tea

TOFU*   12

- *Spanish-Style Scrambled Tofu*
    2 squares firm tofu
    Chopped onion
    Pinch of cumin and oregano
- 1 slice soy cheese
- 1 piece 100 percent rye bread with
  whole-fruit jam
- 10–12 oz. coffee or green tea

CHEESE*   13

- 4 oz. apricot juice or 20–30 grapes
- Raw carrots, celery, zucchini
- 4 oz. farmer's or feta cheese
- Rye Crisps or Rye Vitas
- 10–12 oz. coffee or rose hip tea

CHEESE   14

- 1 apple or pear
- *Grilled Cheese*
    2 pieces sprouted wheat bread
    4 oz. farmer's cheese
- 10–12 oz. peppermint tea or green tea

Blood Type

A

Blood Type A
14-Day Pick-a-Meal Lunch Options

TOFU*   1

- *Stir-Fry Tofu*
  1 square tofu
  Broccoli, carrots, zucchini, asparagus, and bamboo shoots
- Shoyu, tamari, or soy sauce
- 10–12 oz. iced peppermint tea or green tea

TOFU*   2

- Miso soup
- 1 square grilled tofu
- Asparagus and carrots
- Side of brown rice
- 10–12 oz. ginger or green tea

TEMPEH*   3

- *Tempeh Open-Face Sandwich*
  Grilled or baked tempeh
  1 slice soy cheese
  Mushrooms and onions
  1 piece Ezekiel bread
- 10–12 oz. green tea or iced ginger tea

TEMPEH*   4

- *Tempeh in Cheeseless Basil Pesto*
  Grilled tempeh
  1 cup cooked spelt or artichoke pasta
  Cheeseless Basil Pesto (page 232)
- Small side salad
- 10–12 oz. iced peppermint tea or ginger tea

CHICKEN*   5

- 6–8 oz. roasted chicken
- Roasted parsnips and pumpkin
- Mixed greens with pimiento, cucumbers, and scallions
- Herb Mock Vinaigrette Dressing (page 234)
- 10–12 oz. soda water or green tea

SEAFOOD*   6

- 6–8 oz. snapper in lemon and dill
- Spinach or collard greens
- Side of parsnips
- 10–12 oz. green tea or Tazo Refresh Tea (peppermint, spearmint, and tarragon blend)

SEAFOOD*   7

- Italian Minestrone Soup (page 213)
- 6 oz. canned tuna or sockeye salmon
- Raw spinach and arugula
- Pumpkin seeds and alfalfa sprouts
- Creamy Avocado Dressing (page 233)
- 10–12 oz. iced green tea or ginger tea

SEAFOOD*   8

- Grilled grouper with lemon
- Watercress, fennel salad with sliced peaches or nectarines
- Raspberry Mock Vinaigrette Dressing (page 236)
- 10–12 oz. green tea or iced raspberry leaf tea

BEANS   9

- Lentil dahl
- Side of basmati rice
- Blanched asparagus
- 10–12 oz. green tea or iced peppermint tea

* *Anabolic (higher in protein than carbohydrates)*

SOUP AND SANDWICH   10
- Italian Minestrone Soup (page 213)
- *Tuna Sandwich*
  6 oz albacore tuna, celery, minced onions
  (use Creamy Garlic Dressing [page 234] as
  a mayonnaise substitute)
  2 pieces Ezekiel bread
  Lettuce
- 10–12 oz. green tea or spearmint tea

MIXED*   11
- *Chef's Salad*
  1 hard-boiled egg
  2 oz. turkey or chicken
  2 oz. soy cheese
  ¼ cup soy beans
  Raw spinach and arugula
- Creamy Garlic Dressing (page 234)
- 10–12 oz. green tea or iced peppermint tea

TURKEY*   12
- *Turkey Meatball Parmigianâ*
  2 turkey "meatballs" (100 percent turkey meat)
  1 slice mozzarella or soy cheese
- Raw spinach and arugula
- Cucumbers and alfalfa sprouts
- Herb Mock Vinaigrette Dressing (page 234)
- 10–12 oz. bottled water or green tea

TURKEY*   13
- *Mock Waldorf Salad*
  4 oz. sliced turkey
  4–5 chopped walnuts
  ½ chopped apple or pear
- Mesculen salad
- Herb Mock Vinaigrette Dressing (page 234)
- 10–12 oz. green tea or iced peppermint tea

TURKEY*   14
- *Thanksgiving Salad*
  6 oz. cubed turkey
  Appropriate lettuce and dandelion greens,
  red onion, cucumber, and alfalfa sprouts
- Warm Cranberry Dressing (page 237)
- 10–12 oz. alkaline water or green tea

Blood Type

A

Blood Type A
14-Day Pick-a-Meal Dinner Options

TOFU* 1
- Herbed Tofu (page 217)
- 2 oz. appropriate cheese
- Redskin peanuts or macadamia nuts
- Rye Vitas or Rye Crisps
- Small side salad with Miso Dressing (page 235, 236)
- 10–12 oz. ginger tea or iced peppermint tea

TEMPEH* 2
- Grilled marinated tempeh
- Sautéed collard greens, Swiss chard, and kale
- Side of brown rice or quinoa
- 10–12 oz. ginger tea or peppermint tea

CHEESE* 3
- 1 cup butternut, acorn, or other appropriate squash
- 3–4 oz. mozzarella cheese
- Steamed broccoli
- 3–4 oz. turkey chunks
- Small side salad with appropriate dressing
- 10–12 oz. green tea or seltzer water

SEAFOOD* 4
- Fish With Herbs and Lime (page 226)
- Side of broccoli and cauliflower
- Side of millet
- 10–12 oz. green tea or alkaline water

SEAFOOD* 5
- 8 oz. grilled grouper with lemon
- Steamed asparagus and carrots
- Side of quinoa
- 10–12 oz. green tea or alkaline water

SEAFOOD* 6
- 6–8 oz. grilled marinated fresh tuna steak
- 1–2 artichokes, steamed
- Small side salad with soy beans
- Miso Dressing (page 235, 236)
- 10–12 oz. green tea or glass of red wine

SEAFOOD* 7
- Broiled salmon with lemon, white wine, and tarragon
- Steamed broccoli
- Side of beets
- 10–12 oz. green tea or glass of white wine

TURKEY* 8
- Turkey burger
- 1 slice appropriate cheese
- Sliced Spanish onion and avocado
- Small side salad
- Creamy Garlic Dressing (page 234)
- 10–12 oz. alkaline water or iced peppermint tea

TURKEY* 9
- Roasted turkey
- Roasted carrots, parsnips, onions, and beets with rosemary
- Side of cranberries
- Chestnuts or pumpkin seeds
- 10–12 oz. green tea or alkaline water

CORNISH HEN* 10
- 6–8 oz. roasted or grilled Cornish hen
- Side of wild rice
- Small side salad with beets, broccoli, and fennel
- Red Onion Dressing (page 236)
- 10–12 oz. alkaline water or iced peppermint tea

* Anabolic (higher in protein than carbohydrates)

CHICKEN* 11

- 4–6 oz. stir-fry chicken
- Stir-fry appropriate vegetables
- Side of edamame
- Side of brown rice
- 10–12 oz. green tea or bottled water

CHICKEN* 12

- 6–8 oz. broiled chicken in lemon and white wine
- Brown rice and wild rice
  (half and half blend suggested)
- Steamed broccoli
- 10–12 oz. green tea or bottled water

CHICKEN* 13

- Lemon-ginger glazed chicken
- Basmati rice with almond slivers and currants
- Side of brussels sprouts
- 10–12 oz. green tea or ginger tea

BEANS 14

- *Sautéed Swiss Chard and Cannellini Beans*
  Swiss chard sautéed in vegetable stock and
  onions
  ¾ cup cannellini beans
- 1 cup cooked artichoke pasta
- 10–12 oz. green tea or spearmint tea

Blood Type A— Foods That Stimulate Weight Loss

- Vegetable oils—prevent water retention and aid digestion
- Soy foods—metabolize rapidly and aid digestion
- Vegetables—aid digestion and increase intestinal mobility
- Pineapple—increases calorie utilization and intestinal mobility

Blood Type A— Foods That Cause Weight Gain

- Meat—stores as fat, increases digestive toxins, and digests poorly
- Dairy foods—inhibit nutrient metabolism
- Kidney beans, lima beans—slow metabolic rate and interfere with digestive enzymes
- Wheat—overabundance impairs calorie utilization

Note: Inhibited insulin production causes hypoglycemia, a lowering of blood sugar after meals, and leads to less efficient metabolism of foods.

Blood Type

A

Blood Type A
14-Day Pick-a-Meal Snack Options

FRUIT   1
- Large apple with almond butter
- 10–12 oz. green tea

FRUIT*   2
- 1 apple
- 4–6 whole walnuts
- 10–12 oz. green tea or peppermint tea

GRAINS/NUTS   3
- Unsalted redskin peanuts
- 10–12 oz. ginger tea

GRAINS/NUTS*   4
- 4-6 walnuts
- 4-5 figs, dried or fresh
- 10–12 oz. green tea or peppermint tea

GRAINS/NUTS*   5
- Oat-bran muffin
- 1 peach
- 10–12 oz. green tea or chamomile tea

TRAIL MIX   6
- Apple "Pie" Trail Mix (page 238)
- 10–12 oz. green tea or peppermint tea

TRAIL MIX   7
- Peanut Chocolate Trail Mix (page 239)
- 10–12 oz. green tea or spearmint tea

DAIRY*   8
- 6 oz. low-fat yogurt
- 1 peach
- 10–12 oz. green tea or ginger tea

DAIRY*   9
- Fresh strawberries with low-fat yogurt
- 10–12 oz. green tea or chamomile tea

DAIRY*   10
- Fresh blueberries and raspberries with
  low-fat yogurt
- 10–12 oz. green tea or chamomile tea

SMOOTHIES*   11
- Almond Bomb Smoothie (page 210)
  or
- Apricot Cream Smoothie (page 210)

SMOOTHIES*   12
- Chocolate Raspberry Smoothie (page 210)

SMOOTHIES*   13
- Vanilla Cherry Smoothie (page 211)

SMOOTHIES*   14
- Cranberry Crush Smoothie (page 211)

Anabolic (higher in protein than carbohydrates)

Chapter 8

Blood Type B

Blood Type B
Grocery List of Beneficial Foods

Meats—
All Anabolic
- [ ] Lamb
- [ ] Mutton
- [ ] Rabbit
- [ ] Venison

Seafood—
All Anabolic
- [ ] Caviar
  (sturgeon eggs)
- [ ] Cod
- [ ] Grouper
- [ ] Haddock
- [ ] Hake
- [ ] Halibut
- [ ] Mackerel
- [ ] Mahimahi
- [ ] Monkfish
- [ ] Ocean perch
- [ ] Pickerel
- [ ] Pike
- [ ] Porgy
- [ ] Salmon, ocean
- [ ] Sardine
- [ ] Scallops
- [ ] Sea trout
- [ ] Shad
- [ ] Sole
- [ ] Sturgeon
- [ ] Tilapia

Beans/
Legumes
- [ ] Kidney
- [ ] Lima
- [ ] Navy
- [ ] Soy beans, black,
  brown, green
  edamame*

Eggs/Dairy
- [ ] Cottage
  cheese*
- [ ] Farmer's
  cheese*
- [ ] Feta
  cheese*
- [ ] Frozen yogurt
- [ ] Goat cheese*
- [ ] Goat milk
- [ ] Kefir
- [ ] Milk, skim or
  2 percent
- [ ] Mozzarella cheese,
  low fat*
- [ ] Ricotta cheese,
  low fat*
- [ ] Yogurt, low fat
- [ ] Body Genetics
  Protein Shake*

Nuts/Seeds
- [ ] Macadamia

Oils
- [ ] Olive

Cereals
- [ ] Millet
- [ ] Oat bran
- [ ] Oatmeal
- [ ] Puffed millet
- [ ] Puffed rice
- [ ] Rice bran
- [ ] Spelt flakes

Breads
- [ ] Brown rice bread
- [ ] Ezekiel bread
- [ ] Millet bread
- [ ] Oatmeal
- [ ] Rice cakes

Pastas/
Grains
- [ ] Flour, oat, rice
- [ ] Rice pasta
- [ ] Spelt pasta

Vegetables
- [ ] Avocado, Florida
- [ ] Beet leaves
- [ ] Beets
- [ ] Broccoli
- [ ] Brussels sprouts
- [ ] Cabbage, Chinese,
  red, white
- [ ] Carrots
- [ ] Cauliflower
- [ ] Collard greens
- [ ] Eggplant
- [ ] Kale
- [ ] Mushrooms, shii-
  take
- [ ] Mustard greens
- [ ] Parsley
- [ ] Parsnips
- [ ] Peppers, green,
  red, yellow,
  jalepeño
- [ ] Sweet potatoes
- [ ] Yams, all kinds

Fruit
- [ ] Bananas
- [ ] Cranberries
- [ ] Figs, dried, fresh
- [ ] Grapes, black, con-
  cord, green, red
- [ ] Kiwifruit
- [ ] Papaya
- [ ] Pineapple
- [ ] Plum, dark green,
  red

Juice
- [ ] Cabbage
- [ ] Cranberry
- [ ] Grape
- [ ] Papaya
- [ ] Pineapple

Spices/
Condiments
- [ ] Cayenne pepper
- [ ] Curry
- [ ] Ginger
- [ ] Horseradish
- [ ] Parsley

Beverages
- [ ] Green tea
- [ ] Water, alkaline

Herbal Teas
- [ ] Ginger
- [ ] Ginseng
- [ ] Licorice root
- [ ] Parsley
- [ ] Peppermint
- [ ] Raspberry leaf
- [ ] Rose hips
- [ ] Sage

*Anabolic (higher
in protein than
carbohydrates)*

Blood Type B
Grocery List of Neutral Foods

Meats— All Anabolic
- [ ] Beef
- [ ] Buffalo
- [ ] Ground beef
- [ ] Liver
- [ ] Pheasant
- [ ] Turkey
- [ ] Veal

Seafood— All Anabolic
- [ ] Abalone
- [ ] Bluefish
- [ ] Carp
- [ ] Catfish
- [ ] Herring
- [ ] Rainbow trout
- [ ] Red snapper
- [ ] Smelt
- [ ] Snapper
- [ ] Squid
- [ ] Swordfish
- [ ] Tilefish
- [ ] Tuna
- [ ] Whitefish
- [ ] White perch
- [ ] Yellow perch

Beans/ Legumes
- [ ] Broad
- [ ] Cannellini
- [ ] Copper
- [ ] Fava
- [ ] Green
- [ ] Jicama
- [ ] Northern
- [ ] Peas, green, pod, snow
- [ ] Red
- [ ] Snap
- [ ] String
- [ ] Tamarind
- [ ] White

Eggs/Dairy
- [ ] Eggs*
- [ ] Butter
- [ ] Buttermilk
- [ ] Brie*
- [ ] Camembert*
- [ ] Casein*
- [ ] Cheddar*
- [ ] Colby*
- [ ] Cream cheese*
- [ ] Edam*
- [ ] Emmenthal*
- [ ] Gouda*
- [ ] Gruyère*
- [ ] Jarlsberg*
- [ ] Monterey Jack*
- [ ] Muenster*
- [ ] Neufchâtel*
- [ ] Parmesan*
- [ ] Provolone*
- [ ] Soy cheese*
- [ ] Soy milk
- [ ] Swiss*
- [ ] Sherbet
- [ ] Whey*
- [ ] Whole milk

Nuts/Seeds
- [ ] Almond butter*
- [ ] Almonds*
- [ ] Brazil nuts*
- [ ] Chestnuts
- [ ] Hickory*
- [ ] Litchi
- [ ] Pine
- [ ] Pecans
- [ ] Walnuts

Oils
- [ ] Cod liver
- [ ] Linseed (flaxseed)

Cereals
- [ ] Cream of Rice
- [ ] Familia
- [ ] Farina
- [ ] Granola
- [ ] Grape Nuts
- [ ] Oat bran

Breads
- [ ] Gluten-free bread
- [ ] High-protein, no-wheat bread
- [ ] Oat-bran muffins
- [ ] Soy flour bread
- [ ] Spelt

Pastas/ Grains
- [ ] Flour, oat bran, graham, white
- [ ] Quinoa
- [ ] Rice, basmati, brown, white
- [ ] Semolina pasta
- [ ] Spinach pasta

Vegetables
- [ ] Alfalfa sprouts
- [ ] Arugula
- [ ] Asparagus
- [ ] Bok choy
- [ ] Celery
- [ ] Chicory
- [ ] Cucumber
- [ ] Dandelion greens
- [ ] Daikon radish
- [ ] Dill
- [ ] Endive
- [ ] Escarole
- [ ] Fennel

- [ ] Fiddlehead ferns
- [ ] Garlic
- [ ] Ginger
- [ ] Horseradish
- [ ] Kohlrabi
- [ ] Leek
- [ ] Lettuce, Bibb, Boston, iceberg, mesculen, romaine
- [ ] Mushrooms, abalone, domestic, enoki, portobello, tree oyster
- [ ] Okra
- [ ] Onions, green, red, Spanish, yellow
- [ ] Potatoes, red, white
- [ ] Radicchio
- [ ] Rappini
- [ ] Rutabaga
- [ ] Scallions
- [ ] Seaweed
- [ ] Shallots
- [ ] Spinach
- [ ] Squash, all types
- [ ] Turnips
- [ ] Water chestnuts
- [ ] Watercress
- [ ] Zucchini

Fruits
- [ ] Apples
- [ ] Apricots
- [ ] Blackberries
- [ ] Blueberries
- [ ] Boysenberries
- [ ] Cherries
- [ ] Currants, red, black
- [ ] Dates
- [ ] Elderberries
- [ ] Gooseberries
- [ ] Grapefruit
- [ ] Guava
- [ ] Kumquat

- [ ] Lemons
- [ ] Limes
- [ ] Loganberries
- [ ] Mangoes
- [ ] Melon, all types
- [ ] Nectarines
- [ ] Oranges
- [ ] Peaches
- [ ] Pears
- [ ] Prunes
- [ ] Raisins
- [ ] Raspberries
- [ ] Strawberries
- [ ] Tangerines

Juices
- [ ] Apple
- [ ] Apple cider
- [ ] Apricot
- [ ] Black cherry
- [ ] Carrot
- [ ] Celery
- [ ] Cucumber
- [ ] Grapefruit
- [ ] Orange
- [ ] Prune
- [ ] Vegetable

Blood Type

B

Blood Type B
Grocery List of Neutral Foods (cont'd.)

Beverages
- [ ] Black tea, regular, decaf
- [ ] Coffee, regular, decaf
- [ ] Red wine
- [ ] Water and lemon
- [ ] White wine

Herbal Teas
- [ ] Alfalfa
- [ ] Burdock
- [ ] Catnip
- [ ] Cayenne
- [ ] Chamomile
- [ ] Chickweed
- [ ] Dandelion
- [ ] Dong quai
- [ ] Echinacea
- [ ] Elder
- [ ] Hawthorn
- [ ] Horehound
- [ ] Mulberry
- [ ] St. John's wort
- [ ] Sarsaparilla
- [ ] Slippery elm
- [ ] Spearmint
- [ ] Strawberry leaf
- [ ] Thyme
- [ ] Valerian
- [ ] Vervain
- [ ] White birch
- [ ] White oak bark
- [ ] Yarrow
- [ ] Yellow dock

Spices/ Condiments
- [ ] Agar
- [ ] Allspice
- [ ] Anise
- [ ] Apple butter
- [ ] Arrowroot
- [ ] Basil
- [ ] Bay leaf
- [ ] Bergamot
- [ ] Brown rice syrup
- [ ] Brown sugar
- [ ] Caraway
- [ ] Cardamom
- [ ] Carob
- [ ] Chervil
- [ ] Chives
- [ ] Chocolate
- [ ] Clove
- [ ] Coriander (cilantro)
- [ ] Cream of tartar
- [ ] Cumin
- [ ] Dill
- [ ] Dulse
- [ ] Honey
- [ ] Jam/jelly, from appropriate fruit
- [ ] Kelp
- [ ] Maple syrup, pure
- [ ] Mayonnaise
- [ ] Mint
- [ ] Molasses
- [ ] Mustard
- [ ] Mustard, dry
- [ ] Nutmeg
- [ ] Oregano
- [ ] Paprika
- [ ] Pepper, red flakes
- [ ] Peppermint
- [ ] Pickles, dill, kosher, sweet, sour
- [ ] Pimiento
- [ ] Relish

- [ ] Rice syrup
- [ ] Rosemary
- [ ] Saffron
- [ ] Sage
- [ ] Salad dressing
- [ ] Salt
- [ ] Savory
- [ ] Spearmint
- [ ] Stevia**
- [ ] Sucanat**
- [ ] Tabasco sauce
- [ ] Tamarind
- [ ] Tarragon
- [ ] Thyme
- [ ] Turmeric
- [ ] Vanilla
- [ ] Vinegar, apple cider, balsamic, red, white
- [ ] White sugar
- [ ] Wintergreen
- [ ] Worcestershire sauce

* *Anabolic (higher in protein than carbohydrates)*
** *Natural sweetener*

Beneficial, Neutral, and Avoid Foods lists have been adapted and expanded from the following sources: Peter J. D'Adamo, *Eat Right for Your Type* (New York: Putnam Publ. Group, 1997). Steven M. Weissberg and Joseph Christiano, *The Answer is in Your Bloodtype* (Lake Mary, FL: Personal Nutrition USA, 1999).

Blood Type B
List of Foods to Avoid

Meats
- Chicken
- Cornish hens
- Duck
- Goose
- Heart
- Partridge
- Pork, all kinds
- Quail

Seafood
- Anchovy
- Barracuda
- Bass, sea
- Beluga
- Bluegill
- Clams
- Conch
- Crab
- Crayfish
- Eel
- Frog
- Lobster
- Lox (smoked salmon)
- Mussels
- Octopus
- Oysters
- Salmon, farm raised
- Shrimp
- Snail
- Striped bass
- Turtle
- Yellowtail

Beans/ Legumes
- Adzuki
- Black
- Black-eyed peas
- Garbanzo
- Lentils, domestic, green, red
- Pinto

Eggs/Dairy
- American cheese
- Blue cheese
- Ice cream
- String cheese

Nuts/Seeds
- Cashews
- Filberts
- Peanuts
- Peanut butter
- Pine (pignoli)
- Pistachio
- Poppy seeds
- Pumpkin seeds
- Sesame butter (tahini)
- Sesame seeds
- Sunflower butter
- Sunflower seeds

Oils
- Canola
- Corn
- Cottonseed
- Peanut
- Safflower
- Sesame
- Sunflower

Vegetables
- Artichokes, domestic, Jerusalem
- Avocados, California
- Corn, yellow, white
- Mung sprouts
- Olives, black, Greek, green, Spanish
- Pumpkin
- Radishes
- Tempeh
- Tofu
- Tomatoes

Fruit
- Coconut
- Persimmons
- Pomegranates
- Prickly pear
- Rhubarb
- Starfruit

Cereals
- Amaranth
- Barley
- Buckwheat
- Corn flakes
- Cream of Wheat
- Kamut
- Rye
- Seven grain
- Shredded wheat
- Wheat bran
- Wheat germ

Breads
- Corn muffins
- Durum wheat bread
- Fin Crisp
- Gluten flour bread
- Multigrain bread
- Pumpernickel bread
- Rye Crisp
- Rye Vita
- Seven grain
- Wheat bagels
- Wheat-bran muffins
- Whole wheat

Spices/ Condiments
- Allspice
- Almond extract
- Barley malt
- Cinnamon
- Cornstarch
- Corn syrup
- Gelatin, plain
- Ketchup
- Pepper, black, white, ground
- Tapioca

Juice
- Tomato

Beverages
- Liquor
- Seltzer water
- Sodas

Herbal Teas
- Aloe
- Coltsfoot
- Cornsilk
- Fenugreek
- Gentian
- Goldenseal
- Hops
- Linden
- Mullein
- Red clover
- Rhubarb
- Senna
- Shepherd's purse
- Skullcap

Pastas/ Grains
- Artichoke pasta
- Barley flour
- Buckwheat
- Bulgur wheat
- Cornmeal
- Couscous
- Durum wheat
- Gluten flour
- Kasha
- Rye
- Whole-wheat flour
- Wild rice

Blood Type

Blood Type B
14-Day Pick-a-Meal Breakfast Options

SMOOTHIE*　　　　　　　　　　1
- Blueberry Supreme Smoothie (page 210)
- 1 piece Ezekiel or millet bread with apple butter and almond butter
- 10–12 oz. coffee or peppermint tea

SMOOTHIE*　　　　　　　　　　2
- Ginger Apple Smoothie (page 211)
- 1 piece Ezekiel or millet bread
- 1 slice Swiss or provolone cheese
- 10–12 oz. coffee or green tea

SMOOTHIE*　　　　　　　　　　3
- Very Berry Smoothie (page 212)
- 1 piece Ezekiel or millet bread
- Cream cheese and whole-fruit jam
- 10–12 oz. coffee or peppermint tea

DRY CEREAL　　　　　　　　　　4
- 4 oz. prune juice
- Medium bowl of spelt flakes with skim milk
- Sliced kiwifruit and strawberries
- 1 piece spelt bread with almond butter and honey
- 10–12 oz. green tea or alkaline water

DRY CEREAL　　　　　　　　　　5
- 4 oz. carrot juice
- Medium bowl of granola
- Blueberries and almond slivers
- 1 piece Ezekiel bread with whole-fruit jam
- 10–12 oz. coffee or chamomile tea

HOT CEREAL　　　　　　　　　　6
- 3 oz. grape juice
- Medium bowl of oatmeal with appropriate milk
- Cherries, blueberries, or other appropriate fruit
- 4–5 chopped macadamia nuts
- 1 piece Ezekiel bread with whole-fruit jam
- 10–12 oz. coffee or raspberry leaf tea

HOT CEREAL*　　　　　　　　　　7
- 4 oz. grape juice
- Medium bowl of Cream of Rice with skim milk
- ½ Ezekiel bagel with whole-fruit jam and almond butter
- 10–12 oz. peppermint tea or green tea

NUT BUTTER*　　　　　　　　　　8
- ½ grapefruit or 4 oz. grapefruit juice
- 1 Ezekiel bagel
- Cream cheese and whole-fruit jam
- 10–12 oz. coffee or green tea

NUT BUTTER*　　　　　　　　　　9
- 4 oz. carrot, celery, cucumber juice
- 1 piece Ezekiel bread with pecan cream cheese and whole-fruit jam
- 2–3 plums
- 10–12 oz. coffee or alkaline water

EGGS*　　　　　　　　　　10
- 2 eggs, any style
- 2 slices turkey bacon (100 percent turkey)
- Papaya wedge
- 1 piece Ezekiel or millet bread with whole-fruit jam
- 10–12 oz. coffee or green tea

* Anabolic (higher in protein than carbohydrates)

EGGS*   11

- ½ grapefruit
- 2 poached eggs
- Steamed spinach or collard greens
- 1 piece brown rice bread with cream cheese
- 10–12 oz. coffee or green tea

EGGS*   12

- 4 oz. papaya juice
- *Scallion Shiitake Omelet*
    2 eggs, scrambled
    Shiitake mushrooms and scallions
- 1 piece Ezekiel or millet bread with apple butter
- 10–12 oz. coffee or green tea

CHEESE*   13

- 4 oz. ricotta or cottage cheese
- Kiwifruit, pineapple chunks, currants, and almond slivers
- 1 piece Ezekiel bread with whole-fruit jam
- 10–12 oz. Tazo Refresh Tea (spearmint, peppermint, and tarragon blend)

CHEESE*   14

- 4 oz. grapefruit juice or ½ grapefruit
- *Grilled Cheese*
    2 pieces spelt bread
    Mozzarella cheese
- Sliced cucumbers and Florida avocado
- 10–12 oz. Tazo Refresh Tea (spearmint, peppermint, and tarragon blend)

Blood Type

B

Blood Type B
14-Day Pick-a-Meal Lunch Options

MIXED*   1

- *Chef's Salad #1*
  - 1 hard-boiled egg
  - 2 oz. roast beef
  - 2 oz. farmers cheese
  - ¼ cup white beans
  - Sliced beets
  - Mesculen salad
- Honey Mustard Dressing (page 235)
- 10–12 oz. alkaline water or iced peppermint tea

MIXED*   2

- *Chef's Salad #2*
  - 2 oz. mozzarella cheese
  - 3–4 oz. lamb or beef
  - Grilled eggplant, zucchini, and portobello mushrooms
  - Mesculen salad
- Vinegarless Dressing (page 237)
- 10–12 oz. ginger tea or iced peppermint tea

BEEF*   3

- Grilled beef/cheeseburger
- Honey Mustard Dressing (page 235)
- Mixed green salad
- Artichoke hearts, jicama, and carrots
- 10–12 oz. iced ginger tea or green tea

BEEF*   4

- 2 peppers stuffed with ground beef (no tomato sauce)
- Mesculen salad with blanched asparagus, broccoli, radishes, and Brazil nuts
- Herb Mock Vinaigrette Dressing (page 234)
- 10–12 oz. green tea or ginseng tea

SOUP AND SANDWICH   5

- Medium bowl of Onion Soup (page 214)
- Meat loaf with 2 slices spelt bread
- 1 slice cheddar cheese, arugula, and cucumber
- 10–12 oz. alkaline water or iced peppermint tea

SOUP AND SANDWICH*   6

- White Bean and Escarole Soup (page 215)
- Broiled portobello mushroom with goat cheese
- Arugula
- 2 pieces spelt bread
- 10–12 oz. bottled water or iced ginger tea

BEANS*   7

- 4 oz. vegetable juice
- *Soy Beans and Pasta Salad*
  - 4 oz. soy beans
  - 1 cup cooked quinoa or spelt pasta (spirals or elbows)
  - Spanish onions, carrots, broccoli, and bell pepper
- Herb Mock Vinaigrette Dressing (page 234)
- 10–12 oz. alkaline water or iced peppermint tea

SEAFOOD*   8

- *Tuna and Spelt Pasta Salad*
  - 4 oz. canned tuna
  - 1 cup cooked spelt pasta (spirals or elbows)
  - Chopped broccoli, celery, scallions, and carrots
- Bed of mesculen salad
- Herb Mock Vinaigrette Dressing (page 234)
- 10–12 oz. iced ginger tea or green tea

* *Anabolic (higher in protein than carbohydrates)*

SEAFOOD*   9
- Grilled mahimahi or grouper with lemon
- Watercress, fennel salad with sliced peaches or nectarines
- Raspberry Mock Vinaigrette Dressing (page 236)
- 10–12 oz. green tea or Tazo Refresh Tea (spearmint, peppermint, and tarragon blend)

SEAFOOD*   10
- Cucumber soup, cold
- 4 oz. sockeye salmon
- Steamed or sautéed collard greens
- Side of cottage cheese
- 10–12 oz. iced green tea or ginger tea

LAMB*   11
- Grilled lamb chops with mint jelly
- Side of Swiss chard
- Side of brown rice with appropriate mushrooms
- 10–12 oz. soda water or glass of red wine

TURKEY*   12
- *Turkey Meatball Parmigiana*
    2 turkey "meatballs" (100 percent turkey meat)
    1 slice mozzarella or soy cheese
- Raw spinach and arugula
- Cucumbers and alfalfa sprouts
- Herb Mock Vinaigrette Dressing (page 234)
- 10–12 oz. bottled water or green tea

TURKEY*   13
- 6 oz. turkey burger
- 1 slice of nonfat mozzarella cheese
- Sliced Spanish onion and avocado
- Mixed green salad
- Honey Mustard Dressing (page 235)
- 10–12 oz. alkaline water or iced peppermint tea

TURKEY*   14
- *Stuffed Baked Potato*
    Baked sweet potato
    4 oz. turkey chunks
    Cheddar cheese
- Broccoli, steamed
- Small side salad
- Honey Mustard Dressing (page 235)
- 10–12 oz. green tea or seltzer

Blood Type

Blood Type B
14-Day Pick-a-Meal Dinner Options

VEAL* 1
- Sautéed veal cutlets in white wine, mushrooms, lemon, and parsley
- Steamed asparagus
- Mixed green salad with fennel, cucumbers, beets, and red onions
- Vinegarless Dressing (page 237)
- 10–12 oz. green tea or glass of white wine

LIVER* 2
- Liver and onions
- Mesculen salad with cucumbers, celery, avocado, beets, and ½ cup soybeans
- Raspberry Mock Vinaigrette Dressing (page 236)
- 10–12 oz. alkaline water or red wine

BEEF* 3
- 6–8 oz. flank steak or London broil
- Sautéed onions and mushrooms
- Steamed kale
- Small sweet potato with side of cottage cheese
- 10–12 oz. green tea or alkaline water

BEEF* 4
- *Marinated Beef Kabobs*
  Beef cubes, peppers, and onion
- Mixed greens with shredded cabbage, beets, mushrooms, and okra
- Side of quinoa
- 10–12 oz. Tazo Refresh Tea (spearmint, peppermint, and tarragon blend)

BEEF* 5
- Grilled beef cheeseburger (using appropriate cheese)
- Mixed green salad
- Honey Mustard Dressing (page 235)
- Artichoke hearts, carrots, and radish
- 10–12 oz. green tea or iced ginger tea

LAMB* 6
- Lamb chops
- Mesculen salad with mint leaves and steamed asparagus
- Oregano Feta Dressing (page 236)
- 10–12 oz. peppermint tea or glass of red wine

LAMB* 7
- 6 oz. roasted leg of lamb
- Roasted carrots, parsnips, onions, sweet potato, and beets with rosemary
- Side of white beans
- 10–12 oz. peppermint tea or glass of red wine

TURKEY* 8
- 6 oz. roasted turkey
- Roasted carrots, parsnips, onions, sweet potato, and beets with rosemary
- Side of cranberries
- Chestnuts
- 10–12 oz. green tea or alkaline water

TURKEY* 9
- Turkey burger
- Slice of appropriate cheese
- Sliced Spanish onion and avocado
- Small side salad
- Honey Mustard Dressing (page 235)
- 10–12 oz. Tazo Refresh Tea (spearmint, peppermint, and tarragon blend)

* Anabolic (higher in protein than carbohydrates)

RABBIT*   10

• 6 oz. grilled rabbit
• Roasted pumpkin or other squash
• Zucchini
• Side of fava beans with rosemary
• 10–12 oz. alkaline water or red wine

SEAFOOD*   11

• Sautéed scallops in garlic, olive oil, fish stock, or white wine and parsley
• Steamed broccoli and carrots
• Side of quinoa or brown rice
• 10–12 oz. green tea or lemon-lime water

SEAFOOD*   12

• 6–8 oz. salmon with lemon and dill
• Side of asparagus with almond slivers
• Side of basmati rice
• 10–12 oz. green tea or alkaline water

SEAFOOD*   13

• 6 oz. grilled marinated fresh tuna steak
• Sautéed bok choy and broccoli with soy sauce
• Small sweet potato with butter
• 10–12 oz. green tea or strawberry leaf tea

VENISON*   14

• 6–8 oz. venison steak
• Carrots, rutabagas, and sweet potato mixture, roasted or grilled
• Small side salad
• Herb Mock Vinaigrette Dressing (page 234)
• 10–12 oz. green tea

Blood Type B— Foods That Stimulate Weight Loss

• Green vegetables—aid metabolism
• Meat, liver—aid metabolism
• Eggs/low-fat dairy products—aid metabolism
• Licorice tea—counters hypoglycemia

Blood Type B— Foods That Cause Weight Gain

• Corn, lentils—hamper metabolic rate, inhibit insulin efficiency, and cause hypoglycemia
• Peanuts—hamper metabolic efficiency, cause hypoglycemia, and inhibit liver function
• Sesame seeds—hamper metabolic efficiency and cause hypoglycemia
• Buckwheat—inhibits digestion, causes hypoglycemia, and hampers metabolic efficiency
• Wheat—slows digestive and metabolic processes, causes foods to store as fat, and inhibits insulin efficiency

Note: Inhibited insulin production causes hypoglycemia, a lowering of blood sugar after meals, and leads to less efficient metabolism of foods.

Blood Type

B

Blood Type B
14-Day Pick-a-Meal Snack Options

VEGGIES/BEANS* **1**	**TRAIL MIX*** **9**

VEGGIES/BEANS*　　　　1
- Raw vegetables and string beans
- 1 slice appropriate cheese
- 10–12 oz. green tea or spearmint tea

FRUIT　　　　2
- 1 large apple with almond butter
- 10–12 oz. seltzer water

FRUIT*　　　　3
- 1 sliced peach with almond slivers, currants, and honey
- 10–12 oz. green tea

FRUIT*　　　　4
- Small bowl of raspberries and strawberries
- Glass of soy milk

GRAINS/NUTS*　　　　5
- 8–10 almonds
- 10–12 oz. soda water

GRAINS/NUTS　　　　6
- 1 piece Ezekiel bread with almond butter and whole-fruit jam
- 10–12 oz. soda water

GRAINS/NUTS　　　　7
- 2–3 Rye Vitas or Rye Crisps
- Goat or farmer's cheese
- 10–12 oz. green tea

GRAINS/NUTS　　　　8
- 4–6 walnuts
- 4–6 almonds
- 10–12 oz. green tea or coffee

TRAIL MIX*　　　　9
- Basic Trail Mix # 3 (page 239)
- 10–12 oz. green tea or peppermint tea

DAIRY*　　　　10
- 6 oz. low-fat fruit yogurt
- 1–2 Tbsp. granola or Grape Nuts
- 10–12 oz. green tea or ginger tea

DAIRY*　　　　11
- Fresh strawberries with low-fat yogurt
- 10–12 oz. green tea or coffee

DAIRY*　　　　12
- Fresh blueberries and raspberries with low-fat yogurt
- 10–12 oz. green tea or coffee

SMOOTHIES*　　　　13
- Banana Smoothie (page 210)
  or
- Blueberry Supreme Smoothie (page 210)

SMOOTHIES*　　　　14
- Tropical Smoothie (page 211)
  or
- Viennese Coffee Smoothie (page 212)

* Anabolic (higher in protein than carbohydrates)

Chapter 9

Blood Type AB

Blood Type
AB

Blood Type AB
Grocery List of Beneficial Foods

Meats—
All Anabolic
- [ ] Lamb
- [ ] Mutton
- [ ] Rabbit
- [ ] Turkey

Seafood—All
Anabolic
- [ ] Cod
- [ ] Grouper
- [ ] Hake
- [ ] Mackerel
- [ ] Mahimahi
- [ ] Monkfish
- [ ] Ocean perch
- [ ] Pickerel
- [ ] Pike
- [ ] Porgy
- [ ] Rainbow trout
- [ ] Ocean salmon
- [ ] Sailfish
- [ ] Sardine
- [ ] Sea trout
- [ ] Shad
- [ ] Snail
- [ ] Snapper
- [ ] Sturgeon
- [ ] Tilapia
- [ ] Tuna

Beans/
Legumes
- [ ] Lentils, green
- [ ] Navy
- [ ] Pinto
- [ ] Red
- [ ] Soy, brown, black, green edamame*

Eggs/Dairy
- [ ] Cottage cheese, nonfat*
- [ ] Farmer's cheese*
- [ ] Feta cheese*
- [ ] Goat cheese*
- [ ] Mozzarella*
- [ ] Ricotta cheese*
- [ ] Sour cream, nonfat*
- [ ] Yogurt
- [ ] Body Genetics Protein Shake*

Nuts/Seeds
- [ ] Chestnuts
- [ ] Flaxseeds
- [ ] Peanut butter, organic
- [ ] Redskin peanuts, unsalted*
- [ ] Walnuts*

Oils
- [ ] Olive

Cereals
- [ ] Oat bran
- [ ] Oatmeal
- [ ] Puffed rice
- [ ] Puffed millet
- [ ] Rice bran
- [ ] Spelt

Breads
- [ ] Brown rice bread
- [ ] Ezekiel bread
- [ ] Millet bread
- [ ] Rye bread, 100 percent
- [ ] Rye Vita
- [ ] Rye Crisps
- [ ] Sprouted wheat

Pastas/
Grains
- [ ] Millet
- [ ] Oat flour
- [ ] Rice pasta
- [ ] Rye flour, 100 percent
- [ ] Soy flour
- [ ] Spelt pasta

Vegetables
- [ ] Alfalfa sprouts
- [ ] Avocado, Florida
- [ ] Beet leaves
- [ ] Beets
- [ ] Broccoli
- [ ] Broccoli sprouts
- [ ] Cauliflower
- [ ] Celery
- [ ] Collard greens

- [ ] Cucumber
- [ ] Dandelion
- [ ] Eggplant
- [ ] Kale
- [ ] Mushrooms, maitake
- [ ] Mustard greens
- [ ] Parsley
- [ ] Parsnips
- [ ] Sweet potatoes
- [ ] Tempeh*
- [ ] Tofu*
- [ ] Yams, all kinds

Fruit
- [ ] Cherries
- [ ] Cranberries
- [ ] Figs, dried, fresh
- [ ] Gooseberries
- [ ] Grapefruit
- [ ] Grapes, black, concord, green, red
- [ ] Kiwifruit
- [ ] Lemon
- [ ] Loganberries
- [ ] Pineapple
- [ ] Plum, dark green, red

Juice
- [ ] Black cherry
- [ ] Cabbage
- [ ] Carrot
- [ ] Celery
- [ ] Cranberry
- [ ] Grape
- [ ] Papaya

Spices/
Condiments

- [ ] Curry
- [ ] Garlic
- [ ] Horseradish
- [ ] Miso
- [ ] Parsley

Beverages
- [ ] Coffee, regular, decaf
- [ ] Green tea
- [ ] Red wine
- [ ] Water, bottled, filtered

Herbal Teas
- [ ] Alfalfa
- [ ] Burdock
- [ ] Chamomile
- [ ] Echinacea
- [ ] Ginger
- [ ] Ginseng
- [ ] Hawthorn
- [ ] Licorice root
- [ ] Milk thistle
- [ ] Rose hips
- [ ] Strawberry leaf

Anabolic (higher in protein than carbohydrates)

Blood Type AB
Grocery List of Neutral Foods

Meats—
All Anabolic
- [ ] Liver
- [ ] Pheasant

Seafood—
All Anabolic
- [ ] Abalone
- [ ] Bluefish
- [ ] Carp
- [ ] Catfish
- [ ] Caviar
- [ ] Herring, fresh
- [ ] Mussels
- [ ] Scallops
- [ ] Shark
- [ ] Silver perch
- [ ] Smelt
- [ ] Sole
- [ ] Squid
- [ ] Swordfish
- [ ] Tilefish
- [ ] Weakfish
- [ ] White perch
- [ ] Yellow perch

Beans/
Legumes
- [ ] Broad
- [ ] Cannellini
- [ ] Copper
- [ ] Green
- [ ] Jicama
- [ ] Lentils,
    domestic, red
- [ ] Northern
- [ ] Peas, green, pod,
    snow
- [ ] Snap
- [ ] String
- [ ] Tamarind
- [ ] White

Eggs/Dairy
- [ ] Eggs*
- [ ] Casein cheese*
- [ ] Cheddar
    cheese*
- [ ] Colby cheese*
- [ ] Cream cheese*
- [ ] Edam*
- [ ] Emmenthal*
- [ ] Goat milk
- [ ] Gouda*
- [ ] Gruyère*
- [ ] Jarlsberg*
- [ ] Kefir
- [ ] Milk, skim,
    2 percent
- [ ] Monterey
    Jack*
- [ ] Muenster*
- [ ] Neufchâtel*
- [ ] Soy*
- [ ] String*
- [ ] Swiss*

Nuts/Seeds
- [ ] Almond butter*
- [ ] Almonds*
- [ ] Brazil nuts*
- [ ] Cashews
- [ ] Hickory*
- [ ] Litchi
- [ ] Macadamia
- [ ] Pine
- [ ] Pistachios

Oils
- [ ] Canola
- [ ] Cod liver

- [ ] Linseed (flaxseed)
- [ ] Peanut

Cereals
- [ ] Amaranth
- [ ] Barley
- [ ] Cream of Rice
- [ ] Cream of Wheat
- [ ] Familia
- [ ] Farina
- [ ] Granola
- [ ] Grape Nuts
- [ ] Seven grain
- [ ] Shredded wheat
- [ ] Soy flakes
- [ ] Wheat bran
- [ ] Wheat germ

Breads
- [ ] Durum wheat
- [ ] English muffin
- [ ] Gluten-free bread
- [ ] High-protein bread
- [ ] Multigrain bread
- [ ] Oat-bran muffin
- [ ] Pumpernickel
    bread
- [ ] Seven grain
- [ ] Spelt
- [ ] Wheat bagel
- [ ] Wheat bran
- [ ] Wheat-bran muffins
- [ ] Wheat germ
- [ ] Wheat matzos
- [ ] Whole wheat

Pastas/
Grains
- [ ] Brown rice
- [ ] Couscous
- [ ] Flour, barley, bul-
    gur wheat, durum
    wheat, gluten, gra-
    ham, spelt, whole
    wheat
- [ ] Quinoa
- [ ] Semolina pasta
- [ ] Spinach pasta

Vegetables
- [ ] Arugula
- [ ] Asparagus
- [ ] Bamboo shoots
- [ ] Bok choy
- [ ] Brussels sprouts
- [ ] Cabbage, Chinese,
    red, white
- [ ] Carrots
- [ ] Chicory
- [ ] Daikon
- [ ] Endive
- [ ] Escarole
- [ ] Fennel
- [ ] Fiddlehead ferns
- [ ] Kohlrabi
- [ ] Leek
- [ ] Lettuce, Bibb,
    Boston, iceberg,
    mesculen, romaine

- [ ] Mushrooms, aba-
    lone, domestic,
    enoki, portobello,
    shiitake, tree oyster
- [ ] Okra
- [ ] Olives, Greek,
    green, Spanish
- [ ] Onions, green, red,
    Spanish, yellow
- [ ] Potatoes, red, white
- [ ] Radicchio
- [ ] Rappini
- [ ] Rutabaga
- [ ] Scallions
- [ ] Seaweed
- [ ] Shallots
- [ ] Spinach
- [ ] Squash, all types
- [ ] Swiss chard
- [ ] Tomato
- [ ] Turnips
- [ ] Water chestnuts
- [ ] Watercress
- [ ] Zucchini

Blood Type
AB

Blood Type AB
Grocery List of Neutral Foods (cont'd.)

Fruits
- [ ] Apples
- [ ] Apricots
- [x] Blackberries
- [x] Blueberries
- [x] Boysenberries
- [ ] Currants, black, red
- [x] Dates
- [ ] Elderberries
- [ ] Kumquat
- [ ] Limes
- [x] Melon, all types
- [x] Nectarines
- [ ] Papaya
- [x] Peaches
- [ ] Pears
- [ ] Plantains
- [x] Prunes
- [x] Raisins
- [x] Raspberries
- [x] Strawberries
- [x] Tangerines
- [x] Watermelon

Juices
- [x] Apple
- [ ] Apple cider
- [ ] Apricot
- [ ] Cucumber
- [x] Grapefruit
- [ ] Pineapple
- [x] Prune
- [ ] Vegetable

Beverages
- [ ] Club soda
- [ ] Seltzer water
- [x] Water and lemon
- [ ] White wine

Herbal Teas
- [ ] Catnip
- [ ] Cayenne
- [ ] Chickweed
- [x] Dandelion
- [ ] Dong quai
- [ ] Elder
- [ ] Goldenseal
- [ ] Horehound
- [ ] Mulberry
- [ ] Parsley
- [x] Peppermint
- [ ] Raspberry leaf
- [ ] Sage
- [ ] St. John's wort
- [ ] Sarsaparilla
- [ ] Slippery elm
- [x] Spearmint
- [ ] Tarrow
- [ ] Thyme
- [ ] Valerian
- [ ] White birch
- [ ] White oak bark
- [ ] Yellow dock

Spices/Condiments
- [ ] Agar
- [ ] Arrowroot
- [x] Basil
- [x] Bay leaf
- [ ] Bergamot
- [ ] Brown rice syrup
- [x] Brown sugar
- [x] Caraway
- [ ] Cardamom
- [ ] Carob
- [ ] Chervil
- [x] Chives
- [ ] Chocolate
- [x] Cinnamon
- [x] Clove
- [x] Coriander (cilantro)
- [x] Cream of tartar
- [x] Cumin
- [x] Dill
- [ ] Dulse
- [x] Ginger
- [x] Honey
- [ ] Jam/jelly, from appropriate fruit
- [ ] Kelp
- [ ] Maple syrup
- [ ] Marjoram
- [ ] Mint
- [ ] Molasses
- [x] Mustard, dry
- [x] Nutmeg
- [x] Paprika
- [x] Peppermint
- [x] Pimiento
- [ ] Rice syrup
- [x] Rosemary
- [ ] Saffron
- [x] Sage
- [x] Salt
- [ ] Savory
- [ ] Shoyu
- [x] Soy sauce
- [x] Spearmint
- [x] Stevia**
- [ ] Sucanat**
- [x] Tamari
- [ ] Tamarind
- [ ] Tarragon
- [x] Thyme
- [x] Turmeric
- [x] Vanilla
- [x] Vinegar, apple cider, balsamic, red wine
- [x] White sugar
- [ ] Wintergreen

* *Anabolic (higher in protein than carbohydrates)*
** *Natural sweeteners*

Beneficial, Neutral, and Avoid Foods lists have been adapted and expanded from the following sources: Peter J. D'Adamo, *Eat Right for Your Type* (New York: Putnam Publ. Group, 1997); Steven M. Weissberg and Joseph Christiano, *The Answer is in Your Bloodtype* (Lake Mary, FL: Personal Nutrition USA, 1999).

Blood Type AB
List of Foods to (Avoid)

Meats
- Bacon
- Beef
- Buffalo
- Chicken
- Cornish hens
- Duck
- Goose
- Heart
- Partridge
- Pork, all kinds
- Veal
- Venison
- Quail

Seafood
- Anchovy
- Barracuda
- Bass, sea
- Beluga
- Bluegill
- Clam
- Conch
- Crab
- Crayfish
- Eel
- Flounder
- Frog
- Gray sole
- Haddock
- Halibut
- Pickled herring
- Lobster
- Lox
- Octopus
- Oysters
- Salmon, farm-raised
- Shrimp
- Striped bass
- Turtle
- Yellow tail

Beans/ Legumes
- Adzuki
- Black
- Black-eyed peas
- Fava
- Garbanzo
- Kidney
- Lima

Eggs/Dairy
- American cheese
- Blue cheese
- Brie
- Buttermilk
- Camembert
- Ice cream
- Milk, whole
- Parmesan
- Provolone
- Sherbet

Nuts/Seeds
- Filberts
- Poppy seeds
- Pumpkin seeds
- Sesame butter (tahini)
- Sesame seeds
- Sunflower seeds

Oils
- Corn
- Cottonseed
- Safflower
- Sesame
- Sunflower

Cereals
- Buckwheat
- Corn flakes
- Kamut

Breads
- Corn muffins

Pastas/ Grains
- Artichoke pasta
- Barley flour
- Buckwheat
- Corn meal
- Soba noodles

Vegetables
- Artichokes, domestic, Jerusalem
- Avocados, California
- Corn, white, yellow
- Olives, black
- Peppers, red, green, yellow, jalepeño
- Radishes
- Radish sprouts
- Mung sprouts

Fruit
- Bananas
- Coconuts
- Guava
- Mangoes
- Oranges
- Persimmons
- Pomegranates
- Prickly pear
- Rhubarb
- Starfruit (carambola)

Juice
- Any of the fruits and vegetables listed above

Spices/ Condiments
- Allspice
- Almond extract
- Anise
- Barley malt
- Capers
- Cayenne
- Cornstarch
- Corn syrup
- Ketchup
- Pepper, black, cayenne, red flakes, peppercorns, white
- Pickles, dill, kosher, sweet, sour
- Relish
- Tapioca
- Vinegar, white
- Worcestershire sauce

Beverages
- Black tea, regular, decaf
- Liquor
- Sodas

Herbal Teas
- Aloe
- Coltsfoot
- Cornsilk
- Fenugreek
- Gentian
- Hops
- Linden
- Mullein
- Red clover
- Rhubarb
- Senna
- Shepherd's purse
- Skullcap

Blood Type
AB

Blood Type AB
14-Day Pick-a-Meal Breakfast Options

YOGURT   1

- 6 oz. plain yogurt
- 4 figs or dates and walnuts as a topping
- 1 piece Ezekiel or millet bread with whole-fruit jam
- 10–12 oz. green tea or ginger tea

YOGURT   2

- 4 oz. pineapple chunks
- 6 oz. plain yogurt or kefir
- ¼ cup granola as a topping
- 1 piece Ezekiel or millet bread with whole-fruit jam
- 10–12 oz. chamomile tea or sage tea

HOT CEREAL   3

- 3 oz. grape juice
- Medium bowl of oatmeal made with soy milk
- Cherries, blueberries, or other appropriate fruit
- 4–5 chopped macadamia nuts
- 1 pc. Ezekiel bread with whole-fruit jam
- 10–12 oz. coffee or strawberry leaf tea

HOT CEREAL*   4

- 4 oz. apricot juice
- Medium bowl of Cream of Wheat with soy milk
- ½ Ezekiel bagel with whole-fruit jam and organic peanut butter or almond butter
- 10–12 oz. peppermint tea or green tea

PANCAKES   5

- ½ grapefruit
- 3 medium Oat Pancakes With Cranberries and Walnuts (page 207)
- Cranberries, blueberries, or raspberries
- Pure maple syrup or pure honey
- 10–12 oz. chamomile tea or green tea

DRY CEREAL   6

- 4 oz. vegetable juice
- Medium bowl of puffed millet or rice
- 8–10 cherries
- 1 piece brown rice bread with whole-fruit jam
- 10–12 oz. green tea or chamomile tea

DRY CEREAL   7

- 4 oz. cranberry juice
- Medium bowl of Fruit and Nut Granola (page 209)
- ½ cup of raspberries and blueberries
- 1 piece Ezekiel or millet bread with whole-fruit jam
- 10–12 oz. coffee or chamomile tea

NUT BUTTER*   8

- ½ grapefruit or 4 oz. grapefruit juice
- 1 Ezekiel bagel
- Organic peanut butter and whole-fruit jam
- 10–12 oz. coffee or green tea

SCRAMBLED TOFU*   9

- *Scrambled "Egg" Tofu*
  4 oz. tofu with turmeric and minced onions
- 20–30 grapes
- 1 piece brown rice bread with whole-fruit jam
- 10–12 oz. coffee or chamomile tea

EGGS*   10

- 4 oz. vegetable juice
- 2 eggs, poached, boiled, or scrambled
- 1–2 plums or 4–5 figs
- 1 piece Ezekiel or millet bread with whole-fruit jam
- 10–12 oz. coffee or chamomile tea

* Anabolic (higher in protein than carbohydrates)

EGGS*   11

- *Tex-Mex Omelet*
    2 scrambled eggs filled with 2 Tbsp. pinto beans
    1 slice cheddar cheese, sliced tomato, and
    cilantro
- Melon wedge
- 1 piece Ezekiel or millet bread with whole-fruit
  jam
- 10–12 oz. coffee or green tea

CHEESE*   12

- 4 oz. grapefruit juice or ½ grapefruit
- *Grilled Cheese*
    2 pc. seven-grain bread
    4 oz. mozzarella cheese
- Sliced tomato and alfalfa sprouts
- 10–12 oz. peppermint tea or green tea

SMOOTHIE*   13

- Chocolate Raspberry Smoothie (page 210)
- 1 piece Ezekiel or millet bread with almond butter and whole-fruit jam
- 10–12 oz. green tea or peppermint tea

SMOOTHIE*   14

- Cranberry Crush Smoothie (page 211)
- 1 piece 100 percent rye or millet bread with
  organic peanut butter and whole-fruit jam
- 10–12 oz. coffee or green tea

Blood Type

AB

Blood Type AB
14-Day Pick-a-Meal Lunch Options

TURKEY*   1
- 6 oz. turkey burger
- 1 slice mozzarella cheese
- Sliced Spanish onion and avocado
- Small side salad
- Creamy Garlic Dressing (page 234)
- 10–12 oz. alkaline water or iced peppermint tea

TURKEY*   2
- 4 oz. cranberry juice
- 6 oz. sliced turkey
- Small sweet potato
- Small side salad
- Red Onion Dressing (page 236)
- 10–12 oz. green tea or soda water

TURKEY*   3
- *Mock Waldorf Salad*
  - 4 oz. sliced turkey
  - 4–5 chopped walnuts
  - ½ chopped apple or pear
- Mesculen salad
- Herb Mock Vinaigrette Dressing (page 234)
- 10–12 oz. green tea or peppermint tea

CHEESE*   4
- *Antipasto*
  - 4 oz. sliced mozzarella cheese
  - Sliced tomato and fresh basil
- Small side salad
- Red Onion Dressing (page 236)
- 10–12 oz. seltzer or bottled water

CHEESE*   5
- Rye Vitas or Rye Crisps
- 1 kiwifruit and 20 grapes
- Small side salad
- Creamy Avocado Dressing (page 233)
- 10–12 oz. seltzer or green tea

TOFU*   6
- 1 square tofu, steamed
- Steamed broccoli, carrots, zucchini, and Swiss chard
- Miso Dressing (page 235, 236)
- 10–12 oz. seltzer or bottled water

TOFU*   7
- Miso soup
- 1 square grilled tofu
- Asparagus and carrots
- Side of white or brown rice
- 10–12 oz. seltzer or green tea

SEAFOOD*   8
- *Tuna and Spelt Pasta Salad*
  - 4 oz. canned tuna
  - 1 cup cooked spelt pasta (spirals or elbows)
  - Chopped broccoli, celery, scallions, and carrots
- Herb Mock Vinaigrette Dressing (page 234)
- Bed of chopped spinach
- 10–12 oz. green tea or spearmint tea

SEAFOOD*   9
- *Calamari (Squid) Salad*
  - 6 oz. unbreaded calamari sautéed in garlic and olive oil
  - Raw spinach and arugula
  - Tomato, celery, cucumber, and carrots
- 10–12 oz. club soda or chamomile tea

* Anabolic (higher in protein than carbohydrates)

SOUP AND SANDWICH 10
- Creamy Squash Bisque (page 213)
- *Grilled Cheese*
    4 oz. appropriate cheese
    2 pieces Ezekiel or millet bread
- Sliced tomato and alfalfa sprouts
- 10–12 oz. club soda or green tea

SOUP AND SANDWICH 11
- Italian Minestrone Soup (page 213)
- *Tuna Sandwich*
    6 oz. albacore tuna, celery, minced onions
    (use Creamy Garlic Dressing as
    mayonnaise substitute—page 234)
    2 pieces Ezekiel bread with lettuce and tomato
- 10–12 oz. green tea or spearmint tea

BEANS* 12
- 4 oz. vegetable juice
- *Pinto Bean and Pasta Salad*
    4 oz. pinto beans
    1 cup cooked rice pasta (spirals or elbows)
    Spanish onions, carrots, broccoli
- Herb Mock Vinaigrette Dressing (page 234)
- 10–12 oz. club soda or chamomile tea

MIXED* 13
- *Chef's Salad*
    1 hard-boiled egg
    2 oz. turkey
    2 oz. soy cheese
    ¼ cup soybeans
    Raw spinach and arugula
- Green Goddess Dressing (page 234)
- 10–12 oz. club soda or iced peppermint tea

LAMB* 14
- *Lamb Salad*
    6 oz. lamb
    Appropriate lettuce and arugula
    Tomato, cucumber, celery, and avocado
- Creamy Avocado Dressing (page 233)
- Side of white beans
- 10–12 oz. club soda or green tea

Blood Type AB— Foods That Stimulate Weight Loss

- Tofu—stimulates metabolic efficiency
- Seafood—promotes metabolic efficiency
- Dairy products—improve insulin productivity
- Green vegetables—improve metabolic efficiency

Blood Type AB— Foods That Cause Weight Gain

- Red meat—stores as fat, is poorly digested, and creates toxicity in the intestinal tract
- Kidney beans, lima beans—cause hypoglycemia, slow metabolic rate, and inhibit insulin efficiency
- Seeds—inhibit insulin efficiency
- Corn—causes hypoglycemia
- Buckwheat—decreases metabolism
- Wheat—decreases metabolism, is an inefficient use of calories, inhibits insulin efficiency

Note: Inhibited insulin production causes hypoglycemia, a lowering of blood sugar after meals, and leads to less efficient metabolism of foods.

Blood Type

Blood Type AB
14-Day Pick-a-Meal Dinner Options

SEAFOOD*   1
- Fish With Herbs and Lime (page 226)
- Side of broccoli and cauliflower
- Side of millet
- 10–12 oz. green tea or soda water

SEAFOOD*   2
- 8 oz. grilled mahimahi or grouper
- Steamed brussels sprouts and carrots
- Small baked sweet potato
- 10–12 oz. green tea or club soda

SEAFOOD*   3
- *Pan-Seared Salmon in Maple Glaze*
    8 oz. salmon
    ½ tsp. Garam Marsala spice
    1 Tbsp. pure maple syrup
- Steamed or grilled asparagus
- 10–12 oz. green tea or bottled water

SEAFOOD*   4
- *Steamed Mussels and Scallops*
    Mussels and scallops steamed in garlic,
    olive oil, fish stock, and parsley
- Broccoli
- Side of quinoa or couscous
- 10–12 oz. green tea or lemon/lime water

SEAFOOD*   5
- 4–6 oz. canned tuna with celery and onions (use
  Creamy Garlic Dressing as mayonnaise
  substitute—page 234)
- Small side salad
- Oregano-Feta Dressing (page 236)
- Side of couscous
- 10–12 oz. green tea or soda water

RABBIT*   6
- Grilled rabbit
- Roasted pumpkin or other squash
- Zucchini
- Side of appropriate beans with rosemary
- 10–12 oz. bottled water or glass of red wine

LIVER*   7
- Liver and onions
- Mesculen salad with cucumbers, tomatoes,
  celery, avocado, beets, and ½ cup soybeans
- Miso Dressing (page 235, 236)
- 10–12 oz. club soda or glass of red wine

LAMB*   8
- Roasted leg of lamb
- Roasted carrots, parsnips, onions, sweet potato,
  and beets with rosemary
- Side of nonfat cottage cheese
- 10–12 oz. peppermint tea or glass of red wine

TURKEY*   9
- 6 oz. roasted turkey
- Roasted carrots, parsnips, onions, sweet potato,
  and beets with rosemary
- Side of cranberries
- Chestnuts
- 10–12 oz. green tea or seltzer

TURKEY*   10
- Turkey burger
- Slice of appropriate cheese
- Sliced Spanish onion and avocado
- Small side salad
- Creamy Cilantro Lime Dressing (page 234)
- 10–12 oz. alkaline water or iced peppermint tea

CHEESE*   11

- *Stuffed Baked Potato*
    Broccoli, steamed
    Baked sweet potato
    3–4 oz. cheddar cheese
    3–4 oz. turkey chunks
- Small side salad
- Red Onion Dressing (page 236)
- 10–12 oz. green tea or seltzer

BEANS*   12

- Lentil soup
- Mesculen and mustard greens with grilled tofu,
  cucumbers, tomatoes, and alfalfa sprouts
- Oregano-Feta Dressing (page 236)
- 10–12 oz. seltzer or glass of red wine

TOFU*   13

- *Stir-Fry Tofu*
    2 squares tofu
    Broccoli, asparagus, and bamboo shoots
- Shoyu, tamari, or soy sauce
- 10–12 oz. seltzer or green tea

TEMPEH*   14

- *Open-Face Tempeh Sandwich*
    Grilled marinated tempeh
    Avocados, alfalfa sprouts, onions, and tomato
    1 piece Ezekiel or millet bread
- 1 apple or pear
- 10–12 oz. green tea or ginger tea

* Anabolic (higher in protein than carbohydrates)

Blood Type

AB

Blood Type AB
14-Day Pick-a-Meal Snack Options

VEGGIES/BEANS*   1
- Raw vegetables with Creamy Avocado Dressing (page 233); make dressing into a thick dip-like consistency
- 10–12 oz. green tea or spearmint tea

FRUIT   2
- 1 large apple with organic peanut butter
- 10–12 oz. seltzer water

FRUIT*   3
- 10–12 cherries or berries
- 10–12 oz. green tea

FRUIT   4
- Small bowl of raspberries and blueberries
- Glass of soy milk

GRAINS/NUTS*   5
- Unsalted redskin peanuts
- 10–12 oz. soda water

GRAINS/NUTS*   6
- 1 piece Ezekiel bread with almond butter or organic peanut butter and whole-fruit jam
- 10–12 oz. soda water

GRAINS/NUTS   7
- 2–3 Rye Vitas or Rye Crisps
- Goat or farmer's cheese
- 10–12 oz. green tea

GRAINS/NUTS   8
- Oat-bran muffin
- 1 peach
- 10–12 oz. green tea or coffee

TRAIL MIX*   9
- Basic Trail Mix #2 (page 238)
- 10–12 oz. green tea or peppermint tea

DAIRY   10
- 6 oz. low-fat yogurt
- 1 peach
- 10–12 oz. green tea or ginger tea

DAIRY   11
- 6 oz. low-fat kefir
- 1 peach
- 10–12 oz. green tea or ginger tea

DAIRY*   12
- ½ cup ricotta cheese with black currants and honey
- 10–12 oz. green tea

SMOOTHIES*   13
- Apricot Cream Smoothie (page 210)
  or
- Chocolate Raspberry Smoothie (page 210)
  or
- Cranberry Crush Smoothie (page 211)

SMOOTHIES*   14
- Vanilla Cherry Smoothie (page 211)
  or
- Very Berry Smoothie (page 212)
  or
- Viennese Coffee Smoothie (page 212)

* Anabolic (higher in protein than carbohydrates)

Chapter 10

Blood Type O

Blood Type

Blood Type O
Grocery List of Beneficial Foods

Meats—
All Anabolic
- [x] Beef
- [ ] Ground beef
- [ ] Buffalo
- [ ] Heart
- [ ] Lamb
- [ ] Liver
- [ ] Mutton
- [ ] Veal
- [ ] Venison

Seafood—
All Anabolic
- [ ] Bluefish
- [x] Cod
- [ ] Hake
- [ ] Halibut
- [ ] Fresh herring
- [ ] Mackerel
- [ ] Pike
- [ ] Rainbow trout
- [ ] Red snapper
- [x] Salmon
- [ ] Sardines
- [ ] Shad
- [ ] Snapper
- [ ] Sole
- [ ] Swordfish
- [ ] Tilapia
- [ ] Tilefish
- [x] White perch
- [ ] Whitefish
- [ ] Yellow perch
- [ ] Yellowtail

Beans/
Legumes
- [x] Adzuki
- [x] Black-eyed peas
- [x] Pinto beans

Eggs/Dairy
- [x] Mozzarella cheese, nonfat
- [x] Sour cream, nonfat
- [x] Body Genetics Protein Shake*

Nuts/Seeds
- [x] Flaxseeds
- [x] Macadamia nuts
- [x] Pumpkin seeds
- [x] Walnuts*

Oils
- [ ] Linseed (flaxseed)
- [x] Olive

Cereals
- [x] None

Breads
- [ ] Ezekiel bread
- [ ] Millet bread

Pastas/
Grains
- [x] None

Vegetables
- [ ] Artichokes, domestic and Jerusalem
- [ ] Avocado, Florida
- [ ] Beet leaves
- [x] Broccoli
- [ ] Broccoli sprouts
- [ ] Chicory
- [ ] Collard greens
- [ ] Dandelion
- [ ] Escarole
- [ ] Kale
- [ ] Kohlrabi
- [ ] Leek
- [ ] Okra
- [x] Onions, red, Spanish, yellow
- [ ] Parsnips
- [ ] Red peppers
- [x] Romaine lettuce
- [x] Sweet potatoes
- [x] Pumpkin
- [ ] Seaweed
- [x] Spinach
- [ ] Swiss chard
- [ ] Turnips

Fruit
- [ ] Figs, dried and fresh
- [x] Plums, dark, green, red
- [x] Prunes

Juice
- [ ] Black cherry
- [ ] Pineapple
- [x] Prune

Spices/
Condiments
- [ ] Carob
- [x] Cayenne pepper
- [x] Curry
- [ ] Dulse
- [x] Garlic
- [ ] Horseradish
- [ ] Kelp (bladder wrack)
- [x] Parsley
- [ ] Tabasco
- [x] Turmeric

Beverages
- [x] Green tea
- [ ] Seltzer water
- [ ] Soda water
- [ ] Water, alkaline

Herbal Teas
- [ ] Cayenne
- [ ] Chickweed
- [ ] Dandelion
- [ ] Fenugreek
- [ ] Ginger
- [ ] Hops
- [ ] Linden
- [ ] Milk thistle
- [ ] Mulberry
- [ ] Parsley
- [ ] Peppermint
- [ ] Rose hip
- [ ] Sarsaparilla
- [ ] Slippery elm

Anabolic (higher in protein than carbohydrates)

Blood Type O
Grocery List of Neutral Foods

Meats—
All Anabolic
- ☑ Chicken
- ☐ Cornish hens
- ☐ Duck
- ☐ Partridge
- ☐ Pheasant
- ☐ Quail
- ☐ Rabbit
- ☑ Turkey

Seafood—All
Anabolic
- ☐ Abalone
- ☐ Anchovy
- ☐ Beluga
- ☐ Bluegill bass, sea bass
- ☐ Carp
- ☐ Clam
- ☑ Crab
- ☐ Crayfish
- ☐ Frog
- ☐ Flounder
- ☐ Gray sole
- ☐ Grouper
- ☐ Haddock
- ☑ Lobster
- ☐ Mahimahi
- ☐ Mussels
- ☐ Oysters
- ☐ Oysters
- ☐ Salmon
- ☑ Shrimp
- ☑ Tuna

Beans/
Legumes
- ☐ Black
- ☐ Broad
- ☐ Cannellini
- ☐ Fava
- ☐ Garbanzo (chick-peas)

- ☐ Green
- ☐ Jicama
- ☐ Lima
- ☐ Northern
- ☐ Peas, green, snow, pod
- ☐ Red
- ☐ Soy, black, brown, green edamame*
- ☐ Snap
- ☐ String
- ☐ White

Eggs/Dairy
- ☐ Eggs*
- ☐ Butter
- ☐ Farmer's cheese*
- ☐ Feta cheese*
- ☐ Goat cheese*
- ☐ Mozzarella*
- ☐ Soy cheese*
- ☐ Soy milk*

Nuts/Seeds
- ☐ Almonds
- ☐ Almond butter*
- ☐ Chestnuts
- ☐ Filberts*
- ☐ Hickory*
- ☐ Pecan
- ☐ Pine (pignoli)
- ☐ Sesame seeds
- ☐ Sunflower butter
- ☐ Sunflower seeds
- ☐ Tahini (sesame butter)

Oils
- ☐ Canola
- ☐ Cod liver
- ☐ Sesame

Cereals
- ☐ Amaranth
- ☐ Barley
- ☐ Buckwheat
- ☐ Cream of Rice
- ☐ Kamut
- ☐ Kasha
- ☐ Oatmeal
- ☐ Rice bran
- ☐ Puffed rice
- ☐ Puffed millet
- ☐ Spelt flakes

Breads
- ☐ Brown rice bread
- ☐ Buckwheat
- ☐ Fin Crisp
- ☐ Gluten-free bread
- ☐ Millet
- ☐ Rice cake
- ☐ Rye bread, 100 percent
- ☐ Rye Crisp
- ☐ Rye Vita
- ☐ Soy flour bread
- ☐ Spelt bread

Pastas/
Grains
- ☐ Artichoke pasta
- ☐ Barley
- ☐ Buckwheat
- ☐ Kamut
- ☐ Kasha
- ☐ Millet
- ☐ Oatmeal
- ☐ Rice, basmati, brown, white, wild
- ☐ Rye flour
- ☐ Quinoa

Vegetables
- ☐ Arugula
- ☐ Asparagus
- ☐ Bamboo shoots
- ☐ Beets
- ☐ Bok choy
- ☐ Carrots
- ☐ Celery
- ☐ Cucumber
- ☐ Daikon
- ☐ Endive
- ☐ Fennel
- ☐ Fiddlehead ferns
- ☐ Green olives
- ☐ Green onions
- ☐ Lettuce, Bibb, Boston, iceberg, mesculen
- ☐ Mushrooms, enoki, portobello, tree oyster
- ☐ Peppers, green, jalepeño, yellow
- ☐ Radicchio
- ☐ Radishes
- ☐ Rappini
- ☐ Rutabaga
- ☐ Scallion
- ☐ Shallots
- ☐ Sprouts, mung, radish
- ☐ Squash, all types
- ☐ Tempeh*
- ☐ Tofu*
- ☐ Tomato
- ☐ Water chestnut
- ☐ Watercress
- ☐ Yams
- ☐ Zucchini

Fruits
- ☐ Apples
- ☐ Apricots
- ☐ Bananas
- ☐ Blueberries
- ☐ Boysenberries
- ☐ Cherries
- ☐ Cranberries
- ☐ Currants, black, red
- ☐ Dates
- ☐ Elderberries
- ☐ Gooseberries
- ☐ Grapefruit
- ☐ Grapes, black, concord, green, red
- ☐ Guava
- ☐ Kiwifruit
- ☐ Kumquat
- ☐ Lemons
- ☐ Limes
- ☐ Loganberries
- ☐ Mangoes
- ☐ Melons, casaba, Christmas, crenshaw, musk, Spanish
- ☐ Nectarines
- ☐ Papaya
- ☐ Peaches
- ☐ Pears
- ☐ Persimmons
- ☐ Pineapple
- ☐ Pomegranates
- ☐ Prickly pears
- ☐ Raisins
- ☐ Raspberries
- ☐ Starfruit

Blood Type

O

Blood Type O
Grocery List of Neutral Foods (cont'd.)

☐ Strawberries
☐ Watermelon

Juices
☐ Apricot
☐ Carrot
☐ Celery
☐ Cranberry
☐ Cucumber
☐ Grape
☐ Grapefruit
☐ Papaya
☐ Tomato
☐ Vegetable

Beverages
☐ Green tea
☐ Red wine
☐ Water and lemon
☐ White wine

Herbal Teas
☐ Catnip
☐ Chamomile
☐ Dong quai
☐ Elder
☐ Ginseng
☐ Hawthorn
☐ Horehound
☐ Licorice
☐ Mullein
☐ Raspberry leaf
☐ Sage
☐ Skullcap
☐ Spearmint
☐ Thyme
☐ Valerian
☐ Vervain
☐ White birch
☐ White oak bark

☐ Yarrow

Spices/ Condiments
☐ Agar
☐ Allspice
☐ Almond extract
☐ Anise
☐ Apple butter
☐ Arrowroot
☐ Barley malt
☐ Basil
☐ Bay leaf
☐ Bergamot
☐ Brown rice syrup
☐ Brown sugar
☐ Caraway
☐ Cardamom
☐ Chervil
☐ Chives
☐ Chocolate
☐ Coriander (cilantro)
☐ Cumin
☐ Dill
☐ Honey
☐ Jam/jelly from
   appropriate fruit
☐ Maple syrup,
   pure
☐ Marjoram
☐ Mayonnaise
☐ Mint
☐ Miso
☐ Molasses
☐ Mustard, dry
☐ Paprika
☐ Peppercorn
☐ Peppermint
☐ Pimiento

☐ Plain gelatin
☐ Red pepper flakes
☐ Rice syrup
☐ Rosemary
☐ Saffron
☐ Sage
☐ Salt
☐ Savory
☐ Shoyu
☐ Soy sauce
☐ Spearmint
☐ Stevia**
☐ Sucanat**
☐ Tamari
☐ Tamarind
☐ Tapioca
☐ Tarragon
☐ Thyme
☐ Vanilla
☐ White sugar
☐ Wintergreen
☐ Worcestershire
   sauce

* *Anabolic
  (higher in
  protein than
  carbohydrates)*
** *Natural
   sweetener*

Beneficial, Neutral, and Avoid Foods lists have been adapted
and expanded from the following sources: Peter J. D'Adamo,
Eat Right for Your Type (New York: Putnam Publ. Group, 1997).
Steven M. Weissberg and Joseph Christiano, *The Answer is in
Your Bloodtype* (Lake Mary, FL: Personal Nutrition USA, 1999).

Blood Type O
List of Foods to Avoid

Meats
- Goose
- Pork, all

Seafood
- Barracuda
- Catfish
- Caviar
- Conch
- Pickled herring
- Lox, smoked salmon
- Octopus

Beans/ Legumes
- Copper
- Kidney
- Lentils, green domestic, red
- Navy
- Tamarind

Nuts/Seeds
- Brazil nuts
- Cashews
- Litchi
- Peanuts
- Peanut butter
- Pistachios
- Poppy seeds

Oils
- Corn
- Cottonseed
- Peanut
- Safflower

Cereals
- Corn flakes
- Cream of Wheat
- Familia
- Farina
- Grape Nuts
- Oat bran
- Shredded wheat
- Wheat bran
- Wheat germ

Eggs/Dairy
- American cheese
- Blue cheese
- Brie
- Buttermilk
- Camembert
- Casein
- Cheddar
- Colby
- Cottage cheese
- Cream cheese
- Edam
- Emmenthal
- Goat milk
- Gouda
- Gruyère
- Ice cream
- Jarlsberg
- Kefir
- Milk, 2 percent, skim, whole
- Monterey Jack
- Muenster
- Parmesan
- Provolone
- Neufchâtel
- Ricotta
- String cheese
- Swiss cheese
- Whey
- Yogurt, all varieties

Breads
- Corn muffins
- English muffins
- High-protein bread
- Multigrain bread
- Oat-bran muffins
- Pumpernickel
- Seven-grain bread
- Wheat bagels
- Wheat-bran muffins
- Wheat matzos
- Whole-wheat bread

Vegetables
- Avocados, California
- Brussels sprouts
- Cabbage, Chinese, red, white
- Cauliflower
- Corn, white, yellow
- Eggplant
- Mushrooms, domestic, shiitake
- Mustard greens
- Olives, black
- Potatoes, red, white
- Alfalfa sprouts

Fruit
- Blackberries
- Cantaloupe
- Coconut
- Honeydew melon
- Oranges
- Plantains
- Rhubarb
- Tangerine

Juice
- Apple
- Apple cider
- Cabbage
- Orange

Pastas/ Grains
- Bulgur wheat flour
- Cornmeal
- Couscous flour
- Durum wheat flour
- Gluten flour
- Graham flour
- Oat flour
- Semolina and spin-ach pasta
- Soba noodles
- White flour
- Whole-wheat flour

Spices/ Condiments
- Capers
- Cinnamon
- Cornstarch
- Corn syrup
- Ketchup
- Nutmeg
- Pepper, black, white
- Peppercorn
- Pickles, dill, kosher, sweet, sour
- Relish
- Vinegar, apple, red, white, balsamic

Beverages
- Coffee
- Liquor
- Sodas

Herbal Teas
- Black tea, regular, decaf

Blood Type

Blood Type O
14-Day Pick-a-Meal Breakfast Options

SMOOTHIE*   1
- Almond Bomb Smoothie (page 210)
- 1 piece Ezekiel or millet bread with apple butter and tahini
- 10–12 oz. peppermint tea

SMOOTHIE*   2
- Chocolate Raspberry Smoothie (page 210)
- 1 piece 100 percent rye or millet bread with goat cheese
- 10–12 oz. green tea

DRY CEREAL*   3
- Medium bowl of amaranth and spelt flakes (half and half mix is recommended) with soy milk
- ½ mango
- 1 piece Ezekiel bread with almond butter
- 10–12 oz. chamomile tea

DRY CEREAL*   4
- 4 oz. grapefruit juice
- Medium bowl of Kamut Krisps with soy milk
- 1 piece millet bread
- 1 slice soy cheese
- 10–12 oz. chamomile tea

DRY CEREAL   5
- 4 oz. carrot juice
- Medium bowl of puffed millet with soy milk
- 8–10 cherries
- 1 piece millet bread with whole-fruit jam
- 10–12 oz. green tea

HOT CEREAL   6
- 4 oz. pineapple chunks
- Medium bowl of hot rice bran with soy milk
- 1 piece Ezekiel bread with farmer's cheese
- 10–12 oz. green tea

NUT BUTTER*   7
- 4 oz. carrot or tomato juice
- 2 pieces 100 percent rye or Ezekiel bread
- Tahini and honey
- 2 plums
- 10–12 oz. ginger tea

EGGS*   8
- 4 oz. tomato juice
- 2 eggs, poached, boiled, or scrambled
- 2 kiwifruit
- 1 piece Ezekiel or millet bread with whole-fruit jam
- 10–12 oz. chamomile tea

EGGS*   9
- *Tex-Mex Omelet*
     2 eggs, scrambled, filled with ¼ cup pinto beans
- ½ cup salsa
- Melon wedge
- 1 piece Ezekiel or millet bread with whole-fruit jam
- 10–12 oz. green tea

EGGS*   10
- *Curried Scrambled Eggs*
     2 scrambled eggs with ½ tsp. curry powder
- 1 slice nonfat mozzarella cheese
- Melon wedge and strawberries
- 1 piece Ezekiel or millet bread with whole-fruit jam
- 10–12 oz. green tea

Anabolic (higher in protein than carbohydrates)

EGGS* 11
- *Salmon Scrambled Eggs*
  2 scrambled eggs with crumbled salmon pieces
- 2 kiwifruit
- 1 piece Ezekiel or millet bread with whole-fruit jam
- 10–12 oz. chamomile tea

EGGS* 12
- 4 oz. apricot juice
- *Spanish Omelet*
  2 scrambled eggs with onions, mushrooms, and red peppers
- 1 piece Ezekiel bread with butter
- 10–12 oz. peppermint tea

EGGS 13
- 4 oz. grape juice
- *Spinach and Artichoke Omelet*
  2 scrambled eggs
  Leeks, spinach, 2–3 sliced artichoke hearts
- 1 piece Ezekiel bread with whole-fruit jam

CHEESE* 14
- 4 oz. grapefruit juice or 2 grapefruit
- *Grilled Cheese*
  2 pieces spelt bread
  4 oz. mozzarella cheese
- Sliced tomato and Florida avocado
- 10–12 oz. Tazo Refresh Tea (spearmint, pepper-mint, and tarragon blend)

Blood Type

Blood Type O
14-Day Pick-a-Meal Lunch Options

MIXED*   1

• *Chef's Salad #1*
  1 hard-boiled egg
  2 oz. roast beef
  2 oz. farmer's cheese
  ¼ cup pinto beans
  Mesculen salad with sliced beets
• Red Onion Dressing (page 236)
• 10–12 oz. club soda or iced peppermint tea

MIXED*   2

• *Chef's Salad #2*
  1 hard-boiled egg
  2 oz. turkey
  2 oz. soy cheese
  2 oz. roast beef
  Raw spinach and arugula with sliced fennel
• Green Goddess Dressing (page 234)
• 10–12 oz. club soda or iced peppermint tea

BEEF   3

• Medium bowl of beef chili (use pinto beans
  rather than kidney beans)
• Mixed green salad
• Tomato, cucumber, celery, and onions
• 10–12-oz. iced green tea or soda water

BEEF*   4

• *Antipasto*
  4 oz. sliced roast beef
  3 oz. sliced mozzarella cheese
  Sliced tomato, onions, fresh basil
  Roasted red peppers
  Bed of radicchio
• 10–12 oz. seltzer or bottled water

BEEF*   5

• Grilled beef cheeseburger (using appropriate
  cheese)
• Mixed green salad
• Creamy Garlic Dressing (page 234)
• Artichoke hearts, tomato, and radish
• 10–12 oz. iced ginger tea or green tea

BEEF*   6

• 6 oz. sliced roast beef
• Sautéed onions and mushrooms
• 1 slice mozzarella
• Steamed asparagus, broccoli, and carrots
• 10–12 oz. iced spearmint tea or green tea

TOFU*   7

• *Stir-Fry Tofu*
  1 square tofu
  Broccoli, carrots, zucchini, asparagus,
  bamboo shoots
  Shoyu, tamari, or soy sauce
• 10–12 oz. seltzer or green tea

SEAFOOD*   8

• *Tuna and Artichoke Salad*
  1 hard-boiled egg
  6 oz. canned tuna or sockeye salmon
  Artichoke hearts, tomato, onion, avocado
  Mesculen salad and arugula
• Herb Mock Vinaigrette Dressing (page 234)
• 10–12 oz. club soda or iced peppermint tea

* *Anabolic (higher in protein than carbohydrates)*

SEAFOOD*   9

- *Tuna and Spelt Pasta Salad*
    4 oz. canned tuna
    1 cup cooked spelt pasta (spirals or elbows)
    Chopped broccoli, celery, scallions, and
    carrots
    Bed of mesculen salad
- Herb Mock Vinaigrette Dressing (page 234)
- 10–12 oz. green tea or spearmint tea

LAMB*   10

- Grilled lamb chops
- Side of Swiss chard
- Side of brown and wild rice (half and half mixture suggested) with appropriate mushrooms
- 10–12 oz. club soda or glass of red wine

LAMB*   11

- *Lamb Salad*
    6 oz. lamb pieces
    Appropriate lettuce and dandelion greens
    Tomato, cucumber, celery, avocado
- Creamy Avocado Dressing (page 233)
- Side of white beans
- 10–12 oz. club soda or glass of red wine

CHICKEN*   12

- 6–8 oz. roasted chicken
- Roasted parsnips and pumpkin
- Mixed greens with peppers, tomato, okra, and
  scallions
- Creamy Garlic Dressing (page 234)
- 10–12 oz. soda water or green tea

TURKEY*   13

- *Turkey Salad*
    6 oz. cubed turkey
    Appropriate lettuce and dandelion greens
    Avocado, cucumber, beets, and feta cheese
- Warm Cranberry Dressing (page 237)
- 10–12 oz. club soda or peppermint tea

TURKEY*   14

- 6 oz. turkey burger
- 1 slice nonfat mozzarella cheese
- Sliced Spanish onion and avocado
- Mixed greens salad
- Creamy Garlic Dressing (page 234)
- 10–12 oz. alkaline water or iced peppermint tea

Blood Type

Blood Type O
14-Day Pick-a-Meal Dinner Options

SEAFOOD*   1
- Fish With Herbs and Lime (page 226)
- Side of broccoli
- Side of millet
- 10–12 oz. green tea or soda water

SEAFOOD*   2
- 8 oz. grilled mahimahi or grouper
- Steamed broccoli sprouts and carrots
- Small baked sweet potato
- 10–12 oz. green tea or club soda

SEAFOOD*   3
- *Pan-Seared Salmon in Maple Glaze*
    8 oz. salmon
    1 Tbsp. pure maple syrup
- Side of asparagus
- 10–12 oz. green tea or bottled water

SEAFOOD*   4
- 6–8 oz. grilled marinated fresh tuna steak
- Small sweet potato
- Small side salad with appropriate bean
- 10–12 oz. green tea or strawberry leaf tea

BEEF*   5
- 6–8 oz. steak
- Sautéed onions and mushrooms
- Steamed kale
- 10–12 oz. green tea or soda water

BEEF*   6
- *Beef Kabobs*
    Beef cubes, peppers, and onion
- Watercress salad with radish sprouts
- Miso Dressing (page 235, 236)
- Side of millet
- 10–12 oz. green tea or iced ginger tea

* Anabolic (higher in protein than carbohydrates)

LAMB*   7
- Lamb chops
- Mesculen salad with mint leaves, steamed aspara-
  gus, cherry tomatoes, and feta cheese
- Red Onion Dressing (page 236)
- 10–12 oz. peppermint tea or glass of red wine

LAMB*   8
- Roasted leg of lamb
- Roasted carrots, parsnips, onions, sweet potato,
  and beets with rosemary
- Side of white beans
- 10–12 oz. peppermint tea or glass of red wine

TURKEY*   9
- Roasted turkey
- Roasted carrots, parsnips, onions, sweet potato,
  and beets with rosemary
- Warm Cranberry Dressing (page 237)
- 10–12 oz. green tea or seltzer

TURKEY*   10
- Turkey burger
- 1 slice appropriate cheese
- Sliced Spanish onion and avocado
- Small side salad with Creamy Garlic Dressing
  (page 234)
- 10–12 oz. alkaline water or iced peppermint tea

CHICKEN*   11
- 6–8 oz. roasted chicken breast
- 2 steamed artichokes
- Side of carrots and zucchini
- 10–12 oz. green tea or soda water

PHEASANT*   12
- Roasted pheasant
- Baked sweet potato with nonfat sour cream
- Broccoli and cauliflower
- 10–12 oz. bottled water or green tea

VENISON*   13

- 6–8 oz. venison steak
- Carrots, rutabagas, and yam mixture, roasted or grilled
- Small side salad
- Herb Mock Vinaigrette Dressing (page 234)
- 10–12 oz. soda water or green tea

LIVER*   14

- Liver and onions
- Mesculen salad with cucumbers, tomatoes, celery, avocado, beets, and ½ cup of soybeans
- Herb Mock Vinaigrette Dressing (page 234)
- 10–12 oz. club soda or glass of red wine

Blood Type O— Foods That Stimulate Weight Loss

- Red meat—stimulates metabolism
- Broccoli, spinach, and kale—stimulate metabolism
- Seafood, kelp—contain iodine and stimulate thyroid hormone production
- Iodized salt—contains iodine and stimulates thyroid hormone production
- Liver—stimulates metabolism

Blood Type O— Foods That Cause Weight Gain

- Corn—slows the metabolism
- Cabbage, cauliflower, brussels sprouts—inhibit thyroid hormone
- Mustard greens—inhibit thyroid production
- Lentils—inhibit improper nutrient metabolism
- Navy beans, kidney beans—impair calorie utilization
- Wheat gluten—slows the metabolism

Note: Inhibited insulin production causes hypoglycemia, lowering of blood sugar after meals, and leads to less efficient metabolism of foods.

Blood Type

Blood Type O
14-Day Pick-a-Meal Snack Options

FRUIT   1
- 1 large apple with almond butter
- 10–12 oz. seltzer water

FRUIT*   2
- 10–12 cherries or berries
- 10–12 oz. green tea

FRUIT   3
- 1 apple
- 4–6 whole walnuts
- 10–12 oz. green tea or peppermint tea

GRAINS/NUTS*   4
- 8 almonds or walnuts
- 10–12 oz. soda water

GRAINS/NUTS*   5
- Rice cake with almond butter and honey
- 1 peach
- 10–12 oz. green tea or raspberry leaf tea

GRAINS/NUTS*   6
- 4–6 walnuts
- 4–5 figs, dried or fresh
- 10–12 oz. green tea or iced peppermint tea

GRAINS/NUTS*   7
- 8 almonds
- 1 peach
- 10–12 oz. green tea or spearmint tea

TRAIL MIX*   8
- Basic Trail Mix #1 (page 238)
- 10–12 oz. green tea or peppermint tea

TRAIL MIX*   9
- Basic Trail Mix #3 (page 239)
- 10–12 oz. green tea or peppermint tea

TRAIL MIX*   10
- Apple Walnut Trail Mix (page 238)
- 10–12 oz. green tea or ginger tea

SMOOTHIES*   11
- Almond Bomb Smoothie (page 210)

SMOOTHIES*   12
- Chocolate Raspberry Smoothie (page 210)
  or
- Cranberry Crush Smoothie (page 211)

SMOOTHIES*   13
- Maple Magic Smoothie (page 211)
  or
- Purple Passion Smoothie (page 211)

SMOOTHIES*   14
- Vanilla Cherry Smoothie (page 211)
  or
- Very Berry Smoothie (page 212)

* Anabolic (higher in protein than carbohydrates)

Chapter 11

Family Meal Planning

Many people have asked how to make this program work for their families. Many families are a combination of blood types. Families with different blood types *can* make this work. To aid in the process I have created new grocery lists for a few of the possible combinations—A and O families, B and O families, AB and O families. I cross-referenced which foods would be mutually beneficial between the two blood types. Those foods have been asterisked. Then I listed all the other foods that they had in common on their beneficial and neutral lists. As you can see, the grocery lists are full of a variety of foods. I have also provided a seven-day family plan for each "family" combination to give you a head start.

Use the 14-Day Pick-a-Meal Planner and the steps outlined earlier to guide you in feeding your multi–blood type family. The basic principles are the same.

Family Planning AB and O
Grocery List

Meats— All Anabolic

- [ ] Lamb #
- [ ] Liver
- [ ] Mutton #
- [ ] Pheasant
- [ ] Rabbit
- [ ] Turkey

Seafood— All Anabolic

- [ ] Abalone
- [ ] Bluefish
- [ ] Carp
- [ ] Cod #
- [ ] Fresh herring
- [ ] Grouper
- [ ] Hake #
- [ ] Mackerel #
- [ ] Mahimahi
- [ ] Mussels
- [ ] Pike #
- [ ] Rainbow trout #
- [ ] Salmon, ocean #
- [ ] Sardines #
- [ ] Sea trout
- [ ] Shad #
- [ ] Snapper #
- [ ] Sole
- [ ] Swordfish
- [ ] Tilefish
- [ ] Tuna
- [ ] White perch
- [ ] Yellow perch

Beans/ Legumes

- [ ] Broad
- [ ] Cannellini
- [ ] Green
- [ ] Jicama
- [ ] Northern
- [ ] Peas, green, pod, snow
- [ ] Pinto #
- [ ] Red
- [ ] Snap
- [ ] Soy, brown, black, green edamame*
- [ ] String
- [ ] White

Eggs/Dairy

- [ ] Eggs*
- [ ] Farmer's cheese*
- [ ] Feta cheese*
- [ ] Goat cheese*
- [ ] Mozzarella, nonfat*
- [ ] Soy cheese*
- [ ] Soy milk*
- [ ] Body Genetics Protein Shake*

Nuts/Seeds

- [ ] Almond butter*
- [ ] Almonds*
- [ ] Brazil nuts*
- [ ] Flaxseeds #
- [ ] Hickory*
- [ ] Macadamia nuts
- [ ] Pine (pignoli)
- [ ] Walnuts #

Oils

- [ ] Canola
- [ ] Cod liver
- [ ] Linseed (flaxseed)

Cereals

- [ ] Amaranth
- [ ] Barley
- [ ] Puffed millet
- [ ] Puffed rice
- [ ] Rice bran
- [ ] Spelt flakes

Breads

- [ ] Brown rice bread
- [ ] Ezekiel bread #
- [ ] Gluten-free bread
- [ ] Ideal flat bread
- [ ] Millet bread #
- [ ] Rye bread, 100 percent
- [ ] Rye Crisps
- [ ] Rye Vita
- [ ] Spelt bread
- [ ] Wasa bread

Pastas/ Grains

- [ ] Millet
- [ ] Quinoa
- [ ] Spelt flour
- [ ] Spelt pasta

Vegetables

- [ ] Arugula
- [ ] Asparagus
- [ ] Avocado, Florida #
- [ ] Bamboo shoots
- [ ] Beet leaves #
- [ ] Beets #
- [ ] Bok choy
- [ ] Broccoli #
- [ ] Broccoli sprouts #
- [ ] Carrots
- [ ] Celery
- [ ] Chicory
- [ ] Collard greens #
- [ ] Cucumbers #
- [ ] Daikon
- [ ] Dandelion greens #
- [ ] Endive
- [ ] Escarole
- [ ] Fennel
- [ ] Fiddlehead ferns
- [ ] Kale #
- [ ] Kohlrabi
- [ ] Leek
- [ ] Lettuce, Bibb, Boston, iceberg, mesculen, romaine
- [ ] Mushrooms, enoki, portobello, tree oyster
- [ ] Okra
- [ ] Onions, green, red, Spanish, yellow
- [ ] Parsley #
- [ ] Parsnips #
- [ ] Radicchio
- [ ] Rappini
- [ ] Rutabaga
- [ ] Scallions
- [ ] Shallots
- [ ] Spinach
- [ ] Squash, all types
- [ ] Sweet potatoes #
- [ ] Swiss chard
- [ ] Tempeh
- [ ] Tofu
- [ ] Tomato
- [ ] Turnips
- [ ] Water chestnuts
- [ ] Watercress
- [ ] Yams, all kinds
- [ ] Zucchini

Fruits

- [ ] Apples
- [ ] Apricots
- [ ] Blueberries
- [ ] Boysenberries
- [ ] Cherries
- [ ] Cranberries
- [ ] Currants, black, red
- [ ] Dates
- [ ] Elderberries
- [ ] Figs, dried or fresh #
- [ ] Gooseberries
- [ ] Grapefruit
- [ ] Grapes, black, concord, green, red
- [ ] Kiwifruit
- [ ] Kumquat
- [ ] Lemon
- [ ] Limes
- [ ] Loganberries
- [ ] Melon, all types
- [ ] Nectarines
- [ ] Papaya
- [ ] Peaches
- [ ] Pears
- [ ] Pineapple
- [ ] Plantains
- [ ] Plum, dark green, red
- [ ] Prunes
- [ ] Raspberries
- [ ] Strawberries
- [ ] Watermelon

Juices
- [ ] Apricot
- [ ] Black cherry #
- [ ] Carrot
- [ ] Celery
- [ ] Cranberry
- [ ] Cucumber
- [ ] Grape
- [ ] Grapefruit
- [ ] Papaya
- [ ] Pineapple
- [ ] Prune
- [ ] Vegetable

Beverages
- [ ] Red wine
- [ ] Seltzer water
- [ ] Water and lemon
- [ ] White wine

Herbal Teas
- [ ] Catnip
- [ ] Cayenne
- [ ] Chickweed
- [ ] Dandelion
- [ ] Dong quai
- [ ] Elder
- [ ] Horehound
- [ ] Mulberry
- [ ] Parsley
- [ ] Peppermint
- [ ] Sage
- [ ] Sarsaparilla
- [ ] Slippery elm
- [ ] Spearmint
- [ ] Thyme
- [ ] Valerian
- [ ] White birch
- [ ] White oak bark

Spices/ Condiments
- [ ] Agar
- [ ] Arrowroot
- [ ] Basil
- [ ] Bay leaf
- [ ] Bergamot
- [ ] Brown rice syrup
- [ ] Brown sugar
- [ ] Caraway
- [ ] Carob
- [ ] Chervil
- [ ] Chives
- [ ] Chocolate
- [ ] Coriander (cilantro)
- [ ] Cream of tartar
- [ ] Cumin
- [ ] Curry #
- [ ] Dill
- [ ] Dulse
- [ ] Garlic
- [ ] Ginger
- [ ] Honey
- [ ] Horseradish
- [ ] Jam/jelly, from appropriate fruit
- [ ] Kelp
- [ ] Maple syrup, pure
- [ ] Marjoram
- [ ] Mint
- [ ] Miso
- [ ] Molasses
- [ ] Paprika
- [ ] Parsley #
- [ ] Peppermint
- [ ] Pimiento
- [ ] Rice syrup
- [ ] Rosemary
- [ ] Saffron
- [ ] Sage
- [ ] Salt
- [ ] Savory
- [ ] Shoyu
- [ ] Soy sauce
- [ ] Spearmint
- [ ] Stevia**
- [ ] Sucanat**
- [ ] Tamari
- [ ] Tamarind
- [ ] Tarragon
- [ ] Thyme
- [ ] Turmeric
- [ ] Vanilla
- [ ] White sugar

*Anabolic (higher in protein than carbohydrates)
** Natural sweeteners
# Mutually beneficial foods

Blood Type
AB &O

Family Planning AB and O
7-Day Pick-a-Meal Menu Options

DAY 1

Breakfast:
- 4 oz. pineapple juice
- Medium bowl of amaranth flakes with soy milk
- Raspberries and crushed walnuts
- 1 piece Ezekiel bread with whole-fruit jam
- 10–12 oz. green tea

Lunch:
- *Antipasto*
    3–4 oz. mozzarella cheese
    Sliced tomato and fresh basil
    Sliced red onions
- Herb Mock Vinaigrette Dressing (page 234)
- 10–12 oz. green tea

Afternoon Snack:
- Side of edamame
- 10–12 oz. green tea

Dinner:
- 6–8 oz. Rosemary Roasted Lamb With Roasted Vegetables (page 222)
- Side of millet
- Small side salad with beets, broccoli, fennel, and tomato
- Miso Dressing (page 235, 236)
- 10–12 oz. green tea

Evening Snack:
- 1 Body Genetics Protein Shake or Thin Tastic Protein Bar

DAY 2

Breakfast:
- 4 oz. carrot juice
- Medium bowl of spelt flakes with soy milk
- Blueberries and raspberries
- 1 piece millet bread with 1 slice soy cheese
- 10–12 oz. green tea

Lunch:
- *Goat Cheese Salad*
    2 oz. goat cheese
    Lettuce, arugula, walnuts, and radishes
- Raspberry Mock Vinaigrette Dressing (page 236)
- 10–12 oz. green tea

Afternoon Snack:
- Very Berry Smoothie (page 212)

Dinner:
- Trout stuffed with appropriate herbs
- Side of broccoli or asparagus
- Side of millet
- 10–12 oz. green tea

Evening Snack:
- 1 Body Genetics Protein Shake or Thin Tastic Protein Bar

DAY 3

Breakfast:
• *Salmon Scrambled Eggs*
   2 scrambled eggs and crumbled salmon
   pieces
• 2 kiwifruit
• 1 piece spelt bread with whole-fruit jam
• 10–12 oz. green tea

Lunch:
• Onion Soup (page 214)
• *Grilled Cheese Sandwich*
   2–3 oz. farmer's cheese
   2 slices 100 percent rye bread
• Sliced Florida avocado and watercress
• Miso Dressing (page 235, 236)
• 10–12 oz. green tea

Afternoon Snack:
• Brazil nuts, almonds, walnuts (mixed)
• 10–12 oz. green tea

Dinner:
• 8 oz. grilled snapper
• Steamed asparagus and carrots
• Side of quinoa or millet
• 10–12 oz. green tea

Evening Snack:
• 1 Body Genetics Protein Shake or Thin
  Tastic Protein Bar

DAY 4

Breakfast:
• 4 oz. grapefruit juice
• Spinach and Mushroom Frittata (page 216)
• 1 piece 100 percent rye bread with goat
  cheese
• 10–12 oz. green tea

Lunch:
• Tomato Soup (page 214)
• *Tuna Sandwich*
   6 oz. tuna with minced onions and celery
   Lettuce and water chestnuts
   2 pieces 100 percent rye bread
• 10–12 oz. green tea

Afternoon Snack:
• Sliced pears and black currants
• 10–12 oz. green tea

Dinner:
• *Steamed Mussels Over Pasta*
   Mussels in garlic, olive oil, fish stock,
   and parsley
   Side of spelt pasta
• Side salad with appropriate beans
• Herb Mock Vinaigrette Dressing (page 234)
• 10–12 oz. green tea

Evening Snack:
• 1 Body Genetics Protein Shake or Thin
  Tastic Protein Bar

Blood Type
**AB
&O**

DAY 5

Breakfast:
• 4 oz. prune juice
• 2 soft-boiled eggs
• 1 piece spelt bread with almond butter and whole-fruit jam
• 10–12 oz. green tea

Lunch:
• 6–8 oz. turkey cubes
• Lettuce, dandelion greens, and ¼ cup cannellini beans
• Warm Cranberry Dressing (page 237)
• 10–12 oz. green tea

Afternoon Snack:
• Vanilla Cherry Smoothie (page 211)

Dinner:
• 6–8 oz. Marinated Tuna Steaks (page 226)
• Small sweet potato
• Small side salad
• Lemon-Lime Cilantro Dressing (page 235)
• 10–12 oz. green tea

Evening Snack:
• 1 Body Genetics Protein Shake or Thin Tastic Protein Bar

DAY 6

Breakfast:
• 4 oz. vegetable juice
• 2 oz. goat cheese, 1 thin slice ocean salmon (cooked or raw—not lox), sliced onions
• 2 pieces 100 percent rye bread
• 20 grapes
• 10–12 oz. green tea

Lunch:
• 6 oz. turkey burger
• 1 slice mozzarella cheese
• Sliced red onions and avocado
• Small side salad with Red Onion Dressing (page 236)
• 10–12 oz. green tea

Afternoon Snack:
• 6 whole walnuts and 2–3 apricots
• 10–12 oz. green tea

Dinner:
• 6–8 oz. roasted turkey
• Roasted carrots, beets, and onions with rosemary and olive oil
• Side of cranberries
• Small side salad
• Miso Dressing (page 235, 236)
• 10–12 oz. green tea

Evening Snack:
• 1 Body Genetics Protein Shake or Thin Tastic Protein Bar

DAY 7

Breakfast:
• Chocolate Raspberry Smoothie (page 210)
• 1 piece brown rice bread with almond butter
  and whole-fruit jam
• 10–12 oz. green tea

Lunch:
• Herbed Tofu (page 217)
• Rye Vitas or Rye Crisps
• Small side salad with Green Goddess
  Dressing (page 234)
• Wedge of cantaloupe
• 10–12 oz. green tea

Afternoon Snack:
• Small bowl of fresh cranberries and almond
  slivers
• Glass soy milk

Dinner:
• Tofu in Cilantro Sauce (page 218)
• Sautéed Swiss chard, collard greens, and
  kale
• Side of quinoa
• 10–12 oz. green tea

Evening Snack:
• 1 Body Genetics Protein Shake or Thin
  Tastic Protein Bar

Blood Type
**AB
&O**

Family Planning A and O Grocery List

Meats— All Anabolic
- [ ] Chicken
- [ ] Cornish hen
- [ ] Turkey

Seafood— All Anabolic
- [ ] Abalone
- [ ] Carp
- [ ] Cod #
- [ ] Grouper
- [ ] Mackerel #
- [ ] Mahimahi
- [ ] Pike
- [ ] Rainbow trout #
- [ ] Sardines #
- [ ] Snapper #
- [ ] Swordfish
- [ ] Tuna, albacore
- [ ] White perch
- [ ] Whitefish #
- [ ] Yellowtail

Beans & Legumes
- [ ] Adzuki #
- [ ] Black
- [ ] Black-eyed peas
- [ ] Broad
- [ ] Cannellini
- [ ] Fava
- [ ] Green
- [ ] Jicama
- [ ] Peas, green, pod, snow
- [ ] Pinto #
- [ ] Snap
- [ ] Soy, black, brown, green edamame*
- [ ] String
- [ ] White

Eggs/Dairy
- [ ] Eggs*
- [ ] Farmer's cheese*
- [ ] Feta cheese*
- [ ] Goat cheese*
- [ ] Mozzarella, low fat*
- [ ] Soy cheese*
- [ ] Soy milk*
- [ ] Body Genetics Protein Shake*

Nuts/Seeds
- [ ] Almond butter*
- [ ] Chestnuts
- [ ] Filberts*
- [ ] Flaxseeds
- [ ] Hickory*
- [ ] Pine (pignoli)
- [ ] Pumpkin seeds
- [ ] Sesame seeds
- [ ] Sunflower butter
- [ ] Sunflower seeds
- [ ] Tahini (sesame butter)
- [ ] Walnuts*

Oils
- [ ] Canola
- [ ] Cod liver
- [ ] Linseed (flaxseed)
- [ ] Olive

Cereals
- [ ] Amaranth
- [ ] Barley
- [ ] Buckwheat
- [ ] Cream of Rice
- [ ] Kamut
- [ ] Kasha
- [ ] Puffed millet
- [ ] Puffed rice
- [ ] Spelt flakes

Breads
- [ ] Brown rice
- [ ] Ezekiel bread
- [ ] Gluten-free bread
- [ ] Ideal flat bread
- [ ] Millet bread
- [ ] Rice cakes
- [ ] Rye Crisp
- [ ] Rye bread, 100 percent
- [ ] Rye Vita
- [ ] Spelt bread
- [ ] Wasa bread

Pastas/ Grains
- [ ] Artichoke pasta
- [ ] Quinoa
- [ ] Rice, basmati, brown, white, wild
- [ ] Rice flour
- [ ] Rice pasta
- [ ] Rye flour
- [ ] Spelt flour
- [ ] Spelt pasta

Vegetables
- [ ] Artichokes #
- [ ] Arugula
- [ ] Asparagus
- [ ] Avocado, Florida
- [ ] Beet leaves #
- [ ] Beets
- [ ] Bok choy
- [ ] Broccoli #
- [ ] Broccoli sprouts #
- [ ] Carrots
- [ ] Celery
- [ ] Chicory #
- [ ] Collard greens #
- [ ] Cucumber
- [ ] Daikon

- [ ] Dandelion greens #
- [ ] Endive
- [ ] Escarole #
- [ ] Fennel
- [ ] Kale
- [ ] Kohlrabi #
- [ ] Leek #
- [ ] Lettuce, Bibb, iceberg, mesculen, romaine
- [ ] Mushrooms, enoki, portobello, tree oyster
- [ ] Okra #
- [ ] Onions, red, Spanish, yellow
- [ ] Radicchio
- [ ] Radishes
- [ ] Rappini
- [ ] Rutabaga
- [ ] Scallion
- [ ] Seaweed
- [ ] Shallots
- [ ] Spinach #
- [ ] Sprouts, radish
- [ ] Squash, all types
- [ ] Swiss chard #
- [ ] Tempeh*
- [ ] Tofu*
- [ ] Water chestnuts
- [ ] Watercress
- [ ] Zucchini

Fruits
- [ ] Apples
- [ ] Apricot
- [ ] Black currants
- [ ] Blueberries
- [ ] Boysenberries
- [ ] Cherries
- [ ] Cranberries
- [ ] Dates
- [ ] Elderberries
- [ ] Figs, dried and fresh #
- [ ] Gooseberries
- [ ] Grapefruit
- [ ] Grapes, black, concord, green, red
- [ ] Guava
- [ ] Kiwifruit
- [ ] Kumquat
- [ ] Lemons
- [ ] Limes
- [ ] Loganberries
- [ ] Melon, casaba, canang, Christmas, crenshaw, musk, Spanish
- [ ] Nectarines
- [ ] Peaches
- [ ] Pears
- [ ] Persimmons
- [ ] Pineapple
- [ ] Plums, dark green, red #
- [ ] Pomegranates
- [ ] Prickly pears
- [ ] Raisins
- [ ] Raspberries
- [ ] Starfruit
- [ ] Strawberries
- [ ] Watermelon

Juices
- [ ] Apricot
- [ ] Black cherry #
- [ ] Carrot
- [ ] Celery
- [ ] Cranberry
- [ ] Cucumber
- [ ] Grape
- [ ] Grapefruit
- [ ] Pineapple #
- [ ] Prune #
- [ ] Vegetable

Beverages
- [ ] Green tea
- [ ] Red wine
- [ ] Water and lemon
- [ ] White wine

Herbal Teas
- [ ] Chamomile
- [ ] Chickweed
- [ ] Dandelion
- [ ] Dong quai
- [ ] Elder
- [ ] Fenugreek #
- [ ] Ginger #
- [ ] Ginseng
- [ ] Hawthorn
- [ ] Hops
- [ ] Licorice root
- [ ] Linden
- [ ] Milk thistle #
- [ ] Mulberry
- [ ] Mullein
- [ ] Parsley
- [ ] Peppermint
- [ ] Raspberry leaf
- [ ] Sage
- [ ] Sarsaparilla
- [ ] Skullcap
- [ ] Slippery elm #
- [ ] Spearmint
- [ ] Thyme

- [ ] Vervain
- [ ] White birch
- [ ] White oak bark
- [ ] Yarrow

Spices & Condiments
- [ ] Agar
- [ ] Allspice
- [ ] Almond extract
- [ ] Anise
- [ ] Barley malt
- [ ] Basil
- [ ] Bay leaf
- [ ] Bergamot
- [ ] Brown rice syrup
- [ ] Brown sugar
- [ ] Caraway
- [ ] Cardamom
- [ ] Carob
- [ ] Chervil
- [ ] Chives
- [ ] Chocolate
- [ ] Coriander (cilantro)
- [ ] Cumin
- [ ] Curry
- [ ] Dill
- [ ] Dulse
- [ ] Garlic #
- [ ] Ginger
- [ ] Honey
- [ ] Horseradish #
- [ ] Jams/jelly, from appropriate fruit
- [ ] Kelp
- [ ] Maple syrup, pure
- [ ] Mint
- [ ] Paprika
- [ ] Parsley #
- [ ] Peppermint
- [ ] Pimiento
- [ ] Rice syrup
- [ ] Rosemary
- [ ] Saffron

- [ ] Sage
- [ ] Salt
- [ ] Savory
- [ ] Shoyu
- [ ] Soy sauce
- [ ] Spearmint
- [ ] Stevia**
- [ ] Sucanat**
- [ ] Tamari
- [ ] Tamarind
- [ ] Tapioca
- [ ] Tarragon
- [ ] Thyme
- [ ] Turmeric
- [ ] Vanilla
- [ ] White sugar

* Anabolic (higher in protein than carbohydrates)
** Natural sweeteners
 # Mutually beneficial foods

Blood Type
A& O

Family Planning A and O
7-Day Pick-a-Meal Menu Options

DAY 1

Breakfast:
• 4 oz. prune juice
• Medium bowl of Kamut Krisp Flakes with soy milk
• Black currants and sunflower seeds
• 1 piece Ezekiel bread with almond butter
• 10–12 oz. green tea

Lunch:
• *Chef's Salad*
    1 hard-boiled egg
    3–4 oz. chicken
    1 oz. farmer's cheese
    Sliced beets and Florida avocados
    Lettuce and arugula
• Green Goddess Dressing (page 234)
• 10–12 oz. green tea

Afternoon Snack:
• Side of edamame
• 10–12 oz. green tea

Dinner:
• 6–8 oz. Cornish hen in Greek Herb Crust (page 231)
• Side of wild rice with chopped portobello mushrooms
• Small side salad with beets, broccoli, and fennel
• Red Onion Dressing (page 236)
• 10–12 oz. green tea

Evening Snack:
• 1 Body Genetics Protein Shake or Thin Tastic Protein Bar

DAY 2

Breakfast:
• 4 oz. carrot juice
• Medium bowl of puffed millet with soy milk
• 8–10 cherries
• 1 piece millet bread with 1 slice soy cheese
• 10–12 oz. green tea

Lunch:
• *Goat Cheese Salad*
    2 oz. goat cheese
    Raw spinach, arugula, walnuts, and radishes
• Raspberry Mock Vinaigrette Dressing (page 236)
• 10–12 oz. green tea

Afternoon Snack:
• Small bowl of blueberries and raspberries
• Glass of soy milk

Dinner:
• Trout stuffed with appropriate herbs
• Side of broccoli
• Side of quinoa or basmati rice
• 10–12 oz. green tea

Evening Snack:
• 1 Body Genetics Protein Shake or Thin Tastic Protein Bar

DAY 3

Breakfast:
- *Salmon Scrambled Eggs*
  2 scrambled eggs and crumbled salmon pieces
- 2 kiwifruit
- 1 piece spelt bread with whole-fruit jam
- 10–12 oz. green tea

Lunch:
- Creamy Squash Bisque (page 213)
- *Grilled Cheese Sandwich*
  2–3 oz. farmer's cheese
  2 slices 100 percent rye bread
- Sliced Florida avocado and watercress
- 10–12 oz. green tea

Afternoon Snack:
- Apple "Pie" Trail Mix (page 238)

Dinner:
- 6–8 oz. broiled ocean salmon in lemon, white wine, and tarragon
- Steamed broccoli and zucchini
- Side of beets
- 10–12 oz. green tea

Evening Snack:
- 1 Body Genetics Protein Shake or Thin Tastic Protein Bar

DAY 4

Breakfast:
- 4 oz. grapefruit juice
- *Cheese Omelet*
  2 scrambled eggs with soy or goat cheese and scallions
- 1 piece brown rice bread with whole-fruit jam
- 10–12 oz. green tea

Lunch:
- Italian Minestrone Soup (page 213)
- *Tuna Sandwich*
  6 oz. tuna with minced onions and celery
  Lettuce and water chestnuts
  2 pieces 100 percent rye bread
- 10–12 oz. green tea

Afternoon Snack:
- Basic Trail Mix #1 (page 238)

Dinner:
- 8 oz. grilled mahimahi or grouper
- Steamed asparagus and carrots
- Side of quinoa
- 10–12 oz. green tea

Evening Snack:
- 1 Body Genetics Protein Shake or Thin Tastic Protein Bar

Blood Type

DAY 5

Breakfast:
- 4 oz. pineapple juice
- Dandelion Greens and Leek Frittata (page 216)
- 1 piece spelt bread with almond butter and whole-fruit jam
- 10–12 oz. green tea

Lunch:
- 6–8 oz. roasted chicken
- Mixed greens with pimiento, cucumbers, scallions, and radish
- Creamy Avocado Dressing (page 233)
- 10–12 oz. green tea

Afternoon Snack:
- Maple Magic Smoothie (page 211)

Dinner:
- 6–8 oz. grilled swordfish marinated in red wine and appropriate herbs and spices
- Watercress and water chestnut salad with Miso Dressing (page 235, 236)
- Side of artichoke pasta
- 10–12 oz. green tea

Evening Snack:
- 1 Body Genetics Protein Shake or Thin Tastic Protein Bar

DAY 6

Breakfast:
- 4 oz. vegetable juice
- 2 oz. goat cheese, 1 thin slice ocean salmon (cooked or raw—not lox), sliced onions
- 2 pieces 100 percent rye bread
- 20 grapes
- 10–12 oz. green tea

Lunch:
- 6 oz. turkey burger
- 1 slice mozzarella cheese
- Sliced red onions and avocado
- Small side salad with Red Onion Dressing (page 236)
- 10–12 oz. green tea

Afternoon Snack:
- 6 whole walnuts and 4 dried figs
- 10–12 oz. green tea

Dinner:
- 6–8 oz. roasted turkey
- Roasted carrots, beets, and onions with rosemary and olive oil
- Side of cranberries
- 4–6 roasted chestnuts
- 10–12 oz. green tea

Evening Snack:
- 1 Body Genetics Protein Shake or Thin Tastic Protein Bar

DAY 7

Breakfast:
• Almond Bomb Smoothie (page 210)
• 1 piece brown rice bread with almond butter
  and whole-fruit jam
• 10–12 oz. green tea

Lunch:
• *Stir-Fry Tofu*
     1 square tofu, broccoli, carrots, zucchini,
     asparagus, and bamboo shoots
• Shoyu, tamari, or soy sauce
• 1 cup cooked brown rice
• 10–12 oz. green tea

Afternoon Snack:
• 1 slice spelt bread with almond butter and
  whole-fruit jam
• 10–12 oz. green tea

Dinner:
• 6–8 oz. cod or carp in lemon or lime and
  cilantro
• Side of okra
• Side of escarole or kale
• Lemon-Lime Cilantro Dressing (page 235)
• 10–12 oz. green tea

Evening Snack:
• 1 Body Genetics Protein Shake or Thin
  Tastic Protein Bar

Blood Type

**A&
O**

Family Planning B and O
Grocery List

Meats—All Anabolic
- [ ] Beef
- [ ] Buffalo
- [ ] Ground beef
- [ ] Lamb #
- [ ] Liver
- [ ] Mutton #
- [ ] Pheasant
- [ ] Rabbit
- [ ] Turkey
- [ ] Veal
- [ ] Venison #

Seafood—All Anabolic
- [ ] Abalone
- [ ] Bluefish
- [ ] Carp
- [ ] Cod #
- [ ] Grouper
- [ ] Haddock
- [ ] Hake #
- [ ] Halibut #
- [ ] Mackerel #
- [ ] Mahimahi
- [ ] Pike #
- [ ] Rainbow trout
- [ ] Salmon, ocean #
- [ ] Sardine #
- [ ] Sea trout
- [ ] Shad #
- [ ] Snapper
- [ ] Sole #
- [ ] Swordfish
- [ ] Tilefish
- [ ] Tuna
- [ ] White perch
- [ ] Whitefish
- [ ] Yellow perch

Beans/Legumes
- [ ] Broad
- [ ] Cannellini
- [ ] Fava
- [ ] Green
- [ ] Jicama
- [ ] Lima
- [ ] Northern
- [ ] Peas, green, pod, snow
- [ ] Red
- [ ] Snap
- [ ] Soy beans, black, brown, green edamame*
- [ ] String
- [ ] White

Eggs/Dairy
- [ ] Eggs*
- [ ] Butter
- [ ] Soy cheese*
- [ ] Soy milk*
- [ ] Farmer's cheese*
- [ ] Feta cheese*
- [ ] Goat cheese*
- [ ] Mozzarella, low fat* #
- [ ] Body Genetics Protein Shake*

Nuts/Seeds
- [ ] Almond butter*
- [ ] Almonds*
- [ ] Chestnuts
- [ ] Hickory*
- [ ] Pine (pignoli)

Oils
- [ ] Cod liver
- [ ] Olive

Cereals
- [ ] Cream of Rice
- [ ] Puffed millet
- [ ] Puffed rice
- [ ] Rice bran
- [ ] Spelt flakes

Breads
- [ ] Brown rice bread
- [ ] Ezekiel bread*
- [ ] Gluten-free bread
- [ ] Millet bread
- [ ] Rice cakes
- [ ] Soy-flour bread
- [ ] Spelt bread

Pastas/Grains
- [ ] Quinoa
- [ ] Rice, basmati, brown, white
- [ ] Spelt flour
- [ ] Spelt pasta

Vegetables
- [ ] Asparagus
- [ ] Beet leaves #
- [ ] Beets #
- [ ] Broccoli #
- [ ] Carrots
- [ ] Celery
- [ ] Chicory
- [ ] Collard greens #
- [ ] Cucumber
- [ ] Daikon radish
- [ ] Dandelion greens
- [ ] Endive
- [ ] Escarole
- [ ] Fennel
- [ ] Fiddlehead ferns
- [ ] Kale #
- [ ] Kohlrabi
- [ ] Leek
- [ ] Lettuce, Bibb, Boston, iceberg, mesculen, romaine
- [ ] Mushrooms, enoki, portobello, tree oyster
- [ ] Okra
- [ ] Onions, green, red, Spanish, yellow
- [ ] Parsnips #
- [ ] Pepper, green, red, yellow, jalepeño
- [ ] Radicchio
- [ ] Rappini
- [ ] Rutabaga
- [ ] Scallion
- [ ] Squash, all types
- [ ] Sweet potatoes #
- [ ] Turnips
- [ ] Water chestnuts
- [ ] Watercress
- [ ] Yams, all kinds
- [ ] Zucchini

Fruits
- [ ] Apples
- [ ] Apricots
- [ ] Bananas
- [ ] Boysenberries
- [ ] Cherries
- [ ] Cranberries
- [ ] Currants, red, black
- [ ] Dates
- [ ] Elderberries
- [ ] Figs, dried or fresh #
- [ ] Gooseberries
- [ ] Grapefruit
- [ ] Grapes, black, concord, green, red
- [ ] Guava
- [ ] Kiwifruit
- [ ] Kumquat
- [ ] Lemons
- [ ] Limes
- [ ] Loganberries
- [ ] Mangoes
- [ ] Melon, all types
- [ ] Nectarines
- [ ] Papaya
- [ ] Peaches
- [ ] Pineapple
- [ ] Plum, dark green, red #
- [ ] Raisins
- [ ] Raspberries
- [ ] Strawberries

Juices
- [ ] Black cherry
- [ ] Carrot
- [ ] Celery
- [ ] Cranberry
- [ ] Cucumber
- [ ] Grape
- [ ] Grapefruit
- [ ] Papaya
- [ ] Pineapple #
- [ ] Prune
- [ ] Vegetable

Beverages
- [ ] Green tea
- [ ] Red wine
- [ ] Water and lemon
- [ ] Water, alkaline
- [ ] White wine

Herbal Teas
- [ ] Catnip
- [ ] Cayenne
- [ ] Chamomile
- [ ] Chickweed
- [ ] Dandelion
- [ ] Dong quai
- [ ] Elder
- [ ] Ginger #
- [ ] Ginseng
- [ ] Hawthorn
- [ ] Horehound
- [ ] Licorice root
- [ ] Mulberry
- [ ] Parsley #
- [ ] Peppermint #
- [ ] Raspberry leaf
- [ ] Rose hips
- [ ] Sage
- [ ] Sarsaparilla
- [ ] Slippery elm
- [ ] Spearmint
- [ ] Thyme
- [ ] Valerian
- [ ] Vervain
- [ ] White birch
- [ ] White oak bark
- [ ] Yarrow

Spices/ Condiments
- [ ] Agar
- [ ] Allspice
- [ ] Anise
- [ ] Apple butter
- [ ] Arrowroot
- [ ] Basil

- [ ] Bay leaf
- [ ] Bergamot
- [ ] Brown rice syrup
- [ ] Brown sugar
- [ ] Cardamom
- [ ] Carob
- [ ] Cayenne pepper #
- [ ] Chervil
- [ ] Chives
- [ ] Chocolate
- [ ] Coriander (cilantro)
- [ ] Cumin
- [ ] Curry #
- [ ] Dill
- [ ] Dulse
- [ ] Garlic
- [ ] Ginger
- [ ] Honey
- [ ] Horseradish
- [ ] Jam/jelly, from appropriate fruit
- [ ] Kelp
- [ ] Maple syrup, pure
- [ ] Mayonnaise
- [ ] Mint
- [ ] Molasses
- [ ] Paprika
- [ ] Parsley #
- [ ] Peppermint
- [ ] Pimiento
- [ ] Rice syrup
- [ ] Rosemary
- [ ] Saffron
- [ ] Sage
- [ ] Salt
- [ ] Savory
- [ ] Spearmint
- [ ] Stevia**
- [ ] Sucanat**
- [ ] Tabasco sauce
- [ ] Tamarind
- [ ] Tarragon

- [ ] Thyme
- [ ] Turmeric
- [ ] Vanilla
- [ ] White sugar
- [ ] Wintergreen
- [ ] Worcestershire sauce

Anabolic (higher in protein than carbohydrates)
**Natural sweeteners*
 # Mutually beneficial foods

Blood Type
B& O

Family Planning B and O
7-Day Pick-a-Meal Menu Options

DAY 1

Breakfast:
- ½ grapefruit
- Medium bowl of spelt flakes with soy milk and currants
- 1 piece brown rice bread with 1 slice soy cheese
- 10–12 oz. green tea

Lunch:
- 6 oz. turkey burger
- 1 slice mozzarella or farmer's cheese
- Sliced red onions
- Small side salad with Herb Mock Vinaigrette Dressing (page 234)
- 10–12 oz. green tea

Afternoon Snack:
- Sliced peach with almond slivers, currants, and honey
- 10–12 oz. green tea

Dinner:
- Grilled lamb chops
- Side of brown and wild rice with portobello mushrooms
- Side of collard greens
- 10–12 oz. green tea

Evening Snack:
- 1 Body Genetics Protein Shake or Thin Tastic Protein Bar

DAY 2

Breakfast:
- 4 oz. carrot juice
- Medium bowl of puffed millet with soy milk
- 8–10 cherries
- 1 piece millet bread with goat cheese
- 10–12 oz. green tea

Lunch:
- *Mock Waldorf Salad*
    4 oz. sliced turkey
    4–5 chopped walnuts
    ½ chopped apple
- Raspberry Mock Vinaigrette Dressing (page 236)
- 10–12 oz. green tea

Afternoon Snack:
- Side of edamame
- 10–12 oz. green tea

Dinner:
- Trout stuffed with appropriate herbs
- Side of broccoli and carrots
- Side of quinoa or basmati rice
- 10–12 oz. green tea

Evening Snack:
- 1 Body Genetics Protein Shake or Thin Tastic Protein Bar

DAY 3

Breakfast:
- *Salmon Scrambled Eggs*
  2 scrambled eggs and crumbled salmon pieces
- 2 kiwifruit
- 1 piece spelt bread with whole-fruit jam
- 10–12 oz. green tea

Lunch:
- Onion Soup (page 214)
- *Meat Loaf Sandwich*
  1 slice meat loaf with lettuce
  2 slices brown rice bread
- Side of zucchini
- 10–12 oz. green tea

Afternoon Snack:
- Apple Walnut Trail Mix (page 238)

Dinner:
- *Pasta with Salmon*
  6 oz. broiled ocean salmon, broken into pieces
  Side order of spelt pasta with Cheeseless Basil Pesto (page 232)
- Steamed broccoli florets and asparagus
- 10–12 oz. green tea

Evening Snack:
- 1 Body Genetics Protein Shake or Thin Tastic Protein Bar

DAY 4

Breakfast:
- 4 oz. grapefruit juice
- *Cheese Omelet*
  2 scrambled eggs with soy or goat cheese and scallions
- 1 piece brown rice bread with whole-fruit jam
- 10–12 oz. green tea

Lunch:
- Italian Minestrone Soup (page 213)
- *Tuna Sandwich*
  6 oz. tuna with minced onions and celery
  Lettuce and water chestnuts
  2 pieces millet bread
- 10–12 oz. green tea

Afternoon Snack:
- Basic Trail Mix #3 (page 239)

Dinner:
- Veal chops in basil tarragon sauce
- Side of peas and carrots
- Mesculen salad with feta, peppers, red onions, beets, and blanched broccoli
- Herb Mock Vinaigrette Dressing (page 234)
- 10–12 oz. green tea

Evening Snack:
- 1 Body Genetics Protein Shake or Thin Tastic Protein Bar

Blood Type
**B&
O**

DAY 5

Breakfast:
• 4 oz. carrot or vegetable juice
• 2 pieces spelt bread with almond butter and honey
• 2–3 plums or apricots
• 10–12 oz. green tea

Lunch:
• 6–8 oz. turkey cubes
• Lettuce, dandelion greens, and ¼ cup cannellini beans
• Warm Cranberry Dressing (page 237)
• 10–12 oz. green tea

Afternoon Snack:
• 2–3 Almond Honey Cookies (page 239)
• 10–12 oz. green tea

Dinner:
• Sautèed veal cutlets in white wine, portobello mushrooms, lemon, and parsley
• Steamed asparagus
• Mixed green salad with fennel, cucumbers, beets, and red onions
• Herb Mock Vinaigrette Dressing (page 234)
• 10–12 oz. green tea

Evening Snack:
• 1 Body Genetics Protein Shake or Thin Tastic Protein Bar

DAY 6

Breakfast:
• 4 oz. vegetable juice
• *Grilled Cheese*
  2 pieces spelt bread with 2–3 oz. mozzarella cheese
• 1 apple
• 10–12 oz. green tea

Lunch:
• *Feta Burger*
  6 oz. beef burger
  1–2 oz. feta cheese
• Sliced red onions
• Small side salad with Miso Dressing (page 235, 236)
• 10–12 oz. green tea

Afternoon Snack:
• Tropical Smoothie (page 211)

Dinner:
• 6–8 oz. flank steak or London broil
• Sauteed onions and portobello mushrooms
• Mixed greens with beets
• Oregano-Feta Dressing (page 236)
• Small sweet potato
• 10–12 oz. green tea

Evening Snack:
• 1 Body Genetics Protein Shake or Thin Tastic Protein Bar

DAY 7

Breakfast:
• Blueberry Supreme Smoothie (page 210)
• 1 piece brown rice bread with almond butter
  and whole-fruit jam
• 10–12 oz. green tea

Lunch:
• *Lamb Salad*
    6 oz. lamb
    Side of cannellini beans
    Appropriate lettuce, dandelion greens,
    cucumber, celery, fennel, and red onions
• Herb Mock Vinaigrette Dressing (page 234)
• 10–12 oz. green tea

Afternoon Snack:
• 1 slice spelt bread with almond butter and
  whole-fruit jam
• 10–12 oz. green tea

Dinner:
• 6–8 oz. cod or carp in lemon or lime and
  cilantro
• Side of okra
• Side of escarole or kale
• Lemon-Lime Cilantro Dressing (page 235)
• 10–12 oz. green tea

Evening Snack:
• 1 Body Genetics Protein Shake or Thin
  Tastic Protein Bar

Blood Type
**B&
O**

Chapter 12

Pick-a-Meal Recipes

Master Recipe Listing for Blood Type A

- Almond Bomb Smoothie—A, O
- Almond Honey Cookies—ALL
- Apple "Pie" Trail Mix—A, O
- Apple Crisp—A, B, AB
- Applesauce Raisin Muffins—A
- Apricot Cream Smoothie—A, AB, O
- Basic Trail Mix #1—A, O
- Basmati Rice Pudding—A, B, O
- Broiled Portobello Mushrooms—ALL
- Carob Almond Cookies—ALL
- Carrot Bisque—ALL
- Cheeseless Basil Pesto—ALL
- Cherry Clafouti—ALL
- Chicken and Artichokes in Wine Sauce—A, O
- Chicken in Garlic Sauce—A, O
- Chocolate Mousse—A, AB
- Chocolate Raspberry Smoothie—A, AB, O
- Chocolate Ricotta Cream—A, B, AB
- Collard Greens With Nuts—ALL
- Corn-Crusted Fish—A
- Cranberry Crush Smoothie—A, AB, O
- Creamy Avocado Dressing—A, AB, O
- Creamy Cilantro Lime Dressing—A, B, AB
- Creamy Garlic Dressing—A, B, AB
- Creamy Squash Bisque—A, B, AB
- Dandelion Greens and Leek Frittata—ALL
- Earthy Muesli—A
- Fish With Herbs and Lime—ALL
- French Herb Crust—ALL
- Greek Herb Crust—ALL
- Green Goddess Dressing—A, AB, O
- Herb Mock Vinaigrette Dressing—ALL
- Herbed Tofu—A, AB, O
- Honey Chicken With Lime—A
- Italian Herb Crust—ALL
- Italian Minestrone—ALL
- Jerusalem Artichoke Soup—A, O
- Lemon-Lime Cilantro Dressing—ALL
- Licorice Smoothie—ALL
- Maple Magic Smoothie—ALL
- Marinated Tuna Steaks—ALL
- Middle Eastern Dressing—A, B, AB
- Miso Dressing #1—ALL
- Miso Dressing #2—ALL
- Moroccan Spice Rub—A, B, AB
- Onion Soup—ALL
- Oregano Feta Dressing—ALL
- Peaches and Cream Smoothie—A, B, AB
- Peanut Butter Cookies—A, AB
- Peanut Chocolate Trail Mix—A, AB
- Pizza Sauce—A, B, O
- Poached Peaches—ALL
- Purple Passion Smoothie—ALL
- Raspberry Mock Vinaigrette Dressing—ALL
- Red Onion Dressing—ALL
- Rosemary Chicken—A, O
- Sesame Chicken—A, O
- Sesame Turkey Fillets—A, O
- Soy Cheese Sauce—A, AB, O
- Spinach and Mushroom Frittata—A, B, AB
- Spinach Pesto—ALL
- Sunflower Pancakes—A
- Tofu Almondine—A, AB, O
- Tofu Burgers—ALL
- Tofu in Cilantro Sauce—A, AB, O
- Tofu Steak Teriyaki—A
- Traditional Herb Crust—ALL
- Turkish Red Lentil Soup—A, AB
- Vanilla Cherry Smoothie—ALL
- Very Berry Smoothie—ALL
- Viennese Coffee Smoothie—A, B, AB
- Vinegarless Dressing—ALL
- Warm Cranberry Dressing—ALL
- White Bean and Escarole Soup—ALL
- Yummy Rice Pudding—A, B, AB

Master Recipe Listing for Blood Type B

- Almond Honey Cookies—ALL
- Apple Crisp—A, B, AB
- Apple Walnut Trail Mix—B, O
- Banana Oat Muffins—B
- Banana Smoothie—B, O
- Basic Trail Mix #3—B, O
- Basmati Rice Pudding—A, B, O
- Beef and Garlic—B, O
- Beefed-up Cheeseburgers—B, O
- Blueberry Supreme Smoothie—B, O
- Broiled Portobello Mushrooms—ALL
- Carob Almond Cookies—ALL
- Carrot Bisque—ALL
- Cheeseless Basil Pesto—ALL
- Cherry Clafouti—ALL
- Chocolate Ricotta Cream—A, B, AB
- Cocoa Mochaccino Smoothie—B
- Collard Greens With Nuts—ALL
- Creamy Cilantro Lime Dressing—A, B, AB
- Creamy Garlic Dressing—A, B, AB
- Creamy Squash Bisque—A, B, AB
- Crockpot Greek Lamb Salad—B, AB, O
- Dandelion Greens and Leek Frittata—ALL
- Eggplant Casserole—B
- Fish With Herbs and Lime—ALL
- French Herb Crust—ALL
- Ginger Apple Smoothie—B, O
- Greek Herb Crust—ALL
- Hearty Beef Stew—B
- Herb Mock Vinaigrette Dressing—ALL
- Honey Mustard Dressing—B
- Italian Herb Crust—ALL
- Italian Minestrone—ALL
- Lemon-Lime Cilantro Dressing—ALL
- Licorice Smoothie—ALL
- Maple Magic Smoothie—ALL
- Marinated Tuna Steaks—ALL
- Middle Eastern Dressing—A, B, AB
- Miso Dressing #1—ALL
- Miso Dressing #2—ALL
- Moroccan Spice Rub—A, B, AB
- Nutty Granola—B
- Onion Soup—ALL
- Orange Ginger Fish—B
- Orange Marinated Salmon—B
- Oregano Feta Dressing—ALL
- Peaches and Cream Smoothie—A, B, AB
- Pecan Pancakes—B
- Pecan Sandies—B, O
- Pizza Sauce—A, B, O
- Poached Peaches—ALL
- Purple Passion Smoothie—ALL
- Raspberry Mock Vinaigrette Dressing—ALL
- Red Onion Dressing—ALL
- Rosemary Roasted Lamb With Roasted Vegetables—B, AB, O
- Scallops in Garlic Sauce—B, AB
- Spicy Fries—B, AB, O
- Spinach and Mushroom Frittata—A, B, AB
- Spinach Pesto—ALL
- Tofu Burgers—ALL
- Traditional Herb Crust—ALL
- Tropical Smoothie—B, O
- Vanilla Cherry Smoothie—ALL
- Very Berry Smoothie—ALL
- Viennese Coffee Smoothie—A, B, AB
- Vinegarless Dressing—ALL
- Walnut Pancakes—B, O
- Warm Cranberry Dressing—ALL
- White Bean and Escarole Soup—ALL
- Yummy Rice Pudding—A, B, AB

Master Recipe Listing for Blood Type AB

- Almond Honey Cookies—ALL
- Apple Crisp—A, B, AB
- Apple Muesli—AB
- Apricot Cream Smoothie—A, AB, O
- Basic Trail Mix #2—AB
- Bran Muffins—AB
- Broiled Portobello Mushrooms—ALL
- Carob Almond Cookies—ALL
- Carrot Bisque—ALL
- Cheeseless Basil Pesto—ALL
- Cherry Clafouti—ALL
- Chocolate Mousse—A, AB
- Chocolate Raspberry Smoothie—A, AB, O
- Chocolate Ricotta Cream—A, B, AB
- Collard Greens With Nuts—ALL
- Cranberry Crush Smoothie—A, AB, O
- Creamy Avocado Dressing—A, AB, O
- Creamy Cilantro Lime Dressing—A, B, AB
- Creamy Garlic Dressing—A, B, AB
- Creamy Squash Bisque—A, B, AB
- Crockpot Greek Lamb Salad—B, AB, O
- Curried Scallops and Vegetables—AB
- Dandelion Greens and Leek Frittata—ALL
- Fish With Herbs and Lime—ALL
- French Herb Crust—ALL
- Fruit and Nut Granola—AB
- Greek Herb Crust—ALL
- Green Goddess Dressing—A, AB, O
- Herb Mock Vinaigrette Dressing—ALL
- Herbed Tofu—A, AB, O
- Italian Herb Crust—ALL
- Italian Minestrone—ALL
- Lemon-Lime Cilantro Dressing—ALL
- Licorice Smoothie—ALL
- Maple Magic Smoothie—ALL
- Marinated Tuna Steaks—ALL
- Middle Eastern Dressing—A, B, AB
- Miso Dressing #1—ALL
- Miso Dressing #2—ALL
- Moroccan Spice Rub—A, B, AB
- Oat Pancakes With Cranberries and Walnuts—AB
- Onion Soup—ALL
- Oregano Feta Dressing—ALL
- Peaches and Cream Smoothie—A, B, AB
- Peanut Butter Cookies—A, AB
- Peanut Chocolate Trail Mix—A, AB
- Poached Peaches—ALL
- Purple Passion Smoothie—ALL
- Raspberry Mock Vinaigrette Dressing—ALL
- Red Onion Dressing—ALL
- Rice and Salmon—AB, O
- Rosemary Roasted Lamb With Roasted Vegetables—B, AB, O
- Scallops in Garlic Sauce—B, AB
- Soy Cheese Sauce—A, AB, O
- Spicy Fries—B, AB, O
- Spinach and Mushroom Frittata—A, B, AB
- Spinach Pesto—ALL
- Swiss Chard and Feta Frittata—AB, O
- Tofu Almondine—A, AB, O
- Tofu Burgers—ALL
- Tofu in Cilantro Sauce—A, AB, O
- Tomato Italiano Sauce With Tuna—AB, O
- Tomato Soup—AB, O
- Traditional Herb Crust—ALL
- Turkish Red Lentil Soup—A, AB
- Vanilla Cherry Smoothie—ALL
- Very Berry Smoothie—ALL
- Viennese Coffee Smoothie—A, B, AB
- Vinegarless Dressing—ALL
- Warm Cranberry Dressing—ALL
- White Bean and Escarole Soup—ALL
- Yummy Rice Pudding—A, B, AB

Master Recipe Listing for Blood Type O

- Almond Bomb Smoothie—A, O
- Almond Honey Cookies—ALL
- Apple "Pie" Trail Mix—A, O
- Apple Walnut Trail Mix—B, O
- Apricot Cream Smoothie—A, AB, O
- Banana Smoothie—B, O
- Banana Walnut Muffins—O
- Basic Trail Mix #1—A, O
- Basic Trail Mix #3—B, O
- Basmati Rice Pudding—A, B, O
- Beef and Garlic—B, O
- Beefed-up Cheeseburgers—B, O
- Black-Eyed Peas and Fennel—O
- Blueberry Supreme Smoothie—B, O
- Broiled Portobello Mushrooms—ALL
- Cajun Spice Rub—O
- Carob Almond Cookies—ALL
- Carrot Bisque—ALL
- Cheeseless Basil Pesto—ALL
- Cherry Clafouti—ALL
- Chicken and Artichokes—A, O
- Chicken Cacciatore—O
- Chicken Chili Soup—O
- Chicken in Garlic Sauce—A, O
- Chocolate Raspberry Smoothie—A, AB, O
- Collard Greens With Nuts—ALL
- Cranberry Crush Smoothie—A, AB, O
- Creamy Avocado Dressing—A, AB, O
- Crockpot Greek Lamb Salad—B, AB, O
- Dandelion Greens and Leek Frittata—ALL
- Fish With Herbs and Lime—ALL
- French Herb Crust—ALL
- Ginger Apple Smoothie—B, O
- Greek Herb Crust—ALL
- Green Goddess Dressing—A, AB, O
- Herb Mock Vinaigrette Dressing—ALL
- Herbed Tofu—A, AB, O
- Italian Herb Crust—ALL
- Italian Minestrone—ALL
- Jerusalem Artichoke Soup—A, O
- Lemon-Lime Cilantro Dressing—ALL
- Licorice Smoothie—ALL
- Light Beef Stew With Herbs—O
- Maple Magic Smoothie—ALL
- Marinated Tuna Steaks—ALL
- Meat Loaf—O
- Mexican Spice Rub—O
- Miso Dressing #1—ALL
- Miso Dressing #2—ALL
- Onion Soup—ALL
- Oregano Feta Dressing—ALL
- Pecan Sandies—B, O
- Pizza Sauce—A, B, O
- Poached Peaches—ALL
- Purple Passion Smoothie—ALL
- Raspberry Mock Vinaigrette Dressing—ALL
- Red Onion Dressing—ALL
- Rice and Salmon—AB, O
- Rosemary Chicken—A, O
- Rosemary Roasted Lamb With Roasted Vegetables—B, AB, O
- Sesame Chicken—A, O
- Sesame Fish—O
- Sesame Turkey Fillets—A, O
- Shortcut Scampi—O
- Soy Cheese Sauce—A, AB, O
- Spicy Fries—B, AB, O
- Spinach Pesto—ALL
- Stir-Fried Rice—O
- Swiss Chard and Feta Frittata—AB, O
- Tofu Almondine—A, AB, O
- Tofu Burgers—ALL
- Tofu in Cilantro Sauce—A, AB, O
- Tomato Italiano Sauce With Tuna—AB, O
- Tomato Soup—AB, O
- Traditional Herb Crust—ALL
- Tropical Smoothie—B, O
- Vanilla Cherry Smoothie—ALL
- Very Berry Smoothie—ALL
- Vinegarless Dressing—ALL
- Walnut Pancakes—B, O
- Warm Cranberry Dressing—ALL
- White Bean and Escarole Soup—ALL

MUFFINS

APPLESAUCE RAISIN MUFFINS   A

2 cups spelt flour	1 egg white
1 Tbsp. baking powder	½ cup vanilla soy milk
1 tsp. cinnamon	2 Tbsp. canola oil
½ tsp. nutmeg	⅓ cup honey
¼ tsp. cloves	¾ cup unsweetened applesauce
1 egg	½ cup raisins or black currants

Preheat oven to 400 degrees. Line muffin tin with paper liners.

In large bowl, mix together flour, baking powder, cinnamon, nutmeg, and cloves. Mix well. In another bowl, beat egg and egg white. Add soy milk, canola oil, honey, applesauce, and raisins. Mix well.

Fold wet mixture into flour mixture. Mix until combined. Spoon batter into tins, and bake for 20–25 minutes. *Makes 12 muffins.*

BANANA OAT MUFFINS   B

1 cup spelt flour	1 cup mashed ripe bananas
½ tsp. nutmeg	¼ cup pure maple syrup or honey
½ tsp. baking soda	1 tsp. vanilla extract
1 tsp. baking powder	2 Tbsp. olive oil
1 cup rolled oats	¾ cup plain nonfat yogurt
1 egg	½ cup chopped walnuts

Preheat oven to 400 degrees. Line muffin tin with paper liners.

In large bowl, mix together flour, nutmeg, baking soda, and baking powder. Place rolled oats in a food processor and pulverize until texture is similar to cornmeal. Add oats to flour mixture.

In another bowl, beat egg until it is fluffy. Add bananas, honey or maple syrup, vanilla extract, olive oil, yogurt, and walnuts. Mix well. Fold wet mixture into flour mixture. Mix until combined. Spoon batter into tins, and bake for 20–25 minutes. *Makes 12 muffins.*

Unless otherwise noted in Notes section, all recipes are courtesy of Joseph Christiano, author.

BANANA WALNUT MUFFINS   O

3½ cups spelt flour
2 tsp. baking soda
1 tsp. baking powder
1 egg
3 cups mashed ripe bananas

1 cup pure maple syrup
½ tsp. vanilla extract
¼ cup canola oil
1 cup finely chopped walnuts
½ cup carob chips (optional)

Preheat oven to 375 degrees. Line muffin tin with paper liners.

In large bowl, mix together flour, baking soda, and baking powder. In another bowl, beat egg. Add bananas, maple syrup, vanilla extract, canola oil, and walnut to egg. Mix well.

Fold wet mixture into flour mixture. Partially mix, then add carob chips; mix until combined. Spoon batter into tins, and bake for 20–25 minutes. *Makes 14–16 muffins.*

BRAN MUFFINS   AB

1 cup spelt flour
1 tsp. baking powder
½ tsp. cinnamon
¼ tsp. nutmeg
¼ cup flaxseeds
3 egg whites

1 cup skim milk
2 Tbsp. canola oil
¼ cup honey
1 cup All-Bran cereal
½ cup raisins (optional)

Preheat oven to 400 degrees. Line muffin tin with paper liners.

In large bowl, mix together flour, baking powder, cinnamon, and nutmeg. In food processor, grind flaxseeds into cornmeal consistency. Add to other dry ingredients and mix well. In another bowl, beat egg whites well. Add skim milk, canola oil, and honey. Mix well. Soak All-Bran cereal in milk mixture for 10 minutes.

Fold wet mixture into flour mixture. Batter will be slightly lumpy. Mix until combined. Spoon batter into tins, and bake for 20–25 minutes. *Makes 12 muffins.*

PANCAKES

OAT PANCAKES WITH CRANBERRIES AND WALNUTS   AB

1 cup oat flour
½ cup spelt flour
2½ tsp. baking powder
1 egg

1½ tsp. honey
1 cup soy or skim milk
½ cup dried cranberries
½ cup finely chopped walnuts (optional)

Combine flour and baking powder in large bowl. Mix well. In another bowl, lightly beat egg. Add honey and milk to egg. Fold wet mixture into dry mixture. Add cranberries and walnuts. Mix until combined.

Ladle ¼ cup batter onto nonstick griddle. Cook until surface begins to bubble. Flip and allow other side to cook for another 2 minutes. *Makes 12 pancakes; 1 serving = 3 pancakes.*

PECAN PANCAKES   B

1 cup spelt flour   1 tsp. pure maple syrup
½ cup oat flour   1 tsp. vanilla extract
2 tsp. baking powder   1 cup skim or 2 percent milk
1 egg   ½ cup finely chopped pecans

Combine flour and baking powder in large bowl. Mix well. In another bowl, lightly beat egg. Add maple syrup, vanilla extract, and milk to egg. Fold wet mixture into dry mixture. Add pecans, and mix until combined.

Ladle ¼ cup batter onto nonstick griddle. Cook until surface begins to bubble. Flip and allow other side to cook for another 2 minutes. *Makes 12 pancakes; 1 serving = 3 pancakes.*

SUNFLOWER PANCAKES   A

1 cup oat flour   1 tsp. honey
½ cup spelt flour   1 cup soy milk
2½ tsp. baking powder   2 Tbsp. apricot juice
1 egg   ¼ cup sunflower seeds

Combine flour and baking powder in large bowl. Mix well. In another bowl lightly beat egg. Add honey, milk, and apricot juice to egg. Fold wet mixture into dry mixture. Add sunflower seeds. Mix until combined.

Ladle ¼ cup batter onto nonstick griddle. Cook until surface begins to bubble. Flip and allow other side to cook for another 2 minutes. *Makes 12 pancakes; 1 serving = 3 pancakes.*

WALNUT PANCAKES   B, O

1½ cups spelt flour   1 tsp. honey or pure maple syrup
2½ tsp. baking powder   1 cup soy milk
1 egg   ½ cup finely chopped walnuts

Combine flour and baking powder in large bowl. Mix well. In another bowl, lightly beat egg. Add honey or maple syrup and soy milk to egg. Fold wet mixture into dry mixture. Add walnuts, and mix until combined.

Ladle ¼ cup batter onto nonstick griddle. Cook until surface begins to bubble. Flip and allow other side to cook for another 2 minutes. *Makes 12 pancakes; 1 serving = 3 pancakes.*

CEREAL

APPLE MUESLI   AB

2 cups rolled oats

1 cup rye flakes

½ cup coarsely chopped dried apples

½ cup coarsely chopped dried apricots

1 cup raisins or red and black currants

1 cup coarsely chopped almonds

1 cup coarsely chopped walnuts

½ tsp. nutmeg

1 tsp. cinnamon

1 tsp. vanilla or almond extract

4 cups apple cider

Combine all dry ingredients in large bowl. Mix well. Place mixture in airtight storage container. Slowly stir in vanilla or almond extract and apple cider. Place in refrigerator overnight with container sealed tightly. Ready to eat in morning! *Makes 4–5 servings; 1 serving = 1 average cereal bowl.*

EARTHY MUESLI   A

2 cups rolled oats

1 cup rye flakes

1 cup coarsely chopped dates

1 cup raisins or black currants

1 cup coarsely chopped filberts

½ cup coarsely chopped walnuts

½ cup sunflower seeds

½ tsp. nutmeg

1 tsp. cinnamon

1 tsp. vanilla or almond extract

4 cups apple cider

Combine all dry ingredients in large bowl. Mix well. Place mixture in airtight storage container. Slowly stir in vanilla or almond extract and apple cider. Place in refrigerator overnight with container sealed tightly. Ready to eat in morning! *Makes 4–5 servings; 1 serving = 1 average cereal bowl.*

FRUIT AND NUT GRANOLA   AB

½ cup flaxseeds

6 cups rolled oats

½ tsp. cinnamon

½ tsp. nutmeg

¼ cup pure maple syrup

2 Tbsp. canola oil

2 Tbsp. apple juice or water

½ cup finely chopped dried apricots

¼ cup finely chopped walnuts

¼ cup finely chopped almonds

½ cup finely chopped dried figs or raisins

Preheat oven to 300 degrees. Spray 2 cookie sheets with nonstick cooking spray.

In food processor, coarsely grind flaxseeds. In large bowl, combine ground flaxseed, oats, cinnamon, and nutmeg. In small microwave-safe bowl, combine maple syrup, canola oil, and apple juice. Microwave on high for about 1 minute. Stir well. Fold wet ingredients into dry ingredients.

Distribute equal amounts of mixture on both cookie sheets. Pat down lightly. Bake for 20 minutes or until lightly golden brown. Cool thoroughly; add in dried fruit and stir. Transfer to storage bowl. *Makes about 6 servings; 1 serving = 1 average cereal bowl.*

NUTTY GRANOLA   B

½ cup flaxseeds   2 Tbsp. water or apple juice
6 cups rolled oats   1 cup raisins
½ tsp. nutmeg   ¼ cup finely chopped almonds
¼ cup pure maple syrup   ¼ cup finely chopped macadamia
1 tsp. butter   nuts or pecans

Preheat oven to 300 degrees. Spray 2 cookie sheets with nonstick cooking spray.

In food processor, coarsely grind the flaxseeds. In large bowl combine ground flaxseeds, oats, and nutmeg. In small microwave-safe bowl, combine maple syrup, butter, and apple juice. Microwave on high for about 1 minute. Stir well. Fold wet ingredients into dry ingredients.

Distribute equal amounts of mixture on both cookie sheets. Pat down lightly. Bake for 20 minutes or until lightly golden brown. Cool thoroughly. Stir in raisins and nuts. Transfer to storage bowl. *Makes about 6 servings; 1 serving = 1 average cereal bowl.*

SMOOTHIES

For all the recipes below, place ingredients into blender and process until smooth. If they come out too thick for your liking, just add more designated liquid or some water.

ALMOND BOMB   A, O

1 cup soy milk
4 ice cubes
1 tsp. almond extract
1 tsp. almonds, crushed or slivers, as garnish
1 scoop vanilla Body Genetics Protein
   Shake *(blood type specific)*

APRICOT CREAM   A, AB, O

1 cup soy milk
3–4 frozen or canned apricot halves
2–3 ice cubes
2 cups silken soft tofu
1 tsp. vanilla extract *(omit for O)*
1 scoop vanilla Body Genetics Protein
   Shake *(blood type specific)*

BANANA   B, O

1 cup soy milk *(O)*; skim milk *(B)*
3-inch piece frozen banana
1 scoop Body Genetics Protein Shake
   (blood type specific)

BLUEBERRY SUPREME   B, O

1 cup soy milk *(O)*; skim milk *(B)*
3-inch piece of frozen banana
½–¾ cup frozen blueberries
1 Tbsp. fresh lemon juice
1 scoop vanilla Body Genetics Protein
   Shake *(blood type specific)*

CHOCOLATE
RASPBERRY   A, AB, O

1 cup soy milk
½–¾ cup frozen raspberries
½ cup silken soft tofu
1 scoop chocolate Body Genetics Protein
   Shake *(blood type specific)*

COCOA MOCHACCINO   B

1 cup skim milk
2–3 ice cubes
2–3 tsp. instant coffee
3-inch piece frozen banana
1 scoop chocolate Body Genetics
   Protein Shake *(blood type specific)*

CRANBERRY CRUSH A, AB, O

½ cup frozen blueberries

½ cup frozen cranberries

½ cup soft silken tofu

1 tsp. vanilla extract

1 tsp. honey

½ cup cranberry juice

1 scoop Body Genetics Protein Shake
(blood type specific)

GINGER APPLE   B, O

1 cup soy milk *(O)*; skim milk *(B)*

½ cup apple juice

3-inch piece frozen banana

1-inch piece fresh ginger root

1 scoop Body Genetics Protein Shake
(blood type specific)

LICORICE   ALL

1 cup soy milk *(A, O)*; skim milk *(B, AB)*

2–3 ice cubes

¼ tsp. licorice root
(can be adjusted for taste)

½ cup vanilla low-fat yogurt *(A, B, AB)*
or 2 cup silken soft tofu *(A, AB, O)*

1 scoop vanilla Body Genetics Protein
Shake *(blood type specific)*

MAPLE MAGIC   ALL

1 cup soy milk *(A, O)*; skim milk *(B, AB)*

3–4 ice cubes

2 tsp. pure maple syrup

½ cup vanilla low-fat yogurt *(A, B, AB)*
or ½ cup silken soft tofu *(A, AB, O)*

1 scoop vanilla Body Genetics Protein
Shake *(blood type specific)*

PEACHES AND
CREAM   A, B, AB

1 cup soy milk *(A)*; skim milk *(B, AB)*

½ cup vanilla low-fat yogurt

1 sliced frozen peach

2–3 ice cubes

1 scoop Body Genetics Protein Shake
(blood type specific)

PURPLE PASSION   ALL

1 cup concord grape juice

½ cup vanilla low-fat yogurt *(A, B, AB)*
or ½ cup silken soft tofu *(A, AB, O)*

3–4 ice cubes

1 scoop Body Genetics Protein Shake
(blood type specific)

TROPICAL   B, O

1 cup soy milk *(O)*; skim milk *(B)*

2 oz. pineapple chunks

3-inch piece of frozen banana

1 scoop Body Genetics Protein Shake
(blood type specific)

VANILLA CHERRY   ALL

1 cup soy milk *(A, O)*; skim milk *(B, AB)*

½ cup vanilla low-fat yogurt *(A, B, AB)*
or ½ cup silken soft tofu *(A, AB, O)*

2–3 ice cubes

½ cup frozen cherries

1 scoop Body Genetics Protein Shake
(blood type specific)

VERY BERRY   ALL

1 cup soy milk *(A, O)*; skim milk *(B, AB)*
½–¾ cup frozen berries (raspberries,
   blueberries, strawberries)
2–3 ice cubes
1 scoop vanilla Body Genetics Protein
   Shake *(blood type specific)*

VIENNESE COFFEE   A, B, AB

1 cup soy milk *(A)*; skim milk *(B, AB)*
2–3 tsp. instant coffee
½ tsp. cinnamon or nutmeg
3–4 ice cubes
1 scoop vanilla Body Genetics Protein
   Shake *(blood type specific)*

SOUPS

CARROT BISQUE   ALL

1 lb. sliced carrots	2 bay leaves
1 large chopped onion	½–1 tsp. ground peppercorns *(O only)*
¾ cup chopped parsnips	2 Tbsp. olive oil
2 minced shallots	2 Tbsp. mellow white miso
1–2 cloves minced garlic	2–3 tsp. fresh chopped parsley or dill to garnish

In large saucepan, sauté carrots, onion, parsnips, shallots, garlic, bay leaves, and peppercorns in olive oil for 3–4 minutes. Add water to cover vegetables. Water level should be 1½ inches above vegetables. Bring to boil. Reduce to simmer and cook until vegetables are soft.

Ladle 1 cup liquid into bowl. Dissolve miso in this liquid. Add more hot liquid if necessary. Once incorporated, add miso mixture back to soup pot. Stir well. (Miso should never be boiled. It is added at end of preparation of dish and replaces salt in soup.)

Remove from heat. Purée with hand blender to desired consistency. Stir in parsley or dill. Soup can be strained through sieve if you prefer creamier soup. *Makes 4–6 servings.*

CHICKEN CHILI SOUP   O

1 medium chopped onion	Pinch of salt
3 minced shallots	2 tsp. chili powder
2–3 cloves minced garlic	1 tsp. cumin
2 diced carrots	6–8 cups chicken stock
2 stalks diced celery	3 lb. chicken, quartered and skin removed
½ fresh diced red pepper	½ lb. appropriate pasta (spaghetti or linguine)
2 Tbsp. olive oil	2–3 ripe diced tomatoes

In large saucepan, sauté onion, shallots, garlic, carrots, celery, and red pepper in olive oil for 3–4 minutes. Add salt, chili powder, and cumin. Mix well. Add stock and chicken. Bring to boil. Lower heat and simmer for 20 minutes.

In meantime, break dry spaghetti or linguine into 4–5 pieces. Cook al dente. Rinse well and set aside. Remove chicken from soup. Add tomatoes to pot. Shred chicken from bones with fork and replace in pot. Let simmer for 5 more minutes. Add pasta, mix well, and serve. *Makes 4–6 servings.*

CREAMY SQUASH BISQUE A, B, AB

2–3 lbs. winter squash (butternut, acorn, delicata), skin removed and cubed
1 small diced onion
1 tsp. fresh finely minced ginger
1 diced carrot

1 stalk diced celery
2 Tbsp. olive oil
5 cups vegetable stock
½ cup apple juice
½ tsp. nutmeg
Parsley for garnish

Preheat oven to 450 degrees. Cut squash in half. Lay squash cut side down on cookie sheet. Bake for 35–45 minutes. Check doneness with a fork. Set aside to cool for few minutes.

In large saucepan, sauté onions, ginger, carrot, and celery in olive oil for 5–7 minutes, or until onions are translucent. Add stock, apple juice, and nutmeg. Scoop out pulp from squash and add to the mix. Stir well.

Let cook for 10 minutes more. Use hand blender to purée soup into creamy bisque. Toss parsley into soup, and serve immediately. *Makes 6–8 servings.*

ITALIAN MINESTRONE ALL

1 medium diced onion
1–2 cloves minced garlic
2 diced carrots
½ cup winter squash cut in ¼-inch cubes (acorn, butternut, etc.)
2 stalks diced celery
2 Tbsp. olive oil
1 cup fresh packed spinach, kale, or escarole
1 16-oz. can cannellini beans (or other appropriate bean)

1 14-oz. can chopped tomatoes with juice *(omit for A, B)*
¼ cup chopped fresh parsley
6 cups stock (chicken stock—A, O; vegetable stock—B, AB)
½ cup spelt pasta elbows or other small pasta shape
½ cup diced zucchini
1 cup sliced green beans
3–4 sliced basil leaves

In large saucepan, sauté onion, garlic, carrots, squash, and celery in olive oil for 3–4 minutes. Add spinach (escarole or kale), beans, tomatoes, parsley, and stock. Simmer for 10–15 minutes. Meanwhile, cook pasta al dente. Rinse well, and set aside.

Add zucchini, green beans, and cooked pasta. Cook until all vegetables are soft. Stir basil into finished soup. Let cook for 1 minute more. Serve. *Makes 6–8 servings.*

JERUSALEM ARTICHOKE SOUP   A, O

1 lb. Jerusalem artichokes   2 sliced carrots
Lemon juice from half a lemon   3 cups chicken stock
4 Tbsp. butter or olive oil   Pinch of salt
2 sliced leeks, white part only   1 lb. silken tofu

Scrub Jerusalem artichokes well. (If they are scrubbed well you will not need to peel them.) Slice them, and blend with lemon juice in bowl.

In medium saucepan, melt butter. Add leeks, carrots, and artichokes. Cover and cook over low heat for 20–25 minutes. Add 2½ cups chicken stock and pinch of salt. Cover and cook for 30 minutes more.

Purée remaining stock with silken tofu. Add to pot until combined. Soup can be strained through sieve if you prefer smoother soup. *Makes 4 servings.*

ONION SOUP   ALL

1 Tbsp. butter or olive oil   3 cans chicken stock *(A, O)*
2 red onions   or vegetable broth *(B, AB)*
2 white onions   1 bay leaf
2 yellow onions   1 tsp. thyme
2 leeks   1 tsp. savory
3 shallots   ¾ cup red wine
Small head of peeled garlic   Optional: appropriate bread with slice of
                                         appropriate cheese

Melt butter or oil in large soup pot. Sauté onions, leeks, shallots, and garlic on low heat for about 30 minutes. Add broth, seasonings, and wine. Let cook for another 45 to 60 minutes.

Put cheese on bread. Place in bottom of each individual bowl. Pour hot soup into bowl and serve. *Makes 6 servings.*

TOMATO SOUP   AB, O

2 medium chopped onions   8 cups vegetable stock
2–3 cloves minced garlic   4–5 medium chopped tomatoes
3 Tbsp. olive oil   1 bay leaf
1 tsp. dried thyme   1 Tbsp. fresh chopped basil leaves
1 tsp. dried marjoram

In large saucepan, sauté onions and garlic in olive oil for 3–4 minutes. Add thyme and marjoram; mix well. Add vegetable stock, tomatoes, and bay leaf.

Bring to boil. Reduce to simmer for 15–20 minutes. Remove from heat. Purée with hand blender to desired consistency. Stir in basil leaves and serve. *Makes 4–6 servings.*

TURKISH RED LENTIL SOUP   A, AB

2½ cups dry red lentils
1 large minced onion
2 cloves minced garlic
2 diced carrots
1 diced celery stalk

2 Tbsp. olive oil
4–6 cups vegetable stock
½ tsp. salt
Juice from 2 lemons
1 cup chopped fresh spinach or Swiss
  chard, stems and ribs removed

Place lentils in bowl. Cover with cool water. Let stand in water until softened.

In large saucepan, sauté onion, garlic, carrots, and celery in olive oil for 3–4 minutes. Rinse lentils and remove from water. Add to saucepan. Add vegetable stock and salt. Liquid level should be 2 inches above ingredients. Use more water if needed. Bring to boil, then lower to simmer. Let cook for 25–35 minutes, or until lentils are cooked. Remove from heat.

Slowly add half the lemon juice to pot. Let sit for 5 minutes. Taste. Add more lemon juice as desired. For a really lemon taste, add entire amount. Mix in spinach or chard. Heat of soup will wilt greens. *Makes 6–8 servings.*

WHITE BEAN AND ESCAROLE (OR SWISS CHARD) SOUP   ALL

2 Tbsp. olive oil
1 small diced onion
2–3 cloves smashed garlic
1 16-oz. can cannellini beans
  (or other appropriate white bean)
4–5 cups water

2 Tbsp. mellow white miso
½ Tbsp. rosemary, fresh or dried
Salt to taste
½ lb. escarole or Swiss chard,
  trimmed and coarsely chopped

Heat olive oil in large soup pot. Sauté onion and garlic for 3–5 minutes. Add beans and cook until warm.

Heat 1 cup water. Dilute miso in warm water. Set aside.

Purée ⅔ of onions and beans in food processor. Slowly add miso water to thin beans. The consistency should be somewhat loose. Add more water if necessary.

Add puréed beans to soup pot with whole beans and onion. Add balance of water, rosemary, and salt to taste. Bring to simmer. (Note: Miso should never be boiled. It breaks down easily under high temperatures.) Add escarole or Swiss chard. Cook for 10 minutes more. Serve immediately. *Makes 4–6 servings.*

EGGS

DANDELION GREENS AND LEEK FRITTATA   ALL

1½ lb. dandelion greens

5–6 cups water

3–4 Tbsp. olive oil

2 cloves finely minced garlic

1 cup chopped leeks, white part only

6 eggs

2 Tbsp. fresh chopped parsley,
   or 1 Tbsp. dry parsley

Pinch of salt

4 artichoke hearts, sliced
   (B, AB—avoid)

Wash dandelion greens. In large pot, bring water to boil. Put dandelion greens into pot to cook for 3–4 minutes. Remove from pot. Pat away excess water. Coarsely chop. (This will remove some bitterness. If you don't mind bitter taste, skip the parboil stage.)

Using half the oil, sauté garlic and leeks in large nonstick skillet until leeks start to soften. Add dandelion greens to skillet. Cover and let cook for about 10 minutes. Remove from heat. Drain any excess liquid from skillet. Set aside.

Beat eggs, parsley, and salt in large bowl. Add dandelion mixture to egg mixture, along with artichoke hearts (if using). Mix well.

Reheat skillet over medium heat with remaining oil. Be sure oil is hot before adding eggs and greens to skillet. Cover and let cook for 5–8 minutes or until bottom browns. DO NOT turn eggs during cooking process. When cooked, place large plate or platter over top of skillet. Turn over to flip frittata onto plate. Serve warm or cold. *Makes 3–4 servings.*

SPINACH AND MUSHROOM FRITTATA   A, B, AB

3–4 Tbsp. olive oil

2–3 cloves finely minced garlic

1 cup chopped leeks, white part only

4 cups chopped mushrooms
   (blood type specific)

1 lb. spinach

6 eggs

2 Tbsp. fresh chopped parsley,
   or 1 Tbsp. dry parsley

½ tsp. nutmeg

Pinch of salt

Using half the oil, sauté garlic and leeks in large nonstick skillet until leeks start to soften. Add mushrooms, and sauté for 3 minutes. Add spinach to skillet. Cover and let cook for about 10 minutes. Remove from heat. Drain excess liquid from skillet. Set aside.

In large bowl, whisk eggs until fluffy. Add parsley, nutmeg, and salt. Add spinach mixture to egg mixture. Mix well. Reheat skillet over medium heat with remaining oil. Be sure oil is hot before adding eggs and greens to skillet. Cover and let cook for 5–8 minutes or until bottom browns. DO NOT turn eggs during cooking process.

When cooked, place large plate or platter over top of skillet. Turn over to flip frittata onto plate. Serve warm or cold. *Makes 3–4 servings.*

SWISS CHARD AND FETA FRITTATA   AB, O

1 lb. Swiss chard
4 cloves finely minced garlic
1 medium chopped onion
3–4 Tbsp. olive oil
6 eggs

3–4 Tbsp. fresh chopped basil
½ tsp. dried tarragon
Pinch of salt
1 medium sliced tomato
2–3 oz. crumbled feta cheese

Remove stems from chard. Wash well, then coarsely chop. Sauté garlic and onion in large nonstick skillet for 3 minutes using half the oil. Add chard to skillet. Cover and let cook for about 10 minutes. Remove from heat. Drain excess liquid from skillet. Set aside.

Beat eggs, basil, tarragon, and salt in large bowl. Add chard mixture to egg mixture. Mix well. Reheat skillet over medium heat with remaining oil. Be sure oil is hot before adding eggs and chard to the skillet. Layer sliced tomato and sprinkle feta on top. Cover and let cook for 5–8 minutes or until bottom browns. DO NOT turn eggs during cooking process.

When cooked, place large plate or platter over top of skillet. Turn over to flip frittata onto plate. Serve warm or cold. *Makes 3–4 servings.*

TOFU

HERBED TOFU   A, AB, O

1 lb. firm tofu
1 tsp. plum paste (umeboshi paste)
1 tsp. lemon juice
2 tsp. tahini *(AB—use almond butter)*

1–2 tsp. each of 4 or 5 of the following
dried herbs:
oregano, basil (use fresh if possible), parsley
(use fresh if possible), dill, marjoram, tarragon

Drain tofu. Crumble and set aside. In large bowl, cream plum (umeboshi) paste, lemon juice, and tahini together. Add tofu and stir well. Fold in herbs. Chill and serve. *Makes 4–5 servings.*

TOFU ALMONDINE   A, AB, O

⅓ cup soy sherry
⅓ cup soy sauce
⅓ cup fresh lemon juice
3 fresh packed oregano leaves
1 lb. firm or extra-firm tofu

2 cups cooked white rice
4 cups water
1½ cups chopped portobello mushrooms
⅓ cup toasted, coarsely chopped almonds

Combine sherry, soy sauce, lemon juice, and oregano leaves. Set aside ¼ cup of marinade for cooking mushrooms separately.

Drain tofu. Place between several layers of paper-towel thicknesses to absorb extra liquid. Begin to cook rice with water. Place tofu in nonstick skillet over medium-low heat. Add all marinade, except for ¼ cup set aside. Cook tofu until heated through.

In another nonstick skillet, add ¼ cup marinade and mushrooms. Simmer for 10 minutes or until mushrooms are cooked. Serve tofu on top of rice. Garnish with almonds. *Makes 4 servings.*

TOFU BURGERS   ALL

1 lb. extra-firm tofu, drained well   ¼ cup grated carrots
½ cup cooked brown rice   ½ cup low-fat mozzarella or soy cheese
½ cup dry bread crumbs   2 tsp. soy sauce
½ cup chopped scallions   2 tsp. ground walnuts (optional)
2 egg whites

Mash tofu. Mix all ingredients thoroughly. Form burgers. Heat nonstick skillet to medium with spray of olive oil. Cook burgers until golden. *Makes 6 servings.*

TOFU IN CILANTRO SAUCE   A, AB, O

If you have never tried tofu, this is the recipe to start with. Even non–tofu eaters love it! Serve over steamed greens with appropriate grain. It's even good cold as part of a salad.

1 lb. firm or extra-firm tofu   ½–¾ cup fresh cilantro, packed
2 Tbsp. canola or olive oil   and finely chopped
1 tsp. fresh finely minced ginger   1–2 Tbsp. soy, tamari or shoyu sauce
2 cloves finely minced garlic   2–3 Tbsp. water
                                       1–2 Tbsp. honey

Drain tofu well. Let it sit on plate with another plate on top of it. Weigh top plate down with large can of vegetables from your cupboard while you are preparing all other ingredients. This will help excess water to leave tofu. However, be careful not to smash tofu block. Cut tofu into 4 equal squares.

In large nonstick skillet, heat oil on medium heat. Add ginger and garlic. Sauté for 1 minute. Do not burn. Add tofu. Be sure to place tofu directly on ginger and garlic. Let cook for 2–3 minutes. Turn tofu squares over.

Add cilantro, soy sauce, and 2 tablespoons water. Drizzle honey over entire mixture. Cover and let cook for 2–3 minutes. Stir well. Add more water if sauce is too thick. Remove from skillet and serve. *Makes 4 servings.*

TOFU STEAK TERIYAKI   A

1 lb. extra-firm tofu, drained well   4 Tbsp. olive oil
6 Tbsp. sake or white wine   2 chopped scallions
2 medium cloves crushed garlic   2 Tbsp. honey
6 Tbsp. soy sauce   1 Tbsp. arrowroot

Slice tofu into six equal ½-inch strips. Marinate tofu in sake or wine, garlic, soy sauce, 2 tablespoons olive oil, scallions, and honey.

Heat remaining oil in wok over medium heat. Grill tofu in wok until brown on both sides.

Bring leftover marinade to boil. Lower to simmer for 2 minutes. Thicken sauce with arrowroot. *Makes 4–5 servings.*

CHICKEN

CHICKEN AND ARTICHOKES IN WINE SAUCE   A, O

4 boneless chicken breasts,
   skinned and cut in half
¼ cup spelt flour or other
   appropriate flour
4 Tbsp. olive oil
1 tsp. dried thyme
1½ tsp. dried rosemary

Pinch of oregano
2–3 cloves finely minced garlic
½ cup white wine
½ cup chicken broth
3–4 sliced artichoke hearts, packed in water
¼ cup fresh parsley chopped

Rinse chicken and pat dry. Dredge chicken in flour. Heat 2 tablespoons olive oil in large non-stick skillet over medium-high heat. Cook chicken 3 minutes on each side.

Reduce heat. Add dried herbs to skillet with remainder of olive oil. Distribute herbs evenly. Add wine, chicken broth, and artichoke hearts to the pan. Cover and let simmer for 10 minutes. Stir in parsley to finish dish. *Makes 4 servings.*

CHICKEN CACCIATORE   O

1½ lbs. chicken (boneless
   breasts or chicken on bone pieces)
1 tsp. garlic powder
1 tsp. dried thyme
1½ tsp. dried rosemary
1 tsp. dried oregano
½ tsp. dried basil
4 Tbsp. olive oil
2 cloves minced garlic

1 small chopped onion
1 cup chopped green bell peppers
1 15-oz. can diced tomatoes
½ cup dry white or red wine
2 cups coarsely chopped
   portobello mushrooms
4 crushed peppercorns
Salt to taste

Rinse chicken and pat dry. Season both sides of chicken with garlic powder and half the dried herbs. In large skillet, heat olive oil over medium heat. Cook chicken 3–5 minutes on each side or until brown. Remove and set aside.

Sauté garlic, onion, and peppers in remaining olive oil until onions are soft. Add tomatoes with their juice, wine, mushrooms, remaining herbs, peppercorn, and chicken to skillet. Bring to simmer. Cover and cook boneless chicken for 10–20 minutes or chicken pieces for 20–25 minutes. *Makes 4 servings.*

CHICKEN IN GARLIC SAUCE   A, O

1 lb. chicken fillets, cut into
   bite-size chunks
2 cups broccoli florets
1 cup asparagus
2 Tbsp. olive oil

2–4 cloves minced garlic
2 Tbsp. grated fresh ginger
2 Tbsp. fresh lemon juice
½ cup chopped scallions (optional)
Dash of hot chili oil

Rinse chicken in cold water and pat dry.

Steam broccoli florets and asparagus in large covered pot for 5 minutes. Use 1 inch of water on bottom of pot to create steam.

Heat olive oil in large skillet or wok. Sauté garlic and ginger for 1 minute. Add chicken and lemon juice. Cook for 3–4 minutes. Add broccoli and asparagus to skillet (also add scallions if using). Simmer for 4–5 minutes until chicken and vegetables are cooked through. *Makes 3–4 servings.*

HONEY CHICKEN WITH LIME   A

½ tsp. garlic powder
4 boneless, skinless chicken
   breast halves
⅓ cup pineapple juice
¼ cup honey

1 tsp. lime zest
3 Tbsp. fresh lime juice
2 Tbsp. soy sauce
2 tsp. corn starch

Sprinkle garlic powder over chicken; let sit while you prepare sauce.

In small bowl, whisk together pineapple juice, honey, lime zest, lime juice, and soy sauce until well mixed. Brush chicken with sauce. Heat large nonstick skillet to medium heat. Cook each piece of chicken 5 minutes on each side or until done.

Bring leftover marinade to boil. Lower to simmer for 2 minutes. Thicken sauce with cornstarch. *Makes 4 servings.*

ROSEMARY CHICKEN[1]   A, O

6 cloves of crushed garlic
2 Tbsp. fresh or dried rosemary
Juice of 4 limes (about ½ cup)
½ cup olive oil

½ tsp. salt
1 quartered chicken (3½–4 lbs.)
4 rosemary sprigs for garnish
1 lime sliced for garnish

In large bowl, combine garlic, rosemary, lime juice, olive oil, and salt. Place quartered chicken in bowl. Turn to coat all pieces. Cover with plastic wrap and marinate in refrigerator for 3 hours. Turn chicken once during marinating time.

Heat cast-iron skillet to hot. Add chicken pieces, and weight them down with heavy lid or another cast-iron skillet. Cook until crispy, 15 minutes on each side. Serve chicken, garnished with sprig of rosemary and wedge of lime. *Makes 4 servings.*

SESAME CHICKEN A, O

1 lb. chicken, cut up
2 Tbsp. tamari, shoyu or
  light soy sauce
2 Tbsp. water
1 tsp. honey

½ Tbsp. fresh minced ginger
Ground peppercorns to taste *(O only)*
2 Tbsp. canola oil
1 Tbsp. toasted sesame seeds

Rinse chicken in cold water. Pat dry.

In small bowl, combine tamari sauce, water, honey, ginger, and ground peppercorns *(O only)*. Whisk together and set aside.

Heat canola oil in large skillet. Cook chicken 1 minute on each side. Add tamari mixture to chicken. Let cook until mixture comes to slight boil and thickens somewhat. Remove chicken from skillet. Sprinkle with toasted sesame seeds. *Makes 2 servings.*

TURKEY

SESAME TURKEY FILLETS A, O

1 lb. turkey fillets
2 Tbsp. tamari, shoyu or
  light soy sauce
2 Tbsp. water
1 tsp. honey

½ Tbsp. fresh minced ginger
Ground peppercorns to taste *(O only)*
2 Tbsp. canola oil
1 Tbsp. toasted sesame seeds

Rinse turkey fillets in cold water. Pat dry.

In small bowl, combine tamari sauce, water, honey, ginger, and peppercorns *(O only)*. Whisk together and set aside.

Heat canola oil in large skillet. Cook turkey 1 minute on each side. Add tamari mixture to turkey. Let cook until mixture comes to a slight boil and thickens somewhat. Remove turkey from skillet. Sprinkle with toasted sesame seeds. *Makes 2–3 servings.*

LAMB

CROCKPOT GREEK LAMB SALAD   B, AB, O

4 lb. lamb shoulder*

1 Tbsp. lemon zest

¼ cup fresh oregano, or
   2 Tbsp. dried oregano

2–3 whole cloves garlic

Pinch of salt

Lemon juice from 1½ lemons

4 cups fresh spinach or chard

Pasta, blood-type appropriate

1 cup crumbled feta cheese

¼ cup fresh chopped parsley
   or 2 Tbsp. dried parsley

*Ask your butcher to trim the lamb shoulder well. Its less expensive price comes with a great deal more fat. Alternately use a leg of lamb with the bone.

Place lamb in Crockpot with lemon zest, oregano, garlic, and salt. Add lemon juice. Cover lamb with spinach or chard. Cover with lid. Slow-cook on medium for 7 hours. Once lamb is done, remove lamb from pot and let rest. Place drippings in bowl. Let cool; skim fat from top and discard.

Cook pasta while you remove lamb from bone. Meat will be very tender. Discard any bones, gristle, and fat. Chop meat into bite-size pieces. In large bowl, mix lamb pieces with feta, spinach, parsley, and pasta. Slowly ladle some skimmed drippings into bowl. Only use enough to make mixture moist. Add little extra lemon juice if necessary. *Makes 6–8 servings.*

ROSEMARY ROASTED LAMB   B, AB, O
WITH ROASTED VEGETABLES

4 lb. leg of lamb, boned and trimmed
   (ask your butcher to roll and truss
   meat for you)

5–6 sprigs fresh rosemary

8–10 cloves sliced garlic

¾ cup fresh chopped parsley

2–3 Tbsp. olive oil

Pinch of salt

Freshly ground peppercorns to taste *(O only)*

1 medium sweet potato, cut into chunks

1 medium beet cut into chunks

1 medium parsnip or turnip, cut into chunks

2 carrots, cut into chunks

Preheat oven to 400 degrees.

In large bowl, mix all vegetables with 2–3 Tbsp. of olive oil, salt, pepper, rosemary from 2 sprigs, ¼ cup parsley, and small handful of sliced garlic. Vegetables should just be a little wet with oil, not drenched. Set aside.

Place lamb in center of roasting pan and cover with remaining garlic and rosemary. Distribute vegetables around meat. Cook 20 minutes per pound uncovered. *Makes 6 or more servings.*

BEEF

BEEF AND GARLIC B, O

3–4 Tbsp. olive oil

1 lb. boned sirloin steak,
    cut into ¼–inch strips

2–3 cloves minced garlic

3 cups sliced bok choy or broccoli florets

¼ cup sliced green onions

3 Tbsp. light soy, tamari or shoyu sauce

⅓ cup beef stock

In large skillet, heat 2 tablespoons olive oil. Sauté sirloin and garlic until cooked, about 5 minutes. Remove from skillet. Use remaining olive oil to sauté bok choy or broccoli with green onions about 3–4 minutes. Add sirloin and garlic mixture to vegetables. Mix well.

Add light soy sauce and beef stock. Cook for 2 minutes, or until everything is cooked through. *Makes 3–4 servings.*

BEEFED-UP CHEESEBURGERS B, O

2 lbs. lean ground beef

¾ cup finely chopped
    portobello mushrooms

⅓ cup minced onions

1 Tbsp. Worcestershire sauce

1 Tbsp. fresh chopped parsley

½ Tbsp. fresh thyme

1–2 cloves minced garlic (optional)

Dash of hot pepper sauce or cayenne

Pinch of salt

Slice of appropriate cheese (optional)

Preheat broiler.

In large bowl, mix all ingredients together, using your hands to knead well. Shape into 12 burgers. Grill to desired wellness. Top with appropriate cheese of your choice. *Makes 6 servings.*

HEARTY BEEF STEW B

3–4 Tbsp. olive oil

3 sliced carrots

1 cup cubed turnips or parsnips

2 large white potatoes

1 lb. domestic mushrooms

1 medium chopped onion

¼ cup spelt flour

2 lbs. lean cubed beef (top, bottom
    round, or chuck)

Pinch of salt

¼ cup fresh chopped parsley

1 tsp. marjoram

½ cup dark beer

1–1½ cup beef stock

In large Dutch oven or deep saucepan, using 2 tablespoons olive oil, sauté carrots, turnips, potatoes, mushrooms, and onion for 5–7 minutes. Add spelt flour. Mix well. Set aside.

In large skillet, heat remaining olive oil. Season beef with pinch of salt. Sauté until brown but not cooked through. Toss in parsley just before next step.

Add beef and marjoram to vegetable mixture. Pour beer into pot. Then add enough beef stock to bring the level of liquid to 1–1½ inches above ingredients. Cover and simmer until beef is tender, 2–3 hours. Add more liquid if necessary. *Makes 4–6 servings.*

LIGHT BEEF STEW WITH HERBS   O

3 cups fresh or canned chopped
   tomatoes
2 cloves minced garlic
½ tsp. dried basil
½ cup diced celery
½ cup fresh chopped parsley
½ tsp. dried marjoram

½ tsp. dried thyme
4 Tbsp. olive oil
1 lb. lean cubed beef (top, bottom
   round, or chuck)
4–5 crushed peppercorns
1 cup dry white wine
1 tsp. dried rosemary

In large saucepan, simmer tomatoes, garlic, basil, celery, parsley, marjoram, thyme, and 1–2 tablespoons of olive oil for 30 minutes.

Heat remaining olive oil in large skillet. Sauté beef with peppercorns over medium-high heat until brown. Do not cook through. Set meat aside. Pour wine into hot skillet to deglaze the pan of all little bits of meat left behind. Stir, scrapping sides until wine reduces to half.

Add wine mixture, beef, and rosemary to tomato mixture. Cover and simmer for 1½ hours or until meat is tender. *Makes 4 servings.*

MEAT LOAF   O

1½ lbs. lean ground beef
Salt to taste
Pinch of cayenne or hot sauce
½ cup O-friendly bread crumbs
   (Rye Crisp crumbs/oatmeal)
8 oz. tomato sauce
1 egg
¼ cup minced onions
2 cloves minced garlic
   or 1 Tbsp. garlic powder

2 Tbsp. fresh chopped parsley or coriander,
   or 1 Tbsp. dried Italian seasoning
½ cup chopped dates (optional)
½ cup chopped walnuts (optional)
8 oz. shredded mozzarella
1 10-oz. pkg frozen chopped spinach,
   thawed and squeezed, drained well

Preheat oven to 375 degrees.

In large bowl, combine everything except spinach, mozzarella, and 2–3 tablespoons of tomato sauce (use for meat loaf only). Knead well with hands. Place on sheet of foil. Flatten and shape mixture into two rectangular shapes.

Evenly spread mozzarella on top of one meat rectangle, leaving ½-inch border. Spread spinach on top of the cheese. Using foil as an aid, lift second meat rectangle over rectangle with spinach and cheese mixture. Cover completely, and pinch log to seal two rectangles together completely.

Place in pan, seam side down. Brush with remaining tomato sauce. Use foil to create tent over roll. Cook for 20–30 minutes or until done. Let stand for 20 minutes before slicing.

FISH/SEAFOOD

CORN-CRUSTED FISH A

1 cup finely ground cornmeal
1 tsp. dried parsley
1 tsp. dried dill
½ tsp. salt

1½ lb. fresh cod (or any firm, white fish)
1 Tbsp. olive oil
Sliced lemons or limes

Combine cornmeal with parsley, dill, and salt. Mix well. Dredge cod in cornmeal mixture.

Heat skillet with olive oil. Add fish to skillet, and cook over medium heat for 5–7 minutes per side. Use cover so that fish will cook through. (Cooking time will depend on thickness of fish. Fish is done when it begins to flake.)

Just before fish is cooked completely, add a few tablespoons of water to skillet. Allow fish to finish cooking with lid on pan. Remove fish from pan, and garnish with sliced lemons or limes. *Makes 3–4 servings.*

CURRIED SCALLOPS AND VEGETABLES AB

1 lb. bay scallops
1 cup broccoli florets
1 cup asparagus
3 Tbsp. olive oil
2 cloves minced garlic
½ cup chopped onions
1 tsp. curry powder

¾ cup chicken broth
½ cup chopped scallions
Other vegetable options include:
   zucchini and carrot matchsticks
   ½ cup Swiss chard or
     collard green ribbons

Rinse scallops in cold water and pat dry.

Steam broccoli florets and asparagus in large covered pot for 5 minutes. Use 1 inch of water on bottom of pot to create steam.

Heat 2 tablespoons olive oil in large skillet. Sauté scallops, stirring frequently, for 4–5 minutes. Set aside. Use remaining olive oil to sauté garlic and onions with curry powder.

Add chicken broth to onion mixture. Let simmer for 7–10 minutes. Add scallions, broccoli, and asparagus to skillet. Simmer for 2–3 minutes until scallops are cooked and vegetables are heated through. *Makes 3–4 servings.*

FISH WITH HERBS AND LIME[2]   ALL

1½ lb. fresh red snapper or cod
¼ cup lime juice
   (not from concentrate)
4 garlic cloves, pressed or minced
½ cup chopped fresh parsley
½ cup chopped scallions

1 tsp. chopped fresh rosemary,
   or ½ tsp. dried rosemary
1 tsp. fresh thyme,
   or ½ tsp. dried thyme
1 tsp. sweet paprika
1 cup diced fresh tomatoes *(O, AB only)*

Preheat oven to 375 degrees. Rinse fish in cold water and pat dry.

In medium bowl, mix together lime juice, garlic, parsley, scallions, rosemary, thyme, paprika, and tomatoes (if using).

Place fillets in nonstick baking dish (unoiled), and spread topping evenly over fish. Cover tightly with foil, and bake for 25 minutes until fish flakes with a fork. *Makes 3–4 servings.*

MARINATED TUNA STEAKS   ALL

⅓ cup olive oil
¼ cup tamari, shoyu or
   light soy sauce
Lemon juice from half a lemon

2 cloves smashed garlic
2 Tbsp. fresh chopped coriander (cilantro)
1 dollop honey
4 tuna steaks (6 oz. each)

Combine all ingredients except tuna in large Ziploc bag or in shallow bowl. (Ziploc bag makes it easier to move marinade around the fish.) Mix ingredients well. Add tuna to marinade. Cover tuna completely with mixture. Place in refrigerator for 15–30 minutes. Use this time to prepare other parts of your dinner.

Grill or broil tuna steaks on medium heat to desired doneness, 3–4 minutes per side for rare, 5 minutes for medium-well. Let fish sit for 5 minutes before serving. *Makes 3–4 servings.*

ORANGE GINGER FISH   B

(Please note that this recipe works with other firm white fishes.)

Juice from 2 oranges
2 Tbsp. honey
1 Tbsp. tamari or shoyu sauce

1 Tbsp. fresh minced ginger,
   or ½ Tbsp. dried ginger
1½ lb. fresh cod or sole
2 Tbsp. olive oil

Place all ingredients except fish and olive oil in shallow glass bowl and mix well. Add fish. Allow to marinate for 15–20 minutes.

Pan-sear fish in olive oil. Cook covered for 4–5 minutes per side. If fish seems a bit dry, add some of marinade to pot. Remove fish from pan. Reduce any excess liquid in pan, and pour over cooked fish. *Makes 3–4 servings.*

ORANGE MARINATED SALMON
B

(Please note that this recipe works with most firm fishes.)

¾ cup extra-virgin olive oil

¼ cup orange juice
  (not from concentrate)

½ cup chopped scallions

¼ cup white wine

1½ tsp. dried tarragon

1½ lb. salmon fillets

Preheat oven to 375 degrees. In shallow glass bowl combine all ingredients except salmon. Mix well. Rinse fish in cold water and pat dry. Place fish in bowl; marinate for ½ hour at room temperature.

You can cook this fish several different ways: BAKE at 375 degrees for 30 minutes; BROIL for 7–9 minutes or until fish flakes (baste with marinade often); or GRILL on medium-high heat 3–4 minutes each side or until fish flakes. *Makes 3–4 servings.*

RICE AND SALMON
AB, O

2 cups white rice

4 cups water

3 Tbsp. olive oil

1 small chopped onion

3 cloves chopped garlic

2 small cans tomato sauce

3 Tbsp. Spanish olives

1 can of salmon
  or 1 large salmon steak

Put rice and water in saucepan. Bring to a boil. Lower heat to simmer. Cover saucepan and cook for 17 minutes or until done.

In skillet, add olive oil, chopped onion, and garlic. Sauté until onions are translucent. Add tomato sauce, ½ can water, and olives. Let simmer for 10 minutes. Add salmon (including juice in can). Simmer for 10 minutes. Serve over rice. *Makes 1 serving.*

SCALLOPS IN GARLIC SAUCE
B, AB

1 lb. bay scallops

2 cups broccoli florets

1 cup asparagus

1½ Tbsp. olive oil

2–4 cloves minced garlic

2 Tbsp. grated fresh ginger

2 Tbsp. fresh lemon juice

½ cup chopped scallions (optional)

Rinse scallops in cold water, and pat dry.

Steam broccoli florets and asparagus in large covered pot for 5 minutes. Use 1 inch of water on bottom of pot to create steam.

Heat olive oil in large skillet or wok. Sauté garlic and ginger for 1 minute. Add scallops and lemon juice. Cook for 3–4 minutes. Add broccoli and asparagus (and scallions if using) to skillet. Simmer for 4–5 minutes until scallops are cooked and vegetables are heated through. *Makes 3–4 servings.*

SESAME FISH   O

1½ lb. fresh halibut
 (or other firm white fish)
2 Tbsp. toasted sesame seeds
¼ cup olive oil
¼ cup water
⅓ cup lemon juice (not from concentrate)

1 Tbsp. soy, tamari or shoyu sauce
1 Tbsp. honey
2 Tbsp. fresh chopped parsley
2 Tbsp. fresh chopped scallions

Rinse fish in cold water and pat dry.

In small nonstick skillet, heat sesame seeds over medium heat. No oil is necessary. Keep stirring seeds so they do not stick. Let seeds cook until they start to turn a golden color. It will only take 1–2 minutes. Do not burn. Set toasted seeds aside to cool.

Combine olive oil, water, lemon juice, soy sauce, and honey in shallow bowl. Use whisk to mix well. Add sesame seeds, parsley, and scallions. Mix well. Add fish and marinate for ½ hour at room temperature.

Heat large nonstick skillet. Add fish. Allow fish to cook 5–7 minutes per side over medium heat. Cooking time will depend on thickness of fish. Add more marinade mixture to skillet if fish starts to stick or dry out. *Makes 3–4 servings.*

SHORT-CUT SCAMPI (IN FOIL)   O

1 lb. raw medium shrimp,
 shelled and deveined
2 cloves minced garlic or 2 shallots
¼ cup olive oil
¼ cup chicken broth or dry white wine

1 tsp. rosemary
½ tsp. dried parsley
½ tsp. dried basil
1½ Tbsp. lemon juice

Preheat oven to 375 degrees or use BBQ grill for cooking. Rinse shrimp in cold water and pat dry.

In small bowl, whisk together garlic, olive oil, chicken broth or wine, rosemary, parsley, basil, and lemon juice. Pour herb mixture over shrimp and mix well. Divide shrimp into 4 portion sizes.

Lay four layers of aluminum foil, one on top of another, on counter top. Foil needs to be large enough to hold individual portions of shrimp. Bring four corners of foil up over shrimp, and twist to form sealed pouch. Place pouches in oven or on grill for 10–12 minutes. Shrimp will be firm and pink when done. *Makes 3–4 servings.*

VEGETABLES

BROILED PORTOBELLO MUSHROOMS   ALL

1 Tbsp. balsamic vinegar *(A, AB only)* 1 Tbsp. fresh chopped parsley
2 Tbsp. red or white wine *(B, O only)* 1 lb. whole portobello mushrooms,
2 Tbsp. water   stems removed
3–4 Tbsp. olive oil   1 lb. spinach
Pinch of salt   1 oz. goat cheese per mushroom

Preheat broiler.

In small bowl, combine vinegar or wine, water, oil, salt, and parsley. Brush cleaned mushrooms with marinade. Place on baking sheet, cap side up. Broil for 3–5 minutes or until mushrooms soften.

Place trimmed and cleaned spinach in large saucepan of boiling water. Let boil for 3 minutes. Leaves should just turn bright green. Do not overcook. Remove from water, and set aside.

Turn mushrooms over, apply more marinade, and place some crumbled goat cheese inside cap. Let broil until cheese starts to bubble and brown. Remove. Serve mushrooms on bed of spinach. *Makes 4 servings.*

BLACK-EYED PEAS AND FENNEL   O

1 small diced onion   1 16-oz. can black-eyed peas
1 chopped red bell pepper   1 bunch chopped fresh fennel or anise
2–3 Tbsp. canola oil   (white part only)

Sauté onion and red pepper in canola oil until soft. Add peas and heat through. Add fennel with 2–3 Tbsp. of water. Cover and cook for 15 minutes or until fennel is soft. *Makes 3–4 servings.*

COLLARD GREENS WITH NUTS   ALL

1 cup raisins   2 cloves finely minced garlic
1 cup boiling water   1–2 Tbsp. olive oil
¼ cup crushed walnuts   1 lb. collard greens
  or almond slivers

Soak raisins in boiling water for 10 minutes.

In small skillet toast nuts over medium heat for 4–5 minutes. No oil is necessary.

In large saucepan sauté garlic in oil over low heat until soft, about 2–3 minutes. Raise heat to medium. Add collards to garlic. Sauté for 4–5 minutes. Add reserved raisin-soaking water. Cover and let steam for 10–15 minutes or until collards are tender. Stir in raisins and serve. *Makes 4 servings.*

EGGPLANT CASSEROLE   B

1 medium-to-large sliced eggplant   7 oz. pesto with basil
4 zucchinis sliced   Sea salt to taste
8-oz. sliced mozzarella

Preheat oven to 350 degrees.

Layer everything in a large dish, alternating layers of eggplant, zucchini, and mozzarella. Spread a little pesto between each layer. Cover with foil and cook for 35–45 minutes or until eggplant is cooked. *Makes 4 servings.*

SPICY FRIES   B, AB, O

Version 1   *Version 2*
2 lb. potatoes   2 lb. potatoes
  (AB, O use sweet potatoes;   *(AB, O use sweet potatoes;*
  B use white)   *B use white)*
2 Tbsp. olive oil   2 Tbsp. olive oil
1½ Tbsp. paprika   2 Tbsp. fresh rosemary,
1½ tsp. cumin   or 1 Tbsp. dried rosemary
1 tsp. onion powder   1 tsp. garlic powder
                                           1 tsp. onion powder

Preheat oven to 425 degrees.

Wash potatoes, and cut into "fries" shape. Place potatoes in large bowl, and drizzle olive oil over potatoes. Using your hands, mix well. Add spices, and mix again until potatoes are completely covered.

Place potatoes on baking sheet in single layer. Cook for 30–40 minutes, turning occasionally so all sides brown. Sprinkle with salt and serve.

RICE

STIR-FRIED RICE   O

1 tsp. minced garlic   1 cup cut-up cooked beef
1 chopped red bell pepper   (ground beef or steak)
2 chopped green onions   2 Tbsp. soy sauce
2 Tbsp. butter   1 beaten egg
2 cups cooked brown rice

Sauté garlic, red pepper, and onion in butter until tender. Add brown rice, meat, and soy sauce. Stir-fry until hot.

Drizzle egg over rice mixture; stir-fry until egg is cooked. *Makes 4 servings.*

SPICE RUBS AND HERB CRUSTS

One of the easiest ways to increase the flavor of tofu, meat, fish, and poultry is to use dry spice rubs or herb crusts. Any of these mixtures can be used dry, or add 1 teaspoon of water to create a paste. Fresh herbs are suggested unless otherwise specified.[3]

CAJUN SPICE RUB   O

1 Tbsp. paprika
1 tsp. garlic powder
1 tsp. onion powder
½ tsp. dried thyme
½ tsp. oregano
⅛ tsp. cayenne pepper
⅛ tsp. ground red pepper

Makes about 2½ tablespoons.

MEXICAN SPICE RUB   O

1 Tbsp. chili powder
1 Tbsp. fresh chopped cilantro
2 cloves minced garlic
½ tsp. ground cumin
⅛ tsp. ground red pepper

Makes about 2½ tablespoons.

MORROCCAN
SPICE RUB   A, B, AB

1 Tbsp. chopped fresh mint
2 cloves minced garlic
2 tsp. grated fresh ginger
½ tsp. ground cinnamon
½ tsp. ground red pepper *(AB avoid)*

Makes about 3½ tablespoons.

FRENCH HERB CRUST   ALL

3 Tbsp. chopped fresh parsley
1 Tbsp. chopped fresh chives
2 tsp. chopped fresh thyme
2 cloves minced garlic
2 tsp. grated orange rind *(B only)*
2 tsp. grated lemon rind *(A, AB, O)*

Makes about 5 tablespoons.

GREEK HERB CRUST   ALL

2 Tbsp. chopped fresh parsley
1 Tbsp. chopped fresh oregano
1 Tbsp. grated lemon rind
2 cloves minced garlic

Makes about 4 tablespoons.

ITALIAN HERB CRUST   ALL

3 Tbsp. chopped fresh parsley
2 Tbsp. chopped fresh basil
2 cloves minced garlic
2 tsp. grated lemon rind

Makes about 5 tablespoons.

TRADITIONAL
HERB CRUST   ALL

2 Tbsp. chopped fresh parsley
1½ Tbsp. chopped fresh rosemary
2 cloves minced garlic

Makes about 3½ tablespoons.

SAUCES

CHEESELESS BASIL PESTO   ALL

6–8 whole walnuts *(B only)*
6–8 whole almonds *(A, AB, O)*
2–3 cloves garlic
1 Tbsp. light miso *(A, AB, O)*
3 Tbsp. Parmesan cheese *(B only)*

5–6 cups fresh basil leaves,
    packed, trimmed and stemmed
⅓ cup extra-virgin olive oil
Pinch of salt
1 Tbsp. fresh lemon juice

In food processor, pulverize walnuts (or almonds) and garlic. Add in miso (or Parmesan cheese) and pulse lightly. Slowly add basil leaves one cup at a time to processor with a little oil. Continue this process until all oil and basil are incorporated.

Taste pesto and adjust seasoning if necessary with pinch of salt. If you like looser pesto, add more olive oil. However, a paste consistency is OK too. It's up to your personal preference.

Add lemon juice to preserve color of basil. Extra pesto can be frozen in small container. *Makes about ¾–1 cup.*

PIZZA SAUCE   A, B, O

2 tsp. sugar
1 tsp. salt
2 tsp. paprika
1 tsp. oregano powder
1 tsp. dried basil
1 tsp. dried parsley

1 tsp. dried thyme
2 tsp. onion powder
1 tsp. garlic powder
3 drops anise flavoring
½ cup water

In small bowl, combine all dry ingredients and mix well. Stir in anise flavoring and water. Mix well. *Makes about ½–1 cup.*

SOY CHEESE SAUCE   A, AB, O

3 oz. cheddar soy cheese
3 oz. silken tofu
1 Tbsp. soy milk or water

2 Tbsp. vegetable oil
    (linseed, canola, or olive)

Grate soy cheese, and combine everything in microwave-safe bowl. Heat on high for 30 seconds, then blend well with hand blender. Repeat this step until cheese is melted and mixture is completely combined. *Makes 1–1½ cups.*

SPINACH PESTO   ALL

1 bag fresh spinach (350 grams),   4 cloves pressed garlic
  stemmed and trimmed   1 Tbsp. pine nuts (optional—omit for B)
½ cup packed fresh basil leaves   ½ tsp. sea salt
  or a sprinkling of dried basil   1–2 oz. feta cheese
1 Tbsp. extra-virgin olive oil

In large stainless-steel pot, heat ½ inch of water. Toss in spinach and cover. Let steam for 1–2 minutes. Spinach should just be wilted, not completely cooked. Remove from pot and drain immediately.

Place spinach and all other ingredients in food processor. Purée thoroughly. Pesto can be stored in container in freezer or refrigerator. *Makes about 1–1½ cups.*

TOMATO ITALIANO SAUCE WITH TUNA   AB, O

1 small minced onion   2 tsp. dried basil
½ cup fresh chopped parsley   Cayenne to taste
1 chopped red pepper   Salt to taste
2–3 Tbsp. olive oil   1 6-oz. can tuna packed in water
1 large can of crushed Italian tomatoes

Sauté onion, parsley, and red pepper in olive oil until onion is translucent. Add tomatoes and seasonings. In separate dish, chop tuna and add to tomato sauce. Simmer on low for 20 minutes. Serve over pasta. *Makes 8–10 cups.*

SALAD DRESSINGS

CREAMY AVOCADO DRESSING   A, AB, O

4 oz. soft silken tofu   1 tsp. soy sauce
½ ripe avocado   ¼ cup water
  (blood type appropriate)   Salt to taste
Juice of 1 lemon

Place all ingredients in food processor. Purée until smooth. Add water, one tablespoon at a time, to thin as necessary. *Makes 1½ cups.*

CREAMY CILANTRO LIME DRESSING   A, B, AB

1 cup plain low-fat yogurt   1 Tbsp. fresh lime juice
1½ Tbsp. fresh chopped cilantro   1 tsp. honey (optional)
1½ Tbsp. finely minced scallions   Pinch of salt
    or chives

In small bowl or food processor, combine all ingredients until smooth. Add water as needed, 1 teaspoon at a time. Let sit in refrigerator for at least 1 hour so flavors can blend. *Makes 1 cup.*

CREAMY GARLIC DRESSING   A, B, AB

1½ cups plain low-fat yogurt   2 cloves minced garlic
1 Tbsp. almond butter   1 Tbsp. fresh or dried parsley
1 Tbsp. fresh lemon juice   Pinch of salt

In small bowl or food processor, combine all ingredients until smooth. Add water as needed, 1 teaspoon at a time. *Makes 1½ cups.*

GREEN GODDESS DRESSING   A, AB, O

4 oz. silken tofu   ¼ cup fresh chopped parsley
2 Tbsp. Braggs Liquid Amino   2–4 fresh chopped basil leaves
1 tsp. brown rice syrup or honey   1 Tbsp. fresh chopped chives

Bring small saucepan of water to boil. Add tofu; simmer for 5 minutes. Drain well. Set aside to cool for several minutes. Place cooked tofu and all other ingredients in food processor. Purée until smooth. Add water, a teaspoon at a time, to thin if necessary. *Makes 1–1½ cups.*

HERB MOCK VINAIGRETTE DRESSING   ALL

½ cup fresh lemon juice   1 clove pressed garlic
    (about 3–4 lemons)   1 tsp. dried mustard
¼ cup Braggs Liquid Amino   1 tsp. dried basil, or 1 Tbsp. fresh basil
1 cup cold-pressed olive oil   1 tsp. dried tarragon
1 cup cold-pressed canola oil   ½ tsp. dried parsley,
    (or other blood-type appropriate   or 1 tsp. fresh parsley
    oil—not flax)

Combine all ingredients in jar or Tupperware container. Shake vigorously to blend. *Makes 3–4 cups.*

HONEY MUSTARD DRESSING   B

⅓ cup cider vinegar   1–2 Tbsp. honey
1 cup olive oil   Salt to taste
2 Tbsp. Dijon mustard

In a small bowl, whisk together all ingredients. For creamier dressing, add 1 clove roasted garlic. Purée all ingredients in food processor. *Makes 1–1¼ cups.*

LEMON-LIME CILANTRO DRESSING   ALL

1 dollop honey   ¾ cup olive oil
Juice of 1 lemon   2 cloves smashed garlic
Juice of ½ lime   2–3 Tbsp. fresh chopped coriander
¼ cup tamari, shoyu   (cilantro)
   or light soy sauce

Place honey in small bowl. Set bowl in larger bowl of hot water. Heat will loosen honey up. Once it is loose, add citrus juices, tamari, and olive oil. Whisk together well. Add garlic and coriander. Whisk well. Let sit at room temperature for 1 hour so flavors can blend. *Makes 1 cup.*

MIDDLE EASTERN DRESSING   A, B, AB

1½ cups plain low-fat yogurt   1 clove minced garlic
1 Tbsp. almond butter   ½ tsp. ground cumin
1 Tbsp. fresh lemon juice   Pinch of salt

In small bowl or food processor, combine all ingredients until smooth. Add water as needed, 1 teaspoon at a time. *Makes 1½ cups.*

MISO DRESSING #1   ALL

½ cup light miso   ¼ cup lemon juice
½ cup olive oil   1 tsp. dry mustard
½ cup water

Put all ingredients in food processor, and blend well. If you do not have a food processor, bring water to near boil and mix miso until smooth. Whisk in all other ingredients. Let stand at room temperature before serving. *Makes 1¼ cups.*

MISO DRESSING #2   ALL

1 Tbsp. sweet white miso   2 Tbsp. Braggs Liquid Amino
Juice and zest of 1 lemon   ¼ cup olive oil
2 Tbsp. soy sauce   1 tsp. dried basil

Dilute miso in lemon juice and soy sauce using whisk. Add all other ingredients. Whisk to blend. *Makes 1¼ cups.*

OREGANO-FETA DRESSING   ALL

2 oz. feta cheese   1 clove crushed garlic
2 Tbsp. fresh lemon juice   ½ tsp. dried crushed oregano
1 Tbsp. olive oil

Put all ingredients in food processor, and pulse until mixed. *Makes 1 cup.*

RASPBERRY MOCK VINAIGRETTE DRESSING   ALL

6 fresh raspberries   1 cup olive oil
¼ cup apple cider *(A, O avoid)*   1 tsp. finely minced red onions
2 Tbsp. Braggs Liquid Amino   ½ tsp. dried rosemary

Smash raspberries in cider until they are completely broken up. Combine all ingredients in jar or plastic container. Shake vigorously to blend. *Makes 1 cup.*

RED ONION DRESSING   ALL

½ cup fresh lemon juice   1–2 Tbsp. finely chopped red onion
   (about 3–4 lemons)   ½ tsp. dried mustard
¼ cup Braggs Liquid Amino   ½ tsp. dried oregano or parsley
1 cup cold-pressed olive oil   ½ tsp. dried thyme, minced or pressed

Combine all ingredients in jar or plastic container. Shake vigorously to blend. Let sit at room temperature for an hour or so before using to allow flavors to blend. *Makes 1½ cups.*

VINEGARLESS DRESSING   ALL

½ cup fresh lemon juice
  (about 3–4 lemons)
¼ cup Braggs Liquid Amino
1 tsp. garlic powder
1 cup cold-pressed olive oil

1 cup cold-pressed canola oil (or other
  blood-type appropriate oil—not flax)
1 tsp. minced onions
½ tsp. curry or turmeric

Place all ingredients in quart-sized plastic container with lid and pouring feature. Mix ingredients well. If consistency is too thick, add water, or next time use less olive oil and increase other oil. (Add other spices you would like based on your blood type.) Keep refrigerated for 3–4 weeks. *Makes 2¾ cups.*

WARM CRANBERRY DRESSING   ALL

1½ cup fresh, cleaned cranberries
Lemon juice and zest from 1 lemon
  (B—use orange if preferred)
2 Tbsp. brown rice syrup
  or maple syrup
¼ cup olive oil

1 tsp. fresh finely minced ginger
2 Tbsp. soy sauce
½ tsp. plum paste
  (umeboshi paste)
¼ cup crushed walnuts for garnish

In food processor, combine cranberries, lemon juice, zest, and syrup. Mix to a minced consistency. If you like it chunkier, adjust to your preference.

Combine oil, ginger, soy sauce, and plum paste in small saucepan over low heat. Once warm, add cranberry mixture. Let simmer for 5–7 minutes. Remove from heat. Serve and garnish with crushed walnuts. *Makes 1½ cups.*

TRAIL MIXES

Trail mixes are an easy, convenient snack. Make a batch to keep in your cupboard. There are many combinations that can be made from your grocery lists. Below we are providing some sample ideas for trail mixes and a simple guideline for creating your own personalized blend. Remember, your trail mix must use ingredients that are blood-type appropriate.

SUGGESTED TRAIL MIX RECIPE GUIDELINES

Use the measurements given for each component.

½ cup dried fruit	raisins *(ALL)*, apples *(ALL)*, black currants *(ALL)*, red currants *(B, AB, O)*
	(Avoid other dried fruits, which are extremely high in sugar.)
1½ cup nuts (anabolic)	walnuts *(ALL)*, almonds *(ALL)*, Brazil nuts *(B, AB)* hickory *(ALL)*, unsalted redskin peanuts *(A, AB)* filberts (A, O)
¼ cup nonanabolic nuts or seeds	pecans *(B, O)*, cashews *(AB)*, pistachios *(AB)*, macadamia *(AB, O)*, pumpkinseeds *(A, O)*, sesame seeds *(A, O)*, sunflower seeds *(A, O)*
½ cup something chocolate	carob chips *(ALL)*, chocolate chips *(ALL)*

APPLE "PIE" TRAIL MIX   A, O

¼ cup black currants
½ cup almonds
¼ cup dried apple pieces
¼ cup pumpkinseeds
1 cup walnuts

APPLE WALNUT TRAIL MIX   B, O

¼ cup black currants
½ cup almonds
¼ cup dried apple pieces
¼ cup pecans
1 cup walnuts
½ cup carob or chocolate chips

BASIC TRAIL MIX #1   A, O

½ cup raisins
¼ cup sunflower seeds
¾ cup almond slivers
½ cup carob or chocolate chips
1 cup walnuts

BASIC TRAIL MIX #2   AB

½ cup black currants
¼ cup cashews
¾ cup almond slivers
½ cup carob or chocolate chips
¾ cup walnuts

BASIC TRAIL MIX #3   B, O

½ cup black currants
¼ cup pecans
¾ cup almond slivers
½ cup carob or chocolate chips
¾ cup walnuts

PEANUT CHOCOLATE TRAIL MIX   A, AB

¼ cup black currants
½ cup filberts
1 cup unsalted redskin peanuts
½ cup carob or chocolate chip
½ cup almonds

DESSERTS

ALMOND HONEY COOKIES   ALL

1 cup mild, light olive oil
1 2-inch strip lemon peel
½ cup dry white wine
¼ cup honey
1½–2 tsp. grated lemon zest
½ cup sliced almonds or walnuts

1 tsp. almond extract *(A, O only)*,
   or 1 tsp. vanilla extract *(ALL)*
3½ cups spelt flour
   (or other appropriate flour)
1 tsp. cinnamon *(A, AB only)*

In saucepan, gently heat olive oil and lemon peel. Oil should be warm, but not hot enough to "fry" rind. You only need to have oil on heat long enough to warm it. Remove from heat, and place in large mixing bowl to cool. Remove and discard rind once oil has cooled. Add wine, honey, lemon zest, almonds, and extract. Stir gently to mix.

In another bowl, sift together flour and cinnamon. Slowly pour oil mixture into flour mixture, stirring as you go. Once ingredients are incorporated, knead dough with your hands. Let dough rest for 30 minutes in refrigerator.

Preheat oven to 350 degrees. Roll dough into small balls, and flatten with back of a spoon. Bake for 15–20 minutes or until lightly browned. *Makes 12–16 cookies.*

APPLE CRISP   A, B, AB

Filling:

8 medium apples, sliced

½ cup raisins

¼ cup spelt flour

½ tsp. cinnamon *(A, AB only)*

½ cup apple cider

Topping:

1 cup rolled oats

2 Tbsp. spelt flour

⅓ cup light honey

2 Tbsp. canola oil *(A, AB)*

4 Tbsp. butter *(B)*

¾ tsp. cinnamon (optional for *A, AB*)

⅓ cup crushed walnuts (optional)

Preheat oven to 375 degrees. Spray 2-quart baking dish with cooking spray.

In large bowl, place sliced apples and raisins with flour and cinnamon (if using). Toss so apples are coated entirely by flour mixture. Pour into baking dish.

In another bowl, combine all topping ingredients and mix well.

Pour apple cider into baking dish over apples. Crumble topping over apples. Bake for 35–45 minutes or until apples are tender and golden. *Makes 4–6 servings.*

BASMATI RICE PUDDING[4]   A, B, O

1½ cups uncooked white basmati rice

5 cups water

1 Tbsp. butter *(omit for A)*

½ tsp. ground cinnamon *(omit for O)*

½ tsp. ground cardamom

1¾ cups milk *(blood type appropriate)*

½ tsp. salt

⅓ cup black currants

¼ tsp. pure vanilla extract

⅔ cup honey

¼ cup slivered almonds

Rinse and drain basmati rice. In food processor, chop rice into smaller pieces. Soak overnight in enough water to cover grains.

In large pot, combine 5 cups water, drained rice, butter, cinnamon, and cardamom. Cook on medium heat for about 20 minutes or until rice is soft. Add milk, salt, and black currants. Cook to pudding consistency, stirring frequently. Remove from heat, and let cool for 2–4 minutes. Stir in vanilla, honey, and almonds. Serve immediately. *Makes 4–6 servings.*

CAROB ALMOND COOKIES ALL

1½ large apples
   (pears can also be used)
⅓ cup almond butter
2 tsp. canola oil
2 eggs
¼ tsp. unbuffered, corn-free
   vitamin C crystals

1¼ cups brown rice flour,
   or 1 cup brown rice flour and
   ¼ cup spelt or Kamut flour
¾ tsp. baking soda (1 tsp. baking
   powder can be substituted for
   vitamin C and baking soda)
¾ cup carob powder
¼ tsp. salt
30 whole almonds (optional)

Preheat oven to 350 degrees. Spray 2 cookie sheets with cooking spray.

Chop apples into small chunks and put in blender. Add almond butter, oil, eggs, and vitamin C. Purée everything together. You may need to push apples down a few times to get them to purée. If necessary, add a little bit of water.

In separate bowl, combine flour, baking soda (or baking powder), carob powder, salt and almonds (if using). Mix well. Add purée to dry mixture and stir until mixed. Form round teaspoon-size balls, and drop onto cookie sheet. Bake for 10–12 minutes. Cookies are done when toothpick inserted comes out slightly moist. Allow to cool for 5 minutes. Refrigerate extras in airtight container. *Makes 6 servings.*

CHERRY CLAFOUTI ALL

¼ cup spelt flour
   (or other appropriate flour)
½ cup light honey
   (lavender honey works best)
2 eggs, lightly beaten

2 egg yolks
2 cups appropriate milk at
   room temperature
½ tsp. vanilla extract
2 cups pitted fresh cherries

Preheat oven to 375 degrees.

Place flour in a large bowl, making well for eggs and yolks. Using a whisk, slowly pour in milk and mix well. Whisk to a smooth consistency. Add honey and vanilla extract. Mix well.

In 8-inch deep-dish pie pan sprayed with cooking spray, evenly distribute fresh cherries. Carefully pour batter mixture over the fruit. Cook for 40–45 minutes or until brown and puffy. Let cool for 10 minutes before serving. *Makes 6 servings.*

CHOCOLATE MOUSSE   A, AB

1 10-oz. package firm silken   ½ tsp. ground cinnamon
  tofu, drained   1 tsp. instant coffee
¼ cup light honey   2 tsp. cocoa
¼ cup fruit syrup   ½ tsp. vanilla

Place all ingredients in food processor and purée until mixed. Place in airtight container, and refrigerate until well chilled. *Makes 3–4 servings.*

CHOCOLATE RICOTTA CREAM[5]   A, B, AB

1 15-oz. container of low-fat   ¼ tsp. cinnamon
  ricotta cheese   *(B—a dash of nutmeg)*
2 Tbsp. sifted unsweetened   ½ tsp. vanilla extract
  cocoa powder   1 Tbsp. toasted sliced almonds
5 Tbsp. honey   as garnish

Place ricotta in food processor or blender and process for 1 minute. Add all other ingredients. Purée until smooth and creamy. Adjust sweetness and serve. *Makes 6 servings.*

PEANUT BUTTER COOKIES   A, AB

1 cup canola oil   1 cup oat flour (made from freshly
1 cup organic peanut butter   ground whole oats in food processor)
1 cup sucanat
1 tsp. vanilla extract   Optional:
2 eggs   ½–1 cup of the following:
2 cups spelt flour   organic sunspire chocolate chips
1 tsp. baking soda   chopped peanuts
2 Tbsp. soy flour   carob chips

Preheat oven to 350 degrees.

In a large bowl, cream oil, peanut butter, and sucanat. Add vanilla and eggs. Stir in baking soda and flour. Combine until well mixed. Fold in any optional ingredients.

Drop tablespoon-size balls onto cookie sheet. Bake for 10–12 minutes. *Makes 2 dozen cookies.*

PECAN SANDIES[6]   B, O

¼ cup pecan halves

1 cup butter, room temperature

½ cup pure maple syrup

1½ tsp. pure vanilla extract

2 cups spelt flour

1½ cups whole pecans

Whole-fruit jam from appropriate

   fruit (optional)

Preheat oven to 350 degrees. Finely grind pecan halves in food processor or coffee grinding mill. Set aside.

In large bowl, cream butter until fluffy. Add syrup and vanilla, and beat until creamy.

In separate bowl, combine ground pecans and flour. Slowly add to butter mixture. Dough will be soft. Make 1-inch balls of dough. Drop onto cookie sheet sprayed with cooking spray. Make indent with back of spoon. Fill indent with whole pecan pieces and/or whole-fruit jam. Bake for 15 minutes or until edges are brown. *Makes 20 cookies.*

POACHED PEACHES   ALL

3 Tbsp. honey or sucanat

1 cup apple cider or red wine

1 cup water

2 whole cloves

   (optional for *A, B, AB—O omit*)

3 thin slices of lemon rind

½ tsp. vanilla extract

6 ripe fresh peaches, firm, peeled,

   pitted and cut in half (or pears for *A, AB, O*)

¼ cup black currants (optional)

In large saucepan, combine honey, wine or cider, water, cloves, lemon rind, and vanilla. Submerge peaches and currants in liquid. Try to insure liquid covers fruit as much as possible. Bring to boil. Lower to medium heat; cover and simmer for 15–20 minutes, turning fruit frequently, or until the fruit is soft.

Once cooked, remove fruit from liquid. Boil reserved liquid until it reduces by half. Spoon over cooked fruit and serve. *Makes 4 servings.*

YUMMY RICE PUDDING[7]   A, B, AB

2 apples

¼ cup rolled oats

½ cup apple juice

⅓ cup water

½ cup cooked brown rice

¼ tsp. cinnamon

   (B—substitute with dash of nutmeg)

1 Tbsp. brown rice syrup

Dash of allspice *(AB—omit completely)*

Optional Garnishes:

   Sprinkling of toasted almonds or walnuts

   Sprinkling of black currants

Peel, core, and slice apples.

Lightly roast oats by stirring them in saucepan over medium heat until they smell toasty. Add apples and other ingredients. Bring to boil. Cover and simmer for 20 minutes.

Blend in blender until smooth. Garnish with desired elements.

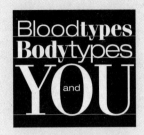

Section III

Body Genetics— Reaching Your Genetic Potential

Chapter 13

Body Genetics

Before we start, let me congratulate you on the wise decision you have made to move forward with your health and physical condition, not allowing the status quo to be an acceptable part of your lifestyle.

Earlier in the book I went into great detail to provide you with food selections uniquely designed for you, introducing you to the concept of eating according to your blood type—teaching you to become an instinctive eater. In this section of the book, I want to share some of the benefits that exercise brings and then help you familiarize yourself with exercise specifics, giving you an exercise program you can use to improve your health, redesign your body, and—ultimately—help you reach your genetic potential.

Exercise is the fitness twin to diet, creating a more efficient BMR and positive body composition. This dynamic duo makes up the major components of a healthy, energetic body. I think it is fair to say most people hate to exercise—at least that has been the feedback I've gotten from sedentary people when the topic arises. The reasons (excuses) given for not exercising are always overshadowed by the reasons why a person should exercise, and rightfully so. I don't want to accuse anyone of being lazy, but most people, when they get off work, want to relax, kick back, and enjoy what little time they have for other sedentary activities. In my book *Never Go Back* (Deland, FL: Body Redesigning, 2007), I share how exercise in and of itself might not be as enjoyable to some because their focus is on the wrong area—the *results*. Try focusing on the *benefit* exercise is to your health, and see if that won't encourage you to stay the course.

The biggest hurdle can be the decision-making process.

Of course, there is always the exception of those few individuals you know who have lived to a ripe old age without exercising and may have even smoked all their lives and drank to excess. For the rest of us, however, for whom lack of exercise can shorten our lives, let's explore some of the benefits that we can receive from exercise—free of charge.

Our bodies have been created for work, physical activity—movement. Heart muscle function is improved by exercise. A conditioned heart is capable of handling physical stress and strain and can recover more quickly (improved resting heart rate). A healthy heart can pump blood more efficiently throughout the body with less strain as a result of exercise. An increase of blood circulation delivers and nourishes every living cell in your body with oxygen, vitamins, minerals, and other nutrients. Exercise strengthens and improves your lung capacity so you can enjoy more stamina and endurance. (When oxygen supply is low, you feel sluggish and lazy—did I say *lazy*?) The hard fact is—exercise creates *more* energy, not less! The following important benefits also result from exercise:

- The digestive system is improved enormously through exercise, which enhances proper bowel function.

- Exercise promotes perspiration, which causes your body to lose excess water retention, salts, and cellular debris (all toxins).

- Exercise stabilizes blood sugar levels, which is good for diabetics and people with insulin problems.

- Exercise will keep you looking and feeling younger and help slow down the aging process.

- Exercise strengthens muscles, ligaments, and cartilage; improves joint mobility and flexibility; and promotes bone density, which prevents the onset of osteoporosis, while improving the quality of your skin by increasing blood flow closer to the surface skin as well as flushing other vital organs.

- Exercise raises your HDL (good cholesterol) and helps reduce your LDL (bad cholesterol). When you exercise, your HDL cholesterol goes up, which in turn helps reduce the LDL (bad cholesterol) and your blood lipids or triglycerides. The net result is a better HDL/cholesterol ratio and lower risk of heart disease, diabetes, stroke, and a host of other potential medical ailments.

BLOOD PRESSURE

Along with the wonderful benefits listed above, it is important to understand that exercise alone may lower blood pressure. This happens for many reasons. First, as you increase your blood flow and oxygen, your blood vessels dilate to accommodate the additional flow required to supply and meet the body's demands. Next, as your HDL (good cholesterol) goes up, it creates a cleansing or vacuuming effect in your blood vessels whereby buildup of plaque or saturated fat is carried away. This allows the heart to pump blood through the arteries more efficiently and with less resistance.

METABOLISM

Your metabolism is also positively affected by exercise. By eating foods that are compatible to your blood type, you will improve your BMR (basal metabolic rate), as we have discussed. However, if you continue to live a sedentary (exercise-less) lifestyle, you are only getting half the results. Exercise is absolutely imperative for weight loss because it also increases your metabolism, your body's ability to burn calories. When you exercise, you are actually revving your metabolism, which helps prevent calories from being stored by the body as fat. Remember—a slow metabolism generates increased body fat (excess weight) and less energy, while a speedy metabolism generates fat loss and more energy!

A slow metabolism also causes a sluggish digestive system, which interferes with proper elimination of waste by-products. This condition leads to toxicity buildup in the bloodstream and fat cells, parasitic infestation, autointoxication, and the potential for colon cancer. A properly operating metabolism helps removes carcinogens from your system more quickly.

The most strenuous exercise in your entire program is getting up from the couch. That decision takes both great mental and physical exertion.

EXERCISE, IN A NUTSHELL

In a nutshell, exercise promotes weight loss; produces a positive body composition; builds muscle; strengthens the immune system; and improves the cardiovascular system, digestive system, and circulatory system, while promoting more energy and stamina, lowering blood pressure and cholesterol, and reversing the effects of aging. What more could you want—for free?

In the minds of many, the concept of exercise is just plain old work. And who needs more work than what they already have in their life? But if you will hang with me long enough, I assure you that you will develop an appreciation for exercise—not only for the results, but also for how it makes you feel about yourself.

Mentally processing all that is involved with exercise can be somewhat paradoxical in nature. What do I mean? The biggest hurdle can be the decision-making process. Let me put it this way: Perhaps you are tired all the time. You have very little, if any, energy—which keeps you from exercising. You need energy to exercise. But here's the paradox—you need to exercise to induce energy!

To have a constant supply of increased energy, you must exercise regularly—for as long as you want the increased energy. Thus enters another paradox—exercising causes muscle fatigue, which makes you feel tired, and the only way to get over being tired is to exercise more! As your body adjusts to exercising regularly, it greatly improves its ability to recover from the new workload. Even though exercise makes you tired for a short time, ultimately it increases your recovery rate, which increases your energy supply quickly throughout each day.

With this increase of energy, you are able to enjoy participating in more physical activities, thus making your lifestyle more energetic. Because your body is now functioning at a greater level of efficiency and performance, it becomes much easier to make exercise a regular part of your life.

If you are like most people, I am sure you would like to feel good all of the time, with energy to spare. It seems obvious to me that it will take a combination of mental and physical exertion to get started—both factors an important part of the decision-making process.

Let me assure you of this one thing: if you are mentally willing to do what is healthy and sound for your immediate and future health, the rest will follow. The most strenuous exercise in your entire program is getting up from the couch. That decision takes both great mental and physical exertion.

Achieving a balance between the mental and physical aspects of exercising, allowing them to work together in concert, will be more difficult than the actual exercises in your entire fitness program. Once you become more familiar with regular exercise, this balance will be easier to maintain. Exercise will begin to play a key role in your journey for living a healthier and more active life as it becomes a regular part of your daily life. We will work together as a team to accomplish your specific goals. So if you are ready, so am I.

> **13-1**
>
> ### Exercise Paradox
>
> - No exercise = no energy
> - No energy = no exercise
> - Mental laziness = procrastination
> - Procrastination = no action
> - Mental effort = mental energy
> - Physical effort = physical energy
> - Mental/physical energy = mental/physical fitness

Throughout the many years I have been involved in the world of health and fitness, I have observed thousands of men and women who were training in health clubs, YMCAs, and other fitness facilities. All of them seemed to be working so very hard and diligently. Yet although many of them wanted desperately to reach their fitness goals, even after weeks—and sometimes months—of relentless effort, they failed to get the results, or they failed to see results fast enough.

Maybe you are one of them. Maybe right now you are saying, "Been there, done that." Maybe you became so discouraged and frustrated with the whole fitness thing that you quit and allowed your fitness goals to elude you. Don't feel alone. That is a common pitfall for many. Over the years, it is those very people—those who feel discouraged, isolated, and failing—who have motivated me to encourage them and you to get back on track, to believe in yourself, and to know that you can reach your fitness goals.

I try to stay on the cutting edge in the world of health and fitness. I like to "push the envelope" by providing advanced exercise techniques and groundbreaking dietary and nutritional programs that are tailored and customized specifically for each individual. My philosophy is to provide the most effective and accurate applications of exercise methodologies, yet making them as simple as possible while being totally productive. Far too many people for far too long have believed that if they did not kill themselves in the gyms, they would not get the results they wanted.

I know that even today there are hundreds of people who desire to improve their physical conditions but have lost their willingness to hang in there or start up again because of some unfortunate experience at a health club. This book will give you a new and fresh attitude about taking control of your life.

In this section of the book, I have provided you with mechanisms for determining your body type, for choosing the strategies that will work best for your body, and for selecting the exercise programs that best suit your body's genetics. I will guide you on your fitness journey so that you will never repeat and experience the negative results you experienced in your past. Your results will come quickly because I am taking you on the fastest route to success by tapping into your genetics.

If getting your body in shape and taking on a healthy lifestyle is a brand-new adventure for you, then I can help you avoid the pitfalls that would interfere and keep you from reaching your goals.

Redesigning Your Body

Besides the obvious health benefits of exercise, how about redesigning your body? Most people gravitate to exercise for improving their shape rather than for health reasons, but the beauty about exercise is you can have the best of both worlds—you can be healthier and look your best.

There is nothing that will get you to reach your genetic potential faster then following a tailored or specialized exercise program that is compatible to your genetics. Exercise specificity is as important to the athlete wanting to enhance his or her sports performance as it is to the nonathletic type and their own personal goals.

Exercise specifics should vary for different body types, but there are some commonalties that should be factored in for making exercise compatible for life. So before I give you a program for your body type, let me make a few suggestions that I have found to be an effective common ground for all body types.

STRENGTH TRAINING

Strength training or resistance training has been my favorite forever, not just because I like that method of training but because it produces maximum results. Today (finally, after all these years) strength training is proven and accepted to be the most effective method of exercise to produce all the aforementioned benefits. It is gender-friendly, used by professional athletes, offered by nearly every commercial fitness club in America, and even implemented in some rehabilitation programs. As stated above, the benefits are numerous. An effective strength-training program is not limited to using heavy weights, as is associated with competitive body-builders, weight lifters, and competitive athletes. When tailored correctly, strength training can be used by men and women of all ages to obtain great results.

Regardless of an individual's body type, I believe everyone should incorporate strength training as part of his or her regular exercise regimen. If you do not exercise and have not made exercise a part of your lifestyle yet, there are probably two reasons for it:

1. You don't feel like exercising after coming home from work or before going to work because you don't have the energy.

2. Since your time is limited anyway, you pass on it because you say don't have enough time.

These are the very reasons why I am highly recommending you begin circuit training. Circuit training will produce maximum results (increased energy included) in the shortest amount of time—less than an hour a day.

TIME FACTOR

Prioritizing your time can almost be an impossibility. We all have busy schedules, so we all are dealing with the cruel realities of the time factor. But I believe you can do anything you want to do—if you are motivated. Think of the things you make yourself do just because you want to.

Now think of circuit training as something you must do! You will soon discover that circuit training requires less time than you thought because the constant tempo allows you to get a total-body workout in as little as thirty minutes. So, along with your motivation and fitness goals, you can learn to make circuit training the perfect method for exercising, particularly if you have little time to spare.

The Universal Exercise Program: Circuit Training

Circuit training is a method of exercise that tones, shapes, and strengthens muscles while stimulating the cardiovascular system. Its unique rhythmic tempo prevents muscle overloading or stimulation, thus not creating maximum muscle development, as do other methods of strength training. By maintaining an elevated training heart rate for a longer period of time because of a rapid tempo of exercise, the muscles are still taxed and conditioned, and fat loss is directly related to using stored body fat (adipose tissue) as its primary source of fuel. While using body fat for energy, you will lose inches and body fat and still maintain lean muscle mass—a positive body composition. When working in concert with your weight loss program, the results will be dramatic.

METHODOLOGY

The following is a typical example of how to perform a *circuit*. Perform an exercise with a weight or resistance mechanism that allows you to get twenty repetitions in thirty seconds. Each exercise is followed by a fifteen- to thirty-second interval period of rest. You should keep moving from one exercise to the next, main-

taining the same tempo of twenty repetitions in thirty seconds.
Repeat this sequence until all the exercises (nine or ten) in your
total body program have been completed. At this point you will
have completed one complete circuit (about ten minutes) and have
worked your total body. Ideally, as your physical fitness conditioning allows, you will want to increase your program to complete two
or three circuits per workout. Due to the constant tempo of exercise
(thirty seconds of exercise and thirty seconds of rest), it is important to stay within the ideal training heart-rate zone for your age.
(See Training Heart Rate Chart on page 295.)

If you are ambitious, highly motivated, or maybe have a deadline to look your best for a special event you have to attend, then
give this a try. Maybe you are just tired of looking frumpy and
feeling fatigued all the time and you want to redesign your body
as quickly as possible. If that is the case, then circuit training
is the ticket. By the way, you can circuit train five days a week
without overtraining.

Circuit training can be done in the privacy of your home or at
health clubs where there are weight machines lined up one after the
other, making it easy to go from one machine to another. You can
use free weights (dumbbells) alone or combine them with weight
machines. Stretch cords work very well because they are portable,
take up no space, and can be done in a spare room in your home or
in a hotel room while traveling.

Always challenge yourself by using enough weight or the proper
amount of resistance that will allow you to perform twenty repetitions in thirty seconds per exercise. This will develop good toned
muscle and shape, and, by constantly moving from one exercise
to the other, you will develop great cardiovascular conditioning and improved stamina. The end results of circuit training are
lower body fat percent, toned and shapely muscles, and increased
energy—something you were lacking in the first place—all accom-
plished in a short period of time. Consider a typical circuit-training
routine using dumbbells.

Circuit-Training Routine

1. Butterflies—chest muscles

Hold dumbbells above your chest with palms facing each other to begin.

With arms slightly bent, slowly lower the dumbbells outward and down until they are level with the chest. Return to starting position and repeat. Keep back arched and chest lifted throughout the exercise. Use good technique and control.

2. Seated Lateral Rises—shoulders

Sit erect with feet flat on the floor while holding dumbbells at a 90-degree angle.

Rotate the dumbbells and your elbows outward and upward until they are parallel to the floor at shoulder height. Return to starting position and repeat. Do not allow the dumbbells to lag behind the elbows.

3. Partial Squats or Knee Bends—thighs

Stand close to a bench (or chair) with feet shoulder width apart. With toes pointed outward, sit down until your buttocks touch the bench.

Return to starting position and repeat. Do not rest on the bench; it's a touch-and-go movement. Hold dumbbells for added resistance.

4. Seated Biceps Curls—upper arm

Sit with arms hanging at full length, holding dumbbells.

With elbows fixed at your sides, curl the dumbbells as high as

possible without moving the elbows from your sides. Keep palms facing upward throughout the exercise. Return to starting position and repeat. Do not swing the dumbbells.

5. Arm Rowing—back

Kneel with right leg on the bench while resting on the right hand.

With dumbbell in left hand at full arm length, pull upward,

keeping your elbow close to your side until even with your hip.

Return to starting position and repeat. Do the same for the opposite side.

6. Lying Triceps Extensions—back of upper arm

Lie flat on your back holding dumbbells at arm's length above your chest with palms facing each other.

While keeping the elbows stationary, bend your elbows and lower dumbbells along your head. Extend the dumbbells and return to starting position; repeat.

7. Lying Side Leg Lifts—hips

Lie on your side with the bottom leg bent.

Raise the top leg as high as possible but less than directly over your body. Keep your toe pointed downward throughout the exercise. Return to starting position and repeat. Do the same for the opposite side. Add ankle weights for added resistance.

8. Reverse Crunch—abdominals

Lie flat on the floor on your back with arms on the floor, palms down. Bend your knees, cross your feet, and hold a 90-degree position with your feet off the floor.

Pressing down on the floor with your palms, curl or roll your lower trunk off the floor about five inches. Return to starting position and repeat. Remain in a tucked position without swinging your legs for momentum.

9. Lunges—buttocks/thighs

Assume a shoulder-width stance. Step forward on your left foot. Squat down until the knee of your back leg touches the floor;

then return to starting position. Repeat. Do the same for the opposite leg. Stay upright. Your knee (on front leg) when squatting in lowest position should not extend past the toes.

10. 90-Degree Side Leg Lifts—hips/buttocks

Bend over at the waist and rest on your palms on bench or chair.

Raise your right leg as high as possible, and then return to

  starting position;

repeat. Do the same for the opposite leg. Raise and lower your leg slowly. Use ankle weights for added resistance.

Note: Start with exercise #1 and perform twenty repetitions. Rest for thirty seconds, and then proceed to exercise #2; perform twenty repetitions. Rest for thirty seconds and proceed to exercise #3, and so on. Be sure to check your heart rate regularly throughout the workout. Your current physical fitness level should dictate how much you do—so listen to your body! Change the sequence of exercises to avoid boredom.

FOR VARIETY

As you can tell, I am convinced of the effectiveness of circuit training for most individuals. But for the sake of variety, based on my years of experience and research, let me share with you some added information that you may find beneficial.

In my studies, I have found that blood type B and O individuals seem to gravitate and respond very well to intense physical exercise. This would include running, aerobics, weight training, stair climbing, tennis, and almost any other physically demanding activity. This is indicated from the studies of blood types and professional occupations, which showed that these blood types chose sports like football, baseball, and hockey along with firefighting and law enforcement professions.

In contrast, blood type A and AB individuals seem to gravitate to exercises that are less strenuous, such as walking, treadmill, golf, dancing, exercise bike, and stretching exercises such as yoga.

These rules are not set in stone, but people tend to gravitate to activities that make them feel good and those they enjoy. I have seen some blood type As and ABs train for competitive bodybuilding shows, contrary to what is typical, while some blood type B and O individuals may enjoy long walks and relaxation exercises. My wife, Lori, and I love to take long walks, and we are both blood types Os. Exercise in many cases comes down to personal preference. Try to match your personal preferences with your physical and emotional requirements as well.

As I stated earlier, I believe circuit training is ideal for *all blood type* individuals, as it is not too intense to overstimulate the blood type AB and A individuals, yet it can provide sufficient muscle stimulation for the blood type B and O individuals.

All body types benefit tremendously from circuit training as well, as it proves to be nearly a universal method of redesigning the body for all people. But the secret for reaching your genetic potential is to implement the circuit training theory with specific exercises that are compatible with your *body genetics.*

Getting the Picture

The path that will eventually lead you to reaching your genetic potential must be paved with a basic understanding of some key body genetic components, along with the proper exercises and methodology of exercises that are compatible with your genetics. This is necessary for success. The one major genetic component that will solidify the pavement on which you walk, and which is absolutely crucial for optimum results, is knowing what you are before you begin the journey. You need to know your body genetics...simply put, you need to know what body type you are.

Your Genes—the Clay

It is estimated that approximately 75 percent of our body typing comes from our genes. As a matter of fact, everything that comprises your genetic baseline was already determined by the time you were born. You didn't put in an order for how you wanted to look, what color you wanted your hair to be, or how tall you wanted to be. Your gene pool had determined what your body type was going to be generations before you even got here.

Your body type—or body genetics—is the foundation of the "house" in which you live. But custom-building your house to your satisfaction requires that you understand what strategies or building plans will work the best.

How many times have you heard someone say, "She has her mother's figure"? Our genetics play a key role in our overall makeup, but most people do not consider genetics when it comes to determining what exercise program is best for them. Your basic genetics can be enhanced and redesigned by using the proper methodology of exercise and diet.

I have four wonderful sisters-in-law who favor their father's genetics more than their mother's. Their musculoskeletal systems—

or body structures—are dominantly inherited from their father's genes. My wife, Lori, has the same basic genetics as her sisters, but because she exercises regularly, she has taken her genetics to another level of aesthetics.

I have three daughters, two of whom are twins. All three daughters have great genetics for building symmetrical bodies through exercise. In fact, some years ago at the age of seventeen, my daughter Jenifer competed in the Miss Buffalo Bodybuilding Championships and won the title from women who were as much as ten years older than she was. She has the proper genetics to work with to become a competitive bodybuilder.

Not everyone has inherited the genetics to be a competitive bodybuilder, but not everyone wants to be one, either. But everyone has a genetic baseline from which to start customizing his or her body. The key to success is found in understanding your body genetics. Then you can maximize your results.

Most of our genetics were determined by our parents—and their parents. But heredity is not completely responsible for your shape. There are things that can be done to redesign and improve the aesthetics and symmetry of your body—regardless of the gene pool from which you came.

Your body type—or body genetics—is the foundation of the "house" in which you live.

Know Your Genetic Limitations

Before I design an exercise program for a client, I do a simple body genetic analysis. In many cases I have never met my clients. Therefore, I conduct my body genetic analysis for many of them by long distance—simply requesting that each person send me a photo for review. I ask the client to wear a swimsuit or a pair of shorts and a top so that I can see the body shape, which allows me to make a valid determination of that person's basic body type. By reviewing each person's photo, I can also determine that person's present condition and the specialized work his or her body will need. After the body analysis, I design the personalized program a client will need to follow in order to balance his or her body's genetics.

When a client visits me for a one-on-one evaluation, the first thing I do is ask that person to stand in front of me so I can make a determination as to his or her body type. It's interesting that after all these years of doing body genetic analyses, I can actually make an immediate determination of a person's body type the minute they walk into a room. But before I can prescribe the exercise program and strategy, I also need to determine each person's current condition. The four primary body sites I choose to be factored into the formula include:

1. The shoulders
2. The chest/bust
3. The waistline
4. The hips/thighs

Using these key sites representing the person's genetic foundation, I can determine the body type and present physical condition. This genetic information will enable me to determine into which body makeover category the person fits based on body type and physical condition. Then I can design their specialized program.

Three Body Makeover Categories

Your genetics and current condition are not identical to that of any other person. To maximize your genetic potential, you will need to focus on one of the three body makeover categories of fine-tuning, minor makeover, or complete makeover.

CATEGORY 1—FINE-TUNING

If a person's body analysis reveals that all four key sites are balanced or symmetrical, that person will require a fine-tuning program. This program helps the individual to enhance natural symmetry by training correctly for her body type. The exercise strategy for this category is probably the easiest of the three categories for two basic reasons. People in this category are blessed with pleasingly balanced body genetics, and they maintain their bodies in good condition rather easily. There may even be a very few people who seem to do very little and get maximum results anyway.

The second reason this category may be easier is because many of the individuals who fit in this category have worked diligently in the past to develop their physique. They balanced and toned their body parts and acquired that symmetrical—or hourglass—body shape through hard work.

If the body analysis for an individual reveals an imbalance or poor symmetry of these key body sites, it will be more difficult to apply the next two body makeover programs. When symmetry—or that hourglass shape—is lacking, a more tailored and specific prescription of exercise will be necessary.

Your genetics and current condition are not identical to that of any other person.

CATEGORY 2—MINOR MAKEOVER

Some people have worked to achieve a level of balance or symmetry between their upper and lower bodies—but are not quite there. These individuals would need to be a part of this second category, focusing on a minor makeover. Some people in this category exercise and have made progress, but they may have hit a plateau. Or they may have naturally pleasing genetics but need to do more work to reach their potential. Their prescription of exercise will differ from the one who requires fine-tuning. It will align more closely to the third category, which is for those needing a major body makeover.

The people in this second category have already begun improving on their body genetics and are in the transformation process or in transition. Their program would be designed to take their advancing condition up another level or two to obtain a totally balanced symmetrical look.

CATEGORY 3—MAJOR BODY MAKEOVER

This category is for people whose condition is usually recognized as being deconditioned—or just plain out of shape. Typically they are people who do not exercise, have a high level of body fat, and are in poor shape. For this reason their bodies have very little or no balance or symmetry of the key body parts. Possibly some do exercise, but they have not been shown how to apply the proper exercise methodology for their body type.

Whatever the case, people in this category need a major body makeover—head to toe. Their exercise prescription will differ from the other two examples because the requirements are obviously different.

Unfortunately, the majority of people's bodies fall into this category. But don't be embarrassed or worry if this is you, because many bodies that have turned out beautifully once needed a major body makeover.

A Solution for Everyone

Sometimes part of my profession makes me feel like an artist or sculptor. For me it is like being given a piece of clay and then working to redesign it into an aesthetic piece of fine art. Taking a body and redesigning it so that it can take on an entirely new transformed shape is truly a reward in itself. By applying the correct strategy of exercise and diet to match individual genetics, a body that is out of balance can develop pleasing body contour. When the main body parts are in balance, or symmetrical, your entire body image takes on a whole new, pleasing look.

I believe this is what almost everyone is looking for when they pursue an exercise program—not the perfect body, but a balanced body. During the initial interview with my clients, I ask them to fill out a questionnaire asking what changes they want to see in their bodies. After years of observing hundreds of clients, I have found that an overwhelming number reply that they want a balanced shape.

A balanced shape is what I refer to as the hourglass or V-shape. Of course, wanting a balanced figure is one thing—obtaining a balanced shape is a totally different story. Most people are not aware of what it takes to obtain that goal. There is a science to body redesigning, but being able to reach that goal requires knowing the methodology of how to get to the goal. And it requires applying that knowledge to your lifestyle—doing it, not just knowing it!

Facing Genetic Limitations

Body genetics is the baseline from which I build for every exercise prescription I prescribe. Even though I have been able to prescribe accurately the right program for a specific body type, each person will have genetic limitations with which he or she will need to contend.

There are genetic limitations that will have to be addressed as your program is designed. Such genetic limitations are found in

> **By applying the correct strategy of exercise and diet to match individual genetics, a body that is out of balance can develop pleasing body contour.**

There is a difference between getting the normal results from increased physical activity and obtaining the specific results you want.

your musculoskeletal system, the God-given genetic structure that is impossible to redesign. These limitations deal with your bone structure, length, and size, and they are unchangeable. For example, let's say that your pelvic bones or hip structure measures 36 inches. There is nothing you and I can do to reduce that measurement, unless we could shave off some of your bone. But if your hips measure 42½ inches on a 36-inch pelvic bone measurement, then I can show you how to reduce those 42 inches down closer to the 36-inch bone measurement.

The same is true for your shoulder width. If your genetic limitations include clavicles that are short, then your narrow shoulder width must be factored into your program design. I can't do anything to make the clavicles longer. But I can show you how to broaden your overall shoulder girth by selecting specific exercises that are compatible to your particular genetic limitations.

These limitations apply to the size and length of your ribs, muscle insertion and origin, and the length and size of your bones. You cannot outsmart your genes, but you can use exercise strategies that are compatible to them. For that reason, identifying your body type—including your genetic limitations—is the first order of business. A further look at your genes will help you to predetermine your outcome, or at least an understanding of what you can expect from your exercise program.

Spinning Your Wheels

There is a difference between getting the normal results from increased physical activity and obtaining the specific results you want. Even a person with a physically sedentary lifestyle, doing no more in the way of exercise than taking the garbage out to the curb once a week, will see results if that person starts exercising regularly. Our bodies were made for physical activity, and they respond accordingly.

But obtaining specific body redesigning results depends on following a specific exercise methodology. The focus of body redesigning must be getting the specific results for which you are looking. You should settle for nothing less.

Let me state this clearly: you should train specifically with exercises designed for your body type. On page 289 you will find a chart designed to help you determine your specific body type. If you have a pear-shaped body, then you should perform exercises designed for the pear shape. This will save you a lot of wasted time and energy, and it will give you a shapelier hourglass figure. You won't simply become a smaller pear. Regardless of whether your body type is a pear, an apple, or a banana, understanding the points I have been making will make your efforts so much easier. Applying these principles will give you the ability to stay focused while on your journey.

By now you should have a real feel for how valuable it is to recognize your body type. My goal is to coach you the best way I know how so you don't have to waste your precious time or get frustrated by not seeing the results you are looking for because you are working hard at exercising that doesn't work for you and your body type.

As your fitness coach, I would like to challenge you to utilize the information in this book about the benefits of circuit training along with understanding the importance of knowing your body type—and combine the two concepts for your lifestyle. By doing so, I am convinced that you will attain the goal(s) you have set for yourself in record time.

Whether you are a pear, an apple, or a banana, there are specific exercises that work best for your body type. (See my body type workout video packages in Appendix C.) Take advantage of your newfound knowledge of exercise methodology and your body genetic structure, and take control of how far your body genetics can go. Should you be one that is blessed with an hourglass figure but may need some fine-tuning, then any of my body type videos will work for you.

As you make the decision to exercise for your body type and eat according to your blood type, you will be joining millions of us who are making the same journey. As part of the requirements for this journey, there are additional necessities or items that you will need to consider for enhancing your progress. In the next chapter I list some basic nutritional necessities for a healthy lifestyle. (For more information, see "Fork in the Road" in Appendix E.)

Let me state this clearly: you should train specifically with exercises designed for your body type.

Chapter 14

Nutrition Support Ideas

As far back as I can remember, I have always taken nutritional supplements. As a young teenager I would save the money I earned from my paper route and snow-shoveling jobs so I could go to the health food store and buy my supplements. I have always viewed purchasing nutritional supplements as an investment in my health. I am walking proof of those health benefits for over forty years, and by the grace of God I have enjoyed a very healthy quality of life—I feel it, it shows, and it will do the same for you.

Supporting your diet with nutritional supplements is vitally important. Just by virtue of genetic engineering or modifying of food sources, pesticides, chemicals, fertilizers, and waste materials being dumped and pumped into our soil, water, and air, nearly all vegetation as we know it today is lacking in the God-given minerals and elements originally planned to help sustain humankind. So even with your best efforts of eating well, you are prone to be deficient in minerals and vitamins. It is a fact that if you were to trace back to the root of nearly every ailment and disease, you would find a mineral deficiency.

That's why, as a naturopathic doctor, I believe it is wise and prudent to first use every natural means possible to get the body to return to normal function so it can heal itself. If medications are to be used, they should be taken for emergency situations after exhausting every natural means available.

When you engage in physical work and recreational activities or embark on a regular exercise program, it is important that you add nutritional supplements and protein to your diet due to the extra demands placed on your body. There are specific supplements you can take when you are planning to lose weight or want to enhance performance for sports. Conditions like heart arrhythmia or elevated cholesterol, to mention just a couple, are benefited with other nutritional supplementation. Consider the stress in your life, the negative side effects of medication, and poor eating habits and choices, and you can see why your body is taking a beating. So I strongly recommend that you consider taking daily supplements.

Fantastic Help With Limitations

Dietary supplements are not formulated to cure illness or disease, but they do provide the environment for assisting your body in the healing process. They can promote cellular health and systemic and organ function, and they can assist in purifying your body through detoxification and removing toxic buildup so your body can heal itself and be restored to normal health as it was designed to do.

However, nutritional supplements have limitations and can't do it all themselves; they need your help. The benefits that come from taking nutritional supplements can be maximized only when working in concert with healthy-living habits. I suggest when deciding to make healthier lifestyle changes that you do not view them as a temporary change but as a way of life. Healthy life choices that work in concert with your nutritional supplements are:

- Diet (eating food compatible to your blood type)
- Drinking enough water (alkaline water)
- Regular exercise
- Proper rest and relaxation
- Daily exposure to sunshine and fresh air
- Physical activities

- Serving and forgiving others
- Positive thoughts

It's all about investing in your health.

Your Need for a Healthy Brain

One more consideration I would like to point out regarding your health is the fact that nearly 90 percent of all disease and sickness comes from the brain. This involves the electrical frequencies and magnetism in your body that are necessary for building healthy, functional molecular structures. The brain operates like an electrical generator, causing electricity to flow throughout your entire body, including the liver.

It is important to know that the liver is dependent upon the brain's electricity. Not only does the liver receive the patterned frequencies from the brain in order to function, but also it receives the invaluable magnetic draw for the uptake of mineral energy, particularly calcium. In other words, in order to assimilate the minerals it desperately needs to function, your liver (and other organs) depends on the electrical circuits from the brain.

When there is a disruption or short circuit in the electrical flow to the liver from the brain, the liver is deprived of this magnetism, which in turn sets the stage for degenerative changes in the liver. Like a domino effect, the rest of the body's organs and systems become affected from these short circuits, and you have what is known as the onset of degenerative diseases.

MENTAL "DIS-EASE"

I gave you this microscopic overview of body chemistry to point out that disease and illness are directly related to the altering or short-circuiting of the electrical flow from the brain, especially to the liver. "Dis-ease" is due to the lack of "perfect peace." Anytime your mind lacks peace, it becomes prey to anxieties, frustrations, guilt, phobias, depression, and so on. The most powerful causes of interference of electrical flow to the body, particularly the liver, are worry, fear, lust, self-centeredness, hatred, and bitterness.

Negative mental exercises are responsible for nearly 90 percent of degenerative disease.[1] This is scientific proof of the truth the Bible recorded thousands of years ago: "For as he thinks in his heart, so is he" (Prov. 23:7, NKJV). This defective thinking or negative thoughts become the enemy of truth, and such defective thinking has an effect on your body chemistry. If the ability of your mind to comprehend or understand truth about your health is blocked, for example, it will in a sense cancel the benefits of your health program.

From a physical perspective, the first stages of mental impairment begin with calcium deficiency. Combine that with a carbohydrate imbalance interfering with oxygen to the brain, and you have the formula for mental distortions, resulting in your thinking being unclear and filled with anxiety and fear. As you can tell, healthy lifestyle changes include a change of mind or attitude that involve your entire makeup—body, soul, and spirit.

Nutrition Support Ideas

We all are in need of nutrition support. Make nutritional supplements a part of your lifestyle, and remember the significance of the word *prevention*. As you experience the many positive healthy benefits from dietary supplementation, you will grow in the wisdom as to why I perceive it as a wise investment in your health.

Below I have given you a brief list of nutrition support ideas and strategies that I believe will cover the bases for most people. They are foundational as far as supporting your diet (compatible with your blood type). Of course, if you have a specific health condition or concern, please consult with your health practitioner or go to my Web site (www.bodyredesigning.com) and click on Healthy Lifestyles Survey. The information you input in the survey will assist me in being most accurate with your specific condition for individualizing your protocol.

The following list also represents what I personally take as a means of prevention as well as for cleansing, strengthening, and fortifying my bodily functions and systems for promoting homeostasis or balance. As my needs change, I make adjustments in what supplements I take. I believe these are necessary and worthy of your consideration for additional support to your healthy lifestyle, as we discussed.

COLON HEALTH: DETOXIFICATION

I strongly recommend that you do a *colon cleanse* as the first step for improving your health. Before you can ever expect an organ, gland, or bodily system to heal and be restored to natural function, you must detoxify your body. As you start making healthy lifestyle changes to avoid or eliminate illness or any health condition, you must first detoxify your colon. I cannot express this fact strongly enough. The healing process cannot take place if your body is toxic.

A dysfunctional colon plays a major role in most degenerative diseases. A dysfunctional colon is related to a slow transit time, which is the time it takes to eliminate food once it has been ingested. This is generally caused by constipation. If you do not have three bowel movements per day, you may be considered clinically constipated. The transit time of a healthy colon is approximately twenty-four to forty-eight hours. As I said earlier in chapter 3, when the transit time is slowed down due to constipation (average American adult transit time is ninety-six hours), a buildup of toxins from impacted fecal matter begins. Mucus and fecal matter that get impacted into the porous walls of the colon not only cause digestive pain and discomfort, but they also lead to more serious conditions such as diverticulitis, IBS, diverticulosis, polyps, and, worse, cancer of the colon.

As the toxins remain in the colon, they eventually get picked up by the bloodstream (a condition called leaky colon) and circulate throughout your body, polluting it and breaking down your quality of health. This condition overloads the liver and causes it to weaken. The health of your colon is directly related to the health of your blood.

Constipation develops from a lack of exercise; not drinking enough water; eating refined flour and refined sugar products, fried foods, and deli food; lack of dietary fiber; and taking medications. (This condition can be improved by making proper lifestyle changes.) Constipation also makes your colon a breeding bed for parasitic infestation. Once these parasites work their way into your colon, they do two things: eat what you ate and excrete their feces into your body while building their breeding colonies. These parasites range from single-cell amoebae to four-inch worms, spreading their toxic refuse throughout your body, which eventually weakens and interrupts your health. Parasitic infestation contributes to a litany of health-related problems like liver dysfunction, degenerative diseases, headaches, achy joints, weakness, weak immune system, skin ailments, poor skin tone, bad breath, and many more.

After you have gone through a colon cleansing, it is necessary to take care of your colon on daily basis to maintain regularity. Since preventing constipation is a daily part of keeping a healthy colon, I strongly suggest that you take a fiber supplement every day of your life. Fiber provides the bulk necessary for speeding up the transit time for proper elimination. It helps prevent the buildup of waste and toxicity in your colon while contributing to lowering your bad cholesterol.

Many people experience *chronic constipation*, a condition that prevents bowel movement for many days or even weeks at a time. Chronic constipation is a very dangerous condition that promotes illnesses, diminishes normal colon function, enhances parasitic infestation, and causes toxicity buildup, which leads to serious poor health conditions (as mentioned above), not to mention the pain and discomfort associated with chronic constipation. If you are suffering with chronic constipation, I recommend an extra-powerful herbal laxative that provides immediate bowel movement to relieve the discomfort and enhance proper colon function and health. (See www .bodyredesigning.com.)

DIGESTIVE ENZYMES

It is true that chewing food slowly and thoroughly will allow food to be broken down more efficiently by allowing the enzymes to do their work, but as we age, the body secretes fewer enzymes that are necessary for proper digestion of food. This condition is common for those who are forty and older, causing digestive disorders, poor nutrient uptake, and eventual poor health. To compensate for the natural decline in enzyme production, consider a complex digestive enzyme supplement with every meal. Digestive enzymes will give your liver and digestive system a break and will also assist in eliminating the discomforts associated with poor enzymatic action. A digestive enzyme complex will enhance your body's ability to break down the food you ingest and allow proper nutrient uptake and assimilation. (See www.bodyredesigning.com.)

MULTIVITAMINS

A multivitamin is a means to supplement the nutrition I get from food sources. A balance of vitamins, minerals, and herbs serves as a healthy safety net for prevention. Going to the next level of specificity, I take multivitamins that are compatible with my blood type. I recommend a daily multivitamin supplement that comes from food extracts and sources that contain vitamins, minerals, antioxidants, and herbs specifically formulated for the nutritional needs of each individual blood type. (See www.bodyredesigning.com.)

MINERALS

Trace minerals are the minute but vital amount of certain minerals that your body does not manufacture; therefore, you need to supply your body with them. We have already discussed the reasons you do not necessarily get them from your food. Without trace minerals, your body cannot absorb vitamins.

I find that a concentrated liquid form is best because I can mix it with water, soups, drinks, or swallow it right from a teaspoon. I have had great success in helping people with dissolving bone spurs and avoiding surgery simply by suggesting they take liquid trace minerals for thirty to sixty days. Strong nails and fast nail growth, better hair condition, and more energy are but a few of the many benefits you will experience when adding trace minerals to your nutritional regimen.

Calcium is priceless. Calcium is an organic mineral and is essential for the function of every organ and gland. It is also necessary for balancing the blood and tissue pH in the body. Calcium is the major mineral our body needs in abundance, yet it is the most difficult mineral to absorb. Calcium needs magnesium and vitamin D_3 (cholecalciferol) to be assimilated properly in the body. Here's a way to save some money: spend one hour in direct sunlight, and you will get approximately 50,000 mg of vitamin D—so get out in the sun.

I prefer taking coral calcium from Okinawa. Calcium carbonate and calcium citrate are probably the easiest to assimilate, especially for women. A pregnant woman requires five to seven times more calcium than a man. (See www.bodyredesigning.com.)

PROTEIN

Protein is essential for your body; your body could not function without it. And you probably are not getting enough protein on a daily basis. The American diet is virtually full of refined white flour products and refined sugars—carbohydrates—all empty and unusable calories. Just by adding protein to your diet and reducing carbohydrates, not only will you see an immediate drop in weight, but you will also experience improved mental alertness and ability to think clearly. If you suffer from hypoglycemia and bouts with low blood sugar, you can restore constant energy and avoid "crashing" in the morning and afternoon when you consume enough protein.

High-protein/no-carbohydrate diets work very well for immediate weight loss, but they can cause you to lose control when carbohydrates are reintroduced to the diet. I wouldn't recommend these diets for a long period of time because your health is dependent on carbohydrates as well.

Of course, the majority of protein should come from food sources, but eating protein is not always palatable or convenient. That's why I recommend considering a protein supplement in the form of a bar or shake. They may serve as a meal replacement or an in-between-meals snack.

When it comes to a protein shake, whey protein is very common because it is not expensive. However, since it is a derivative of dairy (cow's milk), unless you are a blood type B, you should avoid it. Soy protein makes for a great shake and is beneficial for blood type A and AB individuals and neutral for Os and Bs. If you are allergic to soy, don't use it, regardless of your blood type. Rice milk and almond milk are good alternative sources of protein.

I believe you should use a protein shake that is compatible to your blood type so you can get maximum assimilation and usage from it. I prefer using egg white protein powder with water for my shakes. When I travel, I always take my stash with me—protein powder and protein bars. (See www.bodyredesigning.com.)

WATER—LIVING WATER

There are basically three causes for disease and death: free-radical damage to cells, dehydrated cells, and acidosis. When you consider that the human body is made up of trillions of cells, it stands to reason that the healthier the cell, the healthier the individual. The baseline solution of our cells (fluid inside and outside the cell) determines their health and function. When free radicals (impaired molecules) attach themselves to cells in the body, those cells break down. Depending on how long cellular damage has occurred, the degree of ill health will be determined. And depending on where the weakened cells are located in your body, you will suffer disease of the liver, heart, blood, or other body systems.

If the cells do not get proper hydration (water) with bioavailable minerals, an imbalance in the cell occurs; the body falls out of homeostasis. Ultimately, this condition may lead to a variety of diseases and eventually death. Additionally, when the intracellular and extracellular fluid pH level becomes overly acidic for too long, the body will experience organ dysfunction, such as that of the gallbladder or liver. This condition is referred to as acidosis.

The root problem in this case is likely that the individual's pH is out of balance (too acidic) because of a deficiency in sodium. A deficiency of other organic minerals such as calcium, potassium, or magnesium is very common too. When we maintain the proper level of minerals in the body through proper hydration, the body has the mineral reserves to protect itself if the pH should go out of balance for various reasons temporarily. We replenish our body with minerals via diet and nutritional supplements. If the mineral reserves are low or depleted, the body will go into a survival mode to protect itself by creating a buffer. It will go to the next available source of minerals to balance its pH, like calcium.

For example, if the body requires calcium, where do you think it gets it? You guessed it—the bones. In order to protect itself, the body will leach calcium from the bones if a state of acidosis remains too long; however, this "robbing" process causes a lack of calcium in the bones, resulting in osteoporosis.

Think about the healthy athlete or fitness enthusiast who suddenly experiences a heart attack. It seems uncanny, but it happens, and I see it happening more and more. After the victim is dead, an examination is usually conducted to determine if there was some kind of gene or rare genetic disorder that caused the unexpected heart attack. However, the root cause could be simpler than that. If the body chemistry was in a state of acidosis caused by dehydration, that athlete or fitness enthusiast would have developed the perfect condition for a sudden heart attack. How could this happen?

Perhaps the level of acidity was further elevated by adding a high-protein pre-workout meal or snack and routinely eating a high-protein diet with foods that leave an acid ash (acid-ash-like diet) on the tissues, along with the effect of everyday stress. With an ever-increasing acid buildup in the body, the health is constantly challenged. Continuing this lifestyle over time, this healthy-looking athletic man or woman is developing a state of acidosis, which may make him or her the perfect candidate for a heart attack. If you don't learn how to neutralize your pH, the end result will always be damaging to your health, and if it remains undetected, it could become life threatening.

There are a couple of things you can do to neutralize and keep your pH in check. In brief, limit an *acid*-ash-like diet, which is basically the result of eating mostly meats, fish, eggs, and cereals, with very little fruit and vegetables in your diet. This kind of diet will produce acidification of the urine. To neutralize this acid condition, add more *alkaline*-ash-producing foods such as fruit and vegetables.

You can neutralize the acid and balance your pH by drinking ionized or alkaline water, which is one of my daily practices. As imperative as it is for you to hydrate the cells to keep them healthy and properly functioning, it is equally imperative that you know the type of water you drink. For several years, since the infamous craze for drinking bottled water, I have researched what kind of water is in those bottles. I have discovered that nearly all bottled water is acidic, even if it is purified. If you don't believe me, pick out any of the most popular bottled waters at random and compare them to the findings posted on my Web site at www.bodyredesigning.com.

I tested many bottled waters. In fact, I saw the results of nearly all of them, and I was amazed at the claims by doctors and experts who are selling purified water that is acidic. Just think about this for a minute. Since there is a direct link between your blood and tissue pH and cancers and other known diseases, we can conclude that maintaining the proper pH level is crucial.

Since my research of bottled water, I have made a habit of

drinking ionized (alkaline) water exclusively. I have a machine that restructures my tap water into alkaline water. It not only filters out all the chemicals and impurities that make our drinking water unhealthy, but it also retains all the natural bioavailable minerals that are in the water: sodium, calcium, magnesium, and potassium. It reduces the molecular size of the water by half, and through electrolysis, an electrical charge helps drive more alkaline water into my cells. The benefits I get from drinking alkaline water are:

- Neutralizing acid buildup from my workouts
- Neutralizing my pH from foods that leave an acid ash on the tissues
- Hydrating my cells with chemical-free water
- Protects my cells from free-radical damage

The alkaline water is also a natural antioxidant, which counteracts the potential damage to my cells by free radicals. It supplies my body with plenty of bioavailable minerals and assists in balancing my pH. Please, drink water. And make sure you drink alkaline water for your health. (See www.bodyredesigning.com.)

NATURAL ANTIAGING HORMONE (HGH)

There is nothing you can do about the clock on the wall as it continues its relentless, perpetual motion. So when it comes to aging, we all share one thing in common—we're all getting older. However, some of us will make choices that will definitely change the effects of time—we can slow down the aging process.

When I refer to the aging process, I am referring to health-related conditions associated with aging, such as increased body fat, loss of muscle tissue, decreased libido and energy, elevated blood pressure, poor sleep quality, and poor appearance (skin tone), just to mention a few. These common conditions associated with aging can be reversed or slowed down by taking human growth hormone (HGH), preferably in a homeopathic oral form. Other nutritional supplements such as DHEA, melatonin, and HGH support play a vital role as we attempt to slow down the aging process, but allow me to concentrate on HGH for now.

Human growth hormone is critical for our development during childhood and plays a key role in the development of bones, muscles, organs, and the body as a whole. HGH dramatically decreases as you develop to maturity. It is produced naturally by your pituitary gland and other immune cells until you reach your midtwenties. But by the age of eighty, it is virtually nonexistent in your body. The natural aging process affects your overall health and quality of life due to the lack of HGH in your body. Add stress to the formula (which reduces HGH production), and you can see why it's all downhill after you hit thirty to thirty-five years of age.

Since I have been taking this antiaging hormone supplement HGH, I can confirm that it helps me stay leaner, has improved my skin tone, and gives me the satisfaction of knowing I am replacing what my body won't produce anymore. Even my mother takes HGH and comments on the improvement she enjoys in sleeping well each night. If you are over thirty years of age, male or female, I recommend HGH as a part of your nutrition support strategy.

What is listed above is not necessarily mandatory for you to take, because everyone is different. Nor is the list exhaustive, but it does provide a wide spectrum for your consideration. For a complete list of dietary supplements that range from covering the bases to more specific, visit my Web site at www .bodyredesigning.com.

There are no magic bullets, potions, or lotions for improving your health. A healthy life will be a result of creating a balance in your body, soul, and spirit. It encompasses the positive things you do (physical activities), what you ingest (nutrition), the positive thoughts you embrace (forgiveness, compassion for others), keeping a positive attitude (walking in victory), and connecting with your Creator (perfect peace of mind.)

Chapter 15

The Right Program for Your Body Type

As I discussed in chapter 13, *circuit training* is the method of exercise I am recommending that you follow. Please refer to that chapter to help refresh your memory on how to perform a complete circuit correctly. Review the many wonderful benefits of circuit training as well. Assuming you are using circuit training as the baseline to your program, I want to take you to the next level of fitness training. To do this, you need to be training according to your body genetics or body type. Chart 15-6, Determining Your Body Type, on page 289 will help to identify what type your body is.

Once you have determined your body type, you are on the right track for reaching your goals. Now study Troubleshooting the Pear, Apple, or Banana Body Type charts on pages 290–292. These charts will explain trouble areas, inherited genetic problems, and body redesigning strategies for balancing your shape.

In lieu of providing you with an exercise program specifically designed for your body type, I have recorded three different *body type workout* videos that target specific areas for redesigning and creating more symmetry or balance for each body type. (See Appendix C.)

Monitoring Your Progress

It is imperative for you to use some form of tracking device that will assist you to better evaluate your progress. I have included the following to help monitor your progress:

1. Initial Measurements Sheet
2. Progress Report Card
3. Body Fat Test
4. Dietary Analysis

Before you use these charts, read the sections that follow, which describe each of these charts and tell you how to use them.

INITIAL MEASUREMENT SHEET

I have prepared an initial measurements recording sheet for you to use. (See page 286.) It will establish your original measurements before you begin your program, along with directions for taking your own "before" photographs. Recording your initial statistics gives you something with which to compare your progress during your program. Your "before" photo will be followed with an "after" photo.

PROGRESS REPORT CARD

The progress report card on page 287 will ask you a few pertinent questions that apply to your overall program. Just by taking the time to record your results and answer the questions on the sheet, you will stimulate your thinking for making sure you are doing everything you should be. Remember that these are the things I would be asking of you if I were there with you as your personal trainer. Stay accountable—and stay focused.

BODY FAT TEST

Concerning your proper weight profile, your body composition is more important than the way you look in your clothes. I know you are thinking that your appearance is more important, so let me connect the two together. Your lean muscle mass is the true indicator of your success in losing unwanted body fat, especially when it is working in concert with your diet. Your body type workout tape is designed to work in concert with your body genetics so you can look shapelier. This is the connection between the diet, exercise, and body composition rather than simply considering your weight.

Body Fat Test

You can make a reasonable estimate of your fat-to-muscle ratio by using the following charts. Women, measure your hip girth and height, and draw a line from your hip girth to your height. Men, draw a line from your weight to your waist girth. This will give you an approximate measure of your body fat. Subtract that from 100 percent, and you know your muscle rating.

MEN
170-pound man
34" Waist = 18% body fat

WOMEN
5'4" woman
39" hips = 30% body fat

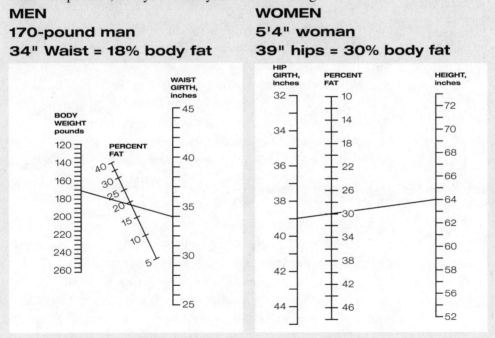

Your BMR (basal metabolic rate) represents your body's ability to burn calories while resting. Exercise not only burns calories while you are active, but it also promotes a higher percentage of lean muscle mass tissue, which in turn allows your body to burn calories efficiently even when you are resting. If your body fat percentage is too high and your lean muscle mass tissue percentage is too low, then your BMR is greatly hindered. So, the focus point for losing weight is found in lowering your body fat percentage and increasing your lean muscle mass tissue through diet and exercise. The end result will be a positive body composition, better calorie burning, and a shapelier body regardless of the weight.

A female is considered clinically obese if her body fat is in excess of 30 percent of her total weight; that figure is 25 percent for the male. The higher the percent of body fat and the lower your lean muscle mass, the slower your metabolism is. It is more difficult to lose weight with a slower metabolism, as we have discussed. By increasing your lean muscle mass through exercise, your body will more efficiently burn calories while you are resting, twenty-four hours per day.

When you are carrying excess body fat, not only are there potential health problems, but also it will be nearly impossible for you to see any significant changes in your shape even after dieting. And as you age, your body loses approximately ½ pound of muscle mass per year. With less muscle mass due to aging and sedentary lifestyles, it is no wonder obesity is accepted as a normal part of aging.

Of course, I would rather you monitor your weight loss success by doing a monthly body fat test, determining your lean muscle mass, than simply showing me how much you weigh. Follow the simple directions on the Body Fat Test chart on page 283 to monitor your progress.

DIETARY ANALYSIS

Recording your consumption of food can be very helpful. Most of us don't realize the amount of little tastes or little bites of food we have consumed throughout each day—especially "avoid" foods. As you track your eating, you will be amazed at how far off the mark of optimal eating you have been—and yet you never saw it happening.

This dietary analysis tracking device on page 288 is best to use before you start out on your journey. That way you get a realistic look at your present eating habits. As you proceed through your exercise journey, repeat the dietary analysis as often as you feel the need to double-check yourself. Each time continue the tracking for three consecutive days. For three days, simply record everything you eat and drink. Record the time you eat each meal or snack. Record the number of cups of coffee and/or cans of soda. If you eat a cookie or have a bowl of ice cream, write down an accurate record of what you ate.

Your dietary analysis will give you an accurate account of whether you are consuming foods that are compatible for your blood type. It will also help you to stay on track. If I were your personal trainer, I would be asking you dietary questions all the time. Tracking your diet will make a big difference in your success or failure—especially when you hit a plateau.

15-2

Rule of Thumb for Healthy Eating

1. Eat when you are hungry.

2. Eat until you are satisfied (not stuffed).

3. Put the brakes on if eating when not hungry, or you will run into emotional eating disorders.

Food can work for you or against you, as we have seen. It can stimulate weight loss, or it can cause weight gain. See the weight loss/gain lists for each blood type, and discover which foods are compatible for weight loss and which are avoid foods, causing weight gain. (Blood type A, see page 143. Blood type B, see page 155. Blood type AB, see page 165. Blood type O, see page 179.)

Now take the time to look over each of the charts on the following pages and fill them in with your specific information. When you are finished, you are ready to determine your body type and move on to start your exercise program.

Initial Measurement Sheet

GENERAL INSTRUCTIONS FOR TAKING YOUR MEASUREMENTS

Always measure and remeasure from the same points for accuracy. Keep the tape measure level.

Body parts	Where to measure	Measurements
1. Shoulders	around the largest point	_____
2. Chest/Bust	midpoint of chest/bust and upper back	_____
3. Arms	largest point while arm is hanging	R_____ L_____
4. Waist	smallest point above navel	_____
5. Hips (female)	midpoint between navel/crotch	_____
6. Thighs	largest upper point	R_____ L_____
7. Calves	largest point	R_____ L_____
8. Wrists	at the bend	R_____ L_____
9. Ankles	at the bend	R_____ L_____
10. Height/Weight	shoes off	H_____ W_____

GENERAL INSTRUCTIONS FOR YOUR "BEFORE" PHOTOGRAPHS

You will need to take "before" photographs to help you determine your body type and your specific exercise program as outlined in this book. Use the following guidelines:

- **Clothing**—Wear something that will allow your physique or figure to be seen clearly (leotards, swimsuit or shorts, and tank top).
- **Photos**—Take three photographs: front, side, and back.
- **Poses**—Stand relaxed with heels together and look straight ahead in each photo.
- **Camera Tips**—Be sure to use a solid-color backdrop, and be sure your figure fills the camera frame from head to toe.

Progress Report Card

Name _____ Date ___/___/____

GENERAL INSTRUCTIONS

Always measure and remeasure from the same points for accuracy. Keep tape level when measuring.

Body parts	Where to measure	Measurements
1. Shoulders	around the largest point	_____
2. Chest/Bust	midpoint of chest/bust and upper back	_____
3. Arms	largest point while arm is hanging	R_____ L_____
4. Waist	smallest point above navel	_____
5. Hips (female)	midpoint between navel/crotch	_____
6. Thighs	largest upper point	R_____ L_____
7. Calves	largest point	R_____ L_____
8. Wrists	at the bend	R_____ L_____
9. Ankles	at the bend	R_____ L_____
10. Height/Weight	shoes off	H_____ W _____

PLEASE ANSWER THE FOLLOWING QUESTIONS

(circle correct answer):

How many times do you train weekly?	1	2	3	4
What is your percentage of eating for your blood type?	60%	70%	80%	90%
Are you keeping a positive attitude?	Often	Sometimes	Never	
In what areas are you having the most difficulty?	Eating	Training		

Explain: _____

_____

_____

What changes have you noticed about yourself since you started the program?

When do you see yourself reaching your goals: Months _____

Are you able to complete ALL the sets and reps per exercise by the end of this month's program? Yes No

Explain: _____

_____

Remember: Commitment is a positive attitude in constant motion.

15-5

Dietary Analysis

Please list ALL the foods and liquids that you consume for three days—*including the amounts.*

DAY 1:

Breakfast _____

Midmorning _____

Noon _____

Midafternoon _____

Dinner _____

After dinner _____

DAY 2:

Breakfast _____

Midmorning _____

Noon _____

Midafternoon _____

Dinner _____

After dinner _____

DAY 3:

Breakfast _____

Midmorning _____

Noon _____

Midafternoon _____

Dinner _____

After dinner _____

Important: Remember to include ALL the "Avoid" foods and junk foods such as Oreos, slices of pizza, cans of soda, etc.

If you take nutritional supplements, please list them:

_____

_____

_____

Determining Your Body Type

15-6

Identifying your body type and your inherited genetic problem areas is very important and *is a must-know*. To determine your body type, simply ask this question:

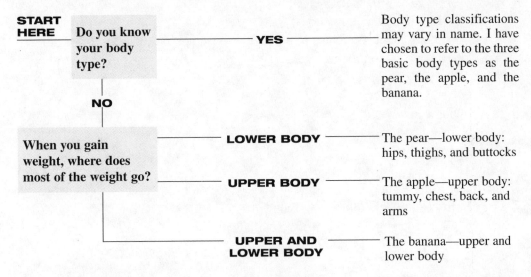

START HERE   **Do you know your body type?** ——————— **YES** ——————— Body type classifications may vary in name. I have chosen to refer to the three basic body types as the pear, the apple, and the banana.

NO

When you gain weight, where does most of the weight go?

——————— **LOWER BODY** ——————— The pear—lower body: hips, thighs, and buttocks

——————— **UPPER BODY** ——————— The apple—upper body: tummy, chest, back, and arms

——————— **UPPER AND LOWER BODY** ——————— The banana—upper and lower body

As you understand your body genetics and problem areas, you are paving the path to success. Now that you have identified your body type, go to pages 290–292 and study your body type further.

Troubleshooting Your Body Type

Now that you have worked through the charts included earlier in this chapter and have completed the Determining Your Body Type chart on this page, it is time to begin your workouts. To better understand the work that is ahead of you, look over the appropriate troubleshooting chart for your body type on pages 290–292.

Troubleshooting the Pear Body Type

TROUBLE AREAS

Weight Distribution Problems

When the pear gains weight, the weight mostly goes to the hips, thighs, and buttocks.

Lower Body

- Most body fat accumulates in the hips, thighs, and buttocks
- Considered bottom heavy

Upper Body

- Generally slender
- Shallow bustline
- Narrow shoulders
- Straight waist

Inherited Genetic Problems

The following are the primary inherent genetic factors:

- Narrow shoulders due to short clavicles
- Shallow and small bustline due to less upper body fat
- Wide pelvic and hip structure
- Excessive adipose fat tissue (cells) on the hips, thighs, and buttocks
- Straight waistline due to narrow or small ribs

BODY REDESIGNING STRATEGIES

Perform exercises designed to:

Upper Body

- Fill out the chest/bust
- Broaden back and add width to the shoulders
- Firm and tone the arms (biceps and triceps)
- Firm the abdominal muscles

Lower Body

- Isolate hips, thighs, and buttocks
- Elongate, firm, and tone
- Reduce lower body major muscles

Avoid any exercises or physical activities that would tend to stimulate the lower body to grow. Concentrate on building muscle mass for the upper body while reducing the lower body.

(See the Body Type Workout videos in Appendix C.)

Troubleshooting the Apple Body Type

TROUBLE AREAS

Weight Distribution Problems

When the apple gains weight, the weight mostly goes to the upper body. The apple lacks upper body/lower body symmetry or balance.

Lower Body

- Generally leaner but lagging in size in comparison to the upper body

Upper Body

- Most body fat stored around the waist, upper back, and arms

Inherited Genetic Problems

The following are the primary inherent genetic factors:

- Excessive adipose tissue (cells) on the upper body, usually in the abdominal region, the chest/bust, back, and arms
- Abdominal muscles usually protrude forward or bulge outward
- Generally longer upper torso and shorter lower torso
- Thin legs and buttocks, in some instances too thin or undersized from a symmetrical viewpoint

BODY REDESIGNING STRATEGIES

Perform exercises that:

Upper Body

- Shape and tone only
- Isolate abdominal muscles

Lower Body

- Build the upper and lower leg muscles
- Build, firm, and tone the buttocks

Avoid exercises that tend to build mass on the upper body. Exercises for the upper body should be done for the sole purpose of firming and toning each muscle group. Concentrate on the abdominal muscles for strengthening and flattening. Incorporate exercises that will stimulate lower body muscles. Using dumbbells will help develop a symmetrical hourglass shape.

(See the Body Type Workout videos in Appendix C.)

Troubleshooting the Banana Body Type

TROUBLE AREAS

Weight Distribution Problems

When the banana gains weight, the weight goes equally to the upper and lower body.

- Mainly lacks curves or shapeliness
- Tends to have a straight-line figure or physique

Inherited Genetic Problems

The following are the primary inherent genetic factors:

- The musculoskeletal system is such that the pelvic bone, ribs, and shoulder width are similar.
- Wide waistline due to above
- Adipose fat tissue (cells) evenly dispersed on the upper and lower body

BODY REDESIGNING STRATEGIES

Perform exercises that:

Upper Body: Firm, tone, and build muscles; strengthen and tone the abdominal muscles.

Lower Body: Elongate the thighs; firm and tone the buttocks.

The banana shape may be somewhat confusing to identify. The idea of having a banana shape makes you think the body would be thin. In most cases this is true, until the banana gains weight. Then the thin banana becomes a full banana, and the weight is dispersed equally in the upper and lower body. Therefore both banana types must incorporate exercises that will even out their shape and add curves and lines. Because the upper and lower are relatively balanced, or symmetrical, the fuller banana will want to add additional cardiovascular workouts to their Body Redesigning program.

(See the Body Type Workout videos in Appendix C.)

Get on Your Mark; Get Set; GO!

Are you ready? No more analyzing to do...no more charts to fill out...no more delays! It's time to begin your workouts. Come on, you can do it!

Your program gives you the best of three worlds. In one workout you will benefit from shaping and toning each muscle group and improving your cardiovascular condition while burning fat calories for the energy to perform the workout. The exercises are targeted to correct the problem areas so your total body symmetry will be more balanced. The first thirty days of training will strengthen your muscles and joints and speed up the recovery factor from exercise. This is the beginning of the strength and toning process, and in a very short time your cardiovascular condition will improve and promote increased endurance and stamina as you are able to progressively pick up the tempo.

By the end of the first thirty days, your metabolism will burn fat calories at a higher rate of efficiency, no longer allowing your body to store calories. Since your metabolism will have been stimulated regularly by following your program, you should start experiencing changes in the way your clothes fit and the way you look in the mirror. I call this process metabolic momentum.

It is not important to me how much weight you lose, and it shouldn't matter to you either. I realize that losing weight is the common monitoring mechanism everybody has used for decades, but you and I have agreed to make changes both physically and mentally. Therefore, keep tabs on how your clothes fit and what the mirror says. The key is your body composition—body fat vs. lean weight, or fat-to-muscle ratio.

At the end of every thirty days you should document your progress so you can make comparisons to where you started. Be sure to fill out your monthly progress report card.

Before You Begin

Here are a few pointers I have listed for your review. So take a moment and read each one before you start your program:

By the end of the first thirty days, your metabolism will burn fat calories at a higher rate of efficiency, no longer allowing your body to store calories.

1. Consult your physician before you begin this or any other exercise program.

2. Before you begin each workout, do the following: Warm up for five to ten minutes using a stationary bike or treadmill, by stepping in place, or by walking. Your exercise program is designed for up to three forty-five-minute workouts per week. This includes your warm-ups and stretching.

3. After each workout, cool down for five to ten minutes, using the stretching exercises on pages 295–296.

4. Cardiovascular training—three thirty- to forty-five-minute cardiovascular workouts per week in addition to your regular workouts are recommended. These can be done on your "off" days. This will assure you of good cardiovascular conditioning and extra fat burning. Suggested aerobic exercises include stationary bike riding, treadmill, power walks, and stair climbers. Remember these important tips: Calculate your Training Heart Rate (THR) using the chart on page 295. (Example: The THR for a forty-year-old should be between 132 beats per minute, or 22 beats per ten seconds at 70 percent maximum heart rate, and 156 beats per minute, or 26 beats per ten seconds at 85 percent maximum heart rate.) Monitor your THR by taking your pulse for ten seconds. Maintain a constant THR throughout each workout.

5. Discontinue exercise if you feel faint or nauseous, if you experience chest pains, or if you have difficulty breathing. If symptoms persist, contact your physician.

Stretching Exercises

To make your exercise program complete, it is vitally important to add some stretching exercises. Stretching helps to elongate the muscles, assists in relieving muscle tightness and soreness, and

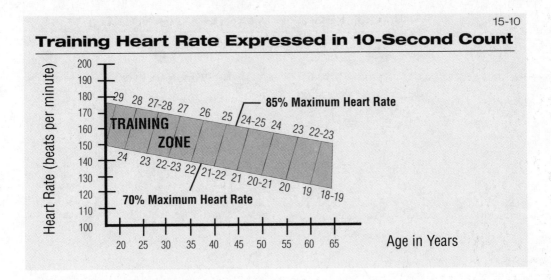

15-10

Training Heart Rate Expressed in 10-Second Count

improves the mobility and range of motion (ROM) of your joints. It is best to stretch after your exercise workout.

Use the following static stretching exercises. Static stretching gently pulls or stretches the intended muscle group. It avoids any form of bouncing or erratic motion. Do not overstretch a muscle group to the point of discomfort. The key is to relax, breathe freely, stretch, hold, and release.

CAT/COW STRETCH (LOWER, MID, AND UPPER BACK)

Position 1: Get down on all fours. Sag your back while lifting your head upward.

Position 2: Arch your back and lower your head. Hold the stretch for fifteen to twenty-five seconds.

Position 3: Lean back on your heels. Hold the stretch for fifteen to twenty-five seconds.

Repeat three to four times.

KNEE/QUAD STRETCH (QUADRICEPS)

Position: Lie face down. Reach back with your left hand and grasp your left ankle. Pull and hold the stretch for fifteen to twenty-five seconds. Repeat for opposite leg.

Repeat three to four times.

DOUBLE LEG STRETCH (LOWER BACK)

Position: Lie on your back with your knees slightly bent. Grasp both legs and gently pull them to your chest, lifting your tailbone off the floor. Hold the stretch for fifteen to twenty-five seconds. Relax, and then repeat three to four times.

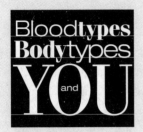

Section IV

Real People,
Real Results

Getting Up in the Morning Is a Joy —Dr. Joe

Before and after photos really say a lot about a person. As I stood in an "all you can eat" line for a Hawaiian buffet, I had my unexpected "Kodak" moment. What I really looked like had never occurred to me prior to that moment. I'm not certain if that moment was defined by the bushel-basket face I had developed, the 305 pounds to which I had zoomed, or the fact that the producers at Sea World were looking for a human Shamu and thought I was a candidate. But my before photo did get my attention.

Two questions loomed before me, immediately demanding answers: How did I get here? How was I going to turn this around?

Whether it was the picture or the realization that I was out of control that motivated me, I made a vow to myself that I would no longer walk around the face of this earth looking like that photo.

I decided to make the necessary changes—in my eating, in my exercise program, and, more importantly, in my mental attitude.

That before picture was taken in April 1981 when I weighed 305 pounds. By December 1981 I had gone down to 220 pounds. I was serious! I've been serious since then—and I've kept the weight off during that time. I might gain a pound or two here or there, but I am careful to never allow myself to go beyond a certain point.

I had been healthy for most of my life. I had the usual health challenges growing up, but nothing out

Before—305 lbs.
April 1981

After—220 lbs.
December 1981

of the ordinary. I did have rheumatic fever as a child, which is interesting considering the fact that I am blood type O (more susceptible to blood disorders), but I did not incur any heart damage. I also managed to get a stomach ulcer at the age of eleven, which is common for blood type O.

I live an active life, and I have been exercising since I was thirteen years of age. Other than a few broken bones and injuries from competitive sports, I've been a pretty healthy camper. But as time passed, I began to deal with one recurring health issue—hypoglycemia. I struggled with it for fifteen years. Anyone who has experienced hypoglycemia, or low blood sugar, knows that it can be a nightmare. It was for me.

My condition became so severe that I could not go for more than one hour without eating. If more time passed, I would "crash." It happened like clockwork—at ten in the morning and three in the afternoon. I would feel lethargic, light-headed, nauseous at times, irritable, and tired. I battled bouts of depression for no known reason. After researching every diet concept, seeking medical advice, and attempting to mix and match the foods I ate, eventually I began testing the concept of eating foods compatible to my blood type. In my research I learned about the link that exists between blood types and food, and I thought I would give it a try.

As blood type O, I discovered that foods like pasta, bread (wheat), and dairy foods should be avoided. Interestingly, some of these foods were the very foods the doctor had told me I should eat for my low-sugar problem. The big hurdle for me to get over as an Italian was the fact that I could no longer eat pasta five times a week. Pasta was my staple—it seemed an impossibility to do without it.

But I figured that if I was going to whip this low-blood-sugar thing, I'd have to give it 100 percent.

As a blood type O, I began adding red meat as a protein source, which is beneficial to my diet. The protein contributed most to the stabilizing of my blood sugar. I eventually started drinking protein drinks as a meal or snack replacement. This further helped to stabilize my blood sugar. Amazingly, I immediately started experiencing gastrointestinal relief—no more gas! I started losing weight (body fat). Most gratifying, I was no longer "crashing."

After eating foods compatible to my blood type for approximately five to ten days, and avoiding foods that were incompatible, not only did I feel better, but I also had constant energy due to the stabilization of my blood sugar. Now my blood sugar remains stable.

My before photo is just a reminder to me of what can happen if I should let things get out of control. When I am consistent at eating food compatible for my blood type, taking my nutritional supplements, and including regular daily exercise and physical activities, I am constantly reminded of the improvement in my appearance, mental outlook, and feelings of accomplishment.

As I make regular exercise and instinctive eating a major part of my life, I am able to enjoy my life to its fullest. I have the energy to work and play. I have no medical bills to pay. Getting up in the morning is a joy. Most importantly, staying healthy makes me more appreciative and grateful to God for uniquely creating the human body to respond naturally and positively to the proper preventative lifestyle.

Wow!   —Carol

I cannot tell you enough...THANK YOU! I am in great health! I feel great! I have lost 11.5 pounds in five weeks. I finally have a sense of direction in my eating habits! This has been a prayer issue for me for quite some time. God answered my prayers when He sent me YOU! Thank you for all of your work and for your ministry! You have no idea, this side of glory, the way you have touched lives! God bless you!

No More GERD   —Judy

My husband and I have taken all the information from your books very seriously and have been using the food plan for our blood type for only a couple weeks. I stopped craving sweet simple carbohydrates, and my husband no longer has GERD or sinus problems. We are convinced that our blood types are crucial to what we eat.

No More Respiratory, No More Asthma Medication   —John

I am type O, apple body type, and sixty-three years old. I switched to eating for my blood type 100 percent. I have cut back on my thyroid medication and am off my asthma and respiratory medications. I no longer have hypoglycemia. I have increased my exercise regimen for the apple body type and have lost four inches around the waist.

Enjoying Good Health   —Linda

In 1981 I was diagnosed with cancer, but now I am enjoying good health. Going through this experience made me appreciate my health and quality of life. When I found out my blood type, I realized that I was eating incorrectly for my type, and my body was reacting to it. Six months after following your book (*Bloodtypes, Bodytypes, and YOU*), my life has changed for the better. I determined in my heart that I would eat beneficial foods and stay away from the avoid foods, and within three days I began to experience the results. I had previously experienced a lot of stomach disorders and was hospitalized on several occasions and discharged because the doctors couldn't determine the cause. Now all the symptoms are gone and my energy is great. In addition to feeling good and having higher energy, I have gone down two dress sizes. *I haven't given up anything except discomfort.*

I Can't Believe the Change!   —Dorothy

I was so skeptical at first about this genetic thing with food and exercise, but I followed the food plans from your book. It has changed my life! The things on the avoid list have always been a problem for me: corn, orange juice, vinegar, peanuts, brussels sprouts, dairy foods, etc. The things I didn't realize were bad for me were wheat, potatoes, and pasta, which I was eating a lot of because I thought they were healthy foods. I have suffered with allergies, thyroid disease, constipation, bloating, gas, and colitis.

I have been on the exercise program for five weeks, and I cannot believe the change. I lost two inches in my waist the first four weeks!

I have not eaten anything on my avoid list, and for the first four weeks I tried to eat only beneficial foods. I felt so good, I just couldn't make myself not continue. Thank you for making this so simple and easy and for giving me the tools to live a healthy life!

Mother and Daughter Lose 218 Pounds in One Year!   —Gail and Jean

I tried other diets, but they did not work. But this was so easy to do. It was not hard at all. When I started, I set a goal to lose weight and be healthier by my fiftieth birthday (August 2004). Heart trouble and high blood pressure run in my family. My mother was having health problems, so I started her eating for her blood type also. After one year I have lost 118 pounds, and my mother has lost 100 pounds. We both have more energy and are in better health. My mother is no longer on medications, and her doctor said, "Whatever you are doing, keep doing it." Both of us follow your 80/20 rule for eating and exercising for our body types. It has been a blessing and is so much better than our old lifestyle.

Before   After   Before   After

Let the Results Speak for Themselves — Pastor Rocky

When I saw Joe Christiano on a television program about three years ago, I decided to buy his book *Bloodtypes, Bodytypes, and YOU*.

I did the typical "Look to see what foods I should avoid based on my blood type" scan of the book. I didn't like everything I saw, but I went ahead and read the book. I decided to at least give it a try. Instead of focusing on the "avoid" foods for being a blood type A, I simply began to switch to more of the beneficial and neutral foods. It was refreshing to try some new foods that I liked. Already in good health, I noticed my energy level increase more than anything. I didn't seem to have the crashing feeling after a meal at all now. My metabolism increased as I noticed more definition in my body. I eat probably 80–90 percent according to my blood type, and I don't feel like I'm depriving myself. I also began to adjust my exercises a little to include those suitable for my body type and renewed my interest in competing in a bodybuilding contest.

So at age forty-two, I entered the 2005 Potomac Cup Drug Free competition. By the grace of God, the support of my wife and daughter, and the advice, expertise, and encouragement of Dr. Joe, I won the lightweight novice division, the forty-and-over pose-down, and finished third in the master's thirty-five division.

I have a passion to see people live up to their full God-given potential in every area: spirit, soul, and body.

Great Results   —Barbara

I just wanted to express my thanks to you for putting this program on the market. My husband (blood type B) and I started this one month ago. We have experienced great results. My husband has lost 16.5 inches over his total body, 7 percent body fat, and 5 pounds. I have lost 28 inches over my total body, 10.25 percent body fat, and 10 pounds. This is all in just the first month. Needless to say, we are continuing with the program and have also shared it with my parents, my brother and his wife, and several friends. Again, thank you for the program.

New Shape   —Caroline

I purchased your exercise tape in June of 2001, and I have continued to follow the exercise for the pear shape. I have dropped from a size 18 to a 12 or 14 and have lost about 36 pounds. This is the first time I have experienced a vast difference in the shape of my lower body. Years ago I walked three miles a day at a fast pace, five to six days a week for two to three years, and did not see the results that I have experienced now. A friend told me that I have a "straight up and down" shape now. Thank you.

Losing Weight Is a No-Brainer —Katherine

I have been on your weight management program since February 2002. I have lost 18 pounds and feel great. I really never looked overweight, but I am 5 feet 4 inches tall, and I weighed 150 pounds. Now I weigh 132 pounds and have lost inches. I went from a size 12 to a size 8. I am forty-six, but I look thirty-six. I have tried it all, and let me tell you, this program is a way of life for me! Thank you for making losing weight a no-brainer.

No More Discomfort   —Judith

I had a lot of digestive problems and some pain in my stomach, which I believe was an ulcer, for years. Since I started eating more food for my blood type, which is A, I am doing much better and NO stomach discomfort! Thank you so much.

It's a Lifestyle Now!   —Stacy and Rod

Stacy: We weren't looking for another diet and exercise program. We've done them all! What we were looking for was a baby. Rod and I have struggled with infertility since 1998 when I was diagnosed with a tumor on my pituitary gland. It wreaked havoc on my hormonal system and caused my progesterone level to be quite low. Conception was very difficult. It also caused weight gain, which added to my depression. Then in August of 1999, my mother passed away from cancer of the brain. My anxiety, stress, and weight were at an all-time high.

Rod and I were both increasingly disgusted with our bodies because of poor eating habits and little or no physical activity. We had low energy and little willpower to resist the foods that were causing our "growing" problem. It seemed overwhelming at times.

When we were introduced to the concept of eating according to our blood type, we were both a bit skeptical. We made the mistake of looking first at the avoid lists and began to protest. But after about a week of eating mostly beneficial and some neutral foods for my blood type, I stopped craving the nachos I had to have! Our energy levels increased incredibly, and combined with the exercises Dr. Joe showed us, we had amazing results.

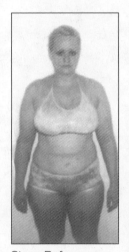 

In twelve weeks we lost fat and inches, gained muscle, and improved our health. Rod lost 42 pounds of fat and normalized his cholesterol (which was high prior to this) and his blood pressure. I lost 30 pounds of fat, gained 5 pounds of muscle, went down three dress sizes, and lost 47 total inches of body size. We like having the three-month goal as a motivation, and when we finish three months, we just start three more. I needed hope again. And I found it by changing my lifestyle. It really is a lifestyle for us now.

Stacy Before   Stacy After

Rob: In just twelve weeks I went from 23 percent body fat to under 10 percent, lost 42 pounds of fat, and went from a tight size 40 pants to a very comfortable 36. I am 6 feet 4 inches tall and weigh 225 pounds, so a size 36 is pretty good!

All the fat loss was great, awesome, and all of that, but the real story is our energy levels and our health. Not only did our energy levels stabilize, but they went through the roof. I am a full-time youth pastor, a part-time Terminator at University Studios in Florida, and a full-time husband. My lifestyle demands a lot from me. My wife is a full-time singer/entertainer and a wonderful wife, so hers is equally demanding. Let's just say that energy is not a problem anymore!

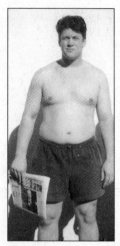

Rod Before

Rod After

We really feel good. We look better, so we feel better about ourselves. All areas of our lives have improved. We are both more confident and less inhibited to try new things. Now that we have done this whole body redesign, we have found that if we can discipline ourselves in one area of our lives, we can do it in any area. Not only are our bodies in better shape, but our lives are also in better shape. We can do anything we put our minds to! We are so proud of each other, and we have a greater respect for each other. Every part of our relationship has improved. We are so glad we met Dr. Joe; he has been a very big help to us!

Others Noticed Something Different
—Debbie

One year ago I was extremely overweight and had no energy. My lifestyle consisted of consuming eight to twelve cans of Diet Pepsi a day and eating a lot of food packed with fat, sugars, and no nutrients.

I began following Dr. Joe's program of eating according to my blood type and exercising according to my body type on a regular basis. I noticed immediate results. Within three weeks, I had blood work done, and my cholesterol had dropped over sixty points. When I went to the doctor's office for the lab results, she burst into the room saying, "I am thrilled at the results of your blood work. Whatever you are doing, keep it up."

Prior to embracing this lifestyle, I had my thyroid removed. My doctor has consistently lowered my medication since I began the program because my body is more in line with the way it should be. Another benefit was the immediate increased energy I felt. I no longer dreaded getting out of bed and dragging myself through the day. The exercise became a part of my daily routine, and very soon I felt something was missing on the days I could not exercise.

I do not have a scale, and I really don't know how much weight I've lost. However, I have lost six dress sizes. Even during Thanksgiving and Christmas holidays I continued to lose sizes. We went to more Christmas parties than we had ever attended, and I ate a lot of food. But I just ate food appropriate for blood type O as much as possible.

Since I have lost so many dress sizes, it is not difficult for others to notice that something is different. I enjoy sharing with them the secrets to my success—eating and exercising according to my type.

Keeping It Off for Eight Years! —Lynn

It is amazing how one person can change your life forever, give you a positive outlook, and help you achieve your goals. I never had a weight problem as a child. That is, until I became a teenager. My hormones kicked in and took my body through many changes, of which 40 to 50 pounds was one of them. I wore baggy clothes so that people wouldn't notice. When people looked at me, I thought they were looking at my weight—not at me as a person. Because of that, I lost a lot of self-confidence.

Throughout high school and college I was very active, playing softball, cheerleading, and dancing, but something was still missing. I tried so many different diet plans, pills, and programs, but nothing helped—it only got worse. I would lose a little weight and then put it right back on. I couldn't find a program that catered to my needs, body, and schedule. I felt overwhelmed and lost.

I had a lot of friends and enjoyed being with people, but deep down inside, I realized I wasn't happy with myself. I knew that one of the most important parts of life was to love me for who I was.

I had many goals in life, and one of them was to compete in the Miss New York USA Pageant. I've been involved in pageants since I was thirteen, but I would not compete if there was a swimsuit competition. I am very goal-oriented, but how could I compete in the pageant when I was overweight?

I had seen Dr. Joe Christiano and read his articles about the work he had done with pageant contestants in several editions of a pageant magazine. The pictures accompanying the articles were amazing. With some of the women, the transition from before to after was unbelievable. I thought if I was going to achieve my goals, a good place to start would be by giving Joe a call. That call changed my life.

I talked extensively with Joe over the phone, and within a few weeks, I was on a regular workout schedule and diet program—not a diet; it was more like an eating regimen.

Dr. Joe and I talked at least once a week for the first month, and then once or twice a month thereafter. At any given time, though, if I felt discouraged or needed encouragement, he was always there to help. He was very encouraging, supportive, and motivating. Whenever I needed him, he was always there—even when I wanted to quit.

I saw results in the first month, and within months after dropping 30 pounds and 17½ inches I was walking down the runway at the Miss New York USA Pageant—my self-esteem and confidence just in taking that walk were amazing.

I was at a standstill; I wasn't losing any more, and I had reached a plateau. That's when Dr. Joe introduced me to eating according to my blood type, a program genetically designed to target my specific blood type. My eating habits changed once again. Foods that before I thought were good for me now actually had a negative effect on my body. This meant that they were not being properly digested.

At the same time, Dr. Joe tweaked my workout program to

target specific areas of my body that needed to be redesigned. What a difference it made. I was losing body fat, not muscle fat. My muscles were more defined and lean. I felt great.

When I wanted to give up, Dr. Joe wouldn't let me. He lent himself to me as a mentor, friend, and personal fitness coach. He never let me become disillusioned with myself. There were pep talks to bolster my self-image and positive encouragement to help me build my self-confidence and continue with my determination to reach my goals. He possessed the very important skill of being a great listener.

My attitude and personality changed dramatically. I learned proper eating habits and ways to work out and challenge my body based on my genetic makeup.

Today, eight years later and thirty-three years old, I still have maintained my weight at 138 pounds. I continue with the techniques I've learned from Dr. Joe and model my life around those techniques. I don't panic if I gain a few pounds for one reason or another because I have a solid foundation of knowledge and expertise to support me. I exercise four to five times a week, including cardio, weights, and various machines. This is very important to me to maintain my weight, but also it's a great stress reliever.

Thank you again for all your support and encouragement. You have truly made a difference in my life.

A Real Winner Would Take the Stairs! —Cindy

I was naïve and inexperienced when I entered my first couple of pageant competitions in 1987—but I was having fun. I won at the mall among only a handful of contestants, which propelled me into my first state competition. Much to my surprise, I placed second runner-up in the Mrs. Florida Pageant, competing with forty-six other contestants. Having no real expectations of major success, I was thrilled. The next year I was able to move up one spot to finish as first runner-up.

In 1989 I decided to try again. I was devastated when my placement stalled at first runner-up again. This was the year I had set my sights on winning. As the weeks and months went by, my devastation turned to sheer determination. I realized that to win at the level of competition in which I found myself (seventy-plus women competing for one prize), relying on my natural physical conditioning was not good enough.

I had heard about Joe Christiano from friends in the pageant arena, and I decided to consult with him. We met, came up with an initial plan of attack, and proceeded. Not only was Joe able to push me to—and past—my limits while at his gym, but he also motivated me to continue pushing myself while training on my own.

Amazingly enough, Joe could tell me all the things I needed to change or improve (diet, exercise, etc.), and I would accept it. Although I did not relish changing my habits (especially giving up candy bars and diet sodas) or pushing myself as hard as he said I should, he commanded a certain respect for what he did. He never asked me to do anything he had not already done himself a thousand times over.

One day Joe decided it was "leg day," which meant *giant sets* of leg extensions, hyperextensions, and lunges—everyone's favorite, right? By the time the training session ended, my legs could barely support me as I walked out the door with my family and toward the elevator. "What do you think you're doing?" Joe asked. I was taken aback for a moment, wondering what he was talking about. "Why are you using the elevator?" he asked me. "A real winner would take the stairs!"

Mrs. Florida 1991

Given the way I felt at that moment, if anyone else had said that to me I would have told him or her to go play in traffic! But no one said that to Joe. He pushed me to the breaking point, but I was better for it. I went into the next competition knowing I was better prepared physically than I ever dreamed I could be.

Joe's personal faith in God and his undying support and friendship toward us were very important. His knowledge, experience, and confidence exuded to a point that I just knew I could do it. With my husband and two-year-old son looking on, and our nine-month-old baby in the hotel room with the babysitter, I finally achieved the title that had eluded me for four years—Mrs. Florida 1991.

Joe immediately began preparing me for the Mrs. America pageant. The fairy-tale ending we had hoped for did not occur. However, I placed a very pleasing third runner-up to the newly crowned Mrs. America and was told that I had the highest score of the swimsuit competition. I was truly honored just to be a part of the national competition, and I readily accepted the choice of the judges—a truly spectacular woman from Indiana.

Having worked with Joe for a period of almost three years at that time, I came to realize that not only was his knowledge of training and nutrition invaluable and always "right-on," but also his ability to provide me with the mental edge I needed was equally important. I could be assured that Joe would always be honest with me—sometimes brutally honest—about what I needed to accomplish my goals. To this day I still follow many of Joe's training and nutritional tips, as they have become an integral part of my life. My "title" dreams now exist in the form of goals in the business world, and the confidence and training values instilled in me by Joe still do, and will always, play an important role in whatever future success I achieve.

Mother, Grandmother, and Swimsuit Fitness Winner at 48!   —Janet

About twenty years ago I wanted to whip my body in shape for a pageant, and that's when I met my now dear friend Dr. Joe. As a mother of two, I had a long way to go to get in shape for a pageant! Little did I know what transition would occur in my body as a result of individualizing my diet and workouts. Although I only weighed about 114 pounds when I started, I had a puffy body and LARGE thighs! I craved carbs all the time and ate a low-fat diet. Yes, I thought low fat was the ticket to getting a great body.

Dr. Joe introduced me to eating foods that were most compatible to my blood type. He told me I had to feed my body and that red meat was a good source of protein for me (blood type O) along with all the other foods in the beneficial and neutral categories. I also used his supplements along with others Dr. Joe recommended to help balance my muscle development and burn fat. Through the years of eating this way and training for my body type, I found that my body has a leaner appearance even if I weigh a little more.

Well, at age forty-eight, I own the title holder of Mrs. Florida United States 2007, plus third place runner-up in the Mrs. United States Pageant. As a bonus, I won the Swimsuit Fitness Award!

I weigh more now than when I started with Dr. Joe twenty years ago, but my body is firmer and in much better shape.

My doctor is always amazed at how good my blood work is when I get my annual physical. In consideration of all my accomplishments, the most important thing to me is that I have the energy to keep up with my three children and four grandchildren every day!

Epilogue

My desire for writing this book has been to communicate, in a reader-friendly way, valuable information that pertains specifically to you. This book can serve as the next best thing to having your own personal nutrition and fitness coach. I have given you the best I can on paper to get you started in the right direction and ultimately to help you reach your goals—the rest is up to you!

I hope something in this book has motivated you and perhaps even challenged your former way of thinking about yourself, your health, and others. Discovering the connection between your genetics and how your body functions should overwhelm you with the realization that you have been wonderfully and incredibly made. You are not just another body on this planet. You possess a uniqueness that sets you apart from anyone else; you are worthy of the best.

Your journey to a healthier lifestyle will not begin by accident but through deliberate actions. Your body has not been designed to be idle; it is designed to be physically active. So, you must determine that there is no such thing as living a sedentary lifestyle any longer. Your mind can be clear and alert so it can function at its maximum capacity when you eat correctly and exercise regularly. When it is free of negative thoughts like anger, jealousy, hatred, anxiety, doubt, fear, lust, and self-centeredness, your body will begin the healing process and prolong the onset of diseases. In the world around you will be people who are attracted to you by the example you live, not by what you say.

Though our paths may never cross, may our commitment to a healthier, more energetic life be the common ground we walk. Continue on the journey, stay the course, stay positive, and remember—you are an inspiration in transition!

Life is like a tennis match—in order to win, you must serve first!

Be healthy in your body, soul, and spirit.

Notes

Introduction

1. Weight-Control Information Network (WIN), "Statistics Related to Overweight and Obesity," National Institute of Diabetes and Digestive and Kidney Diseases (NIDDK), http://win.niddk.nih.gov/statistics/index.htm (accessed December 18, 2007).

2. Rob Wilkins and Mike O'Hearn, "Obesity! Public Enemy Number One," *Natural Muscle Magazine*, January 2000, 28.

Chapter 1: Genetics—Your Foundation for Success

1. Jesper L. Anderson, Peter Schjerling and Bengt Saltin, "Muscle, Genes and Athletic Performance," *Scientific American*, September 2000, 49–55.

2. Ibid.

3. *USA Today*, "Diabetes Risk Written on a Gene," August 28, 2000, 6D.

4. Associated Press, "Discovery Opens Door to Treat Obesity, Diabetes," *Orlando Sentinel*, September 20, 2000, A3.

5. Nancy McVicar, "Genome Work Spurs Grant for Miami School," *Orlando Sentinel* (August 30, 2000), D5.

6. Jonathan Safarti, "Blood Types and Their Origins (Answering the Critics)," *TJ: Journal of Creation* 11, no. 1 (April 1997): 31–32, viewed at AnswersinGenesis.org, http://www.answersingenesis.org/tj/v11/i1/blood_types.asp (accessed December 18, 2007).

7. Michael Denton, *Evolution: A Theory in Crisis* (Bethesda, MD: Adler and Adler, 1985), 16, as quoted in a dissertation by Dr. Carl E. Baugh, "Conventional Explanation for Human Antiquities in Question," http://www.creationevidence.org/carlbaugh/diss1.htm (accessed January 15, 2008).

8. Steven M. Weissberg and Joseph Christiano, *The Answer is in Your Bloodtype* (Lake Mary, FL: Personal Nutrition USA, 1999), 57.

9. Bernard Jensen, PhD, ND, *The Chemistry of Man* (Escondido, CA: Bernard Jensen International, 1983), 17.

10. Wessberg and Christiano, *The Answer is in Your Bloodtype*, 28–36.

11. Ibid., 37–43.

12. Ibid., 44–47.

13. Ibid., 48–53.

Chapter 2: Bridging the Gap

1. Marc S. Lewis, PhD, Commencement Address, University of Texas at Austin, May 19, 2000, http://www-personal.umich.edu/~cnegrut/wisdom/speeches/0013-lewis.htm (accessed January 18, 2008).

2. No source available for this story.

Chapter 3: Your Colon: Good Health From the Inside Out

1. DigestivePlus.com, "Constipation," http://www.digestivesplus.com/constipation.html (accessed January 21, 2008).

2. Cathy Hainer, "Back in the Bloom of Health: A Year After Diagnosis, Reporter Is Cancer-Free," *USA Today*, January 11, 1999, https://secure.pqarchiver.com/USAToday/access/37952581 .html?dids=37952581:37952581&FMT=FT&FMTS=ABS:FT&date=Jan+11%2C+1999&author =Cathy+Hainer&pub=USA+TODAY&edition=&startpage=01.D&desc=Back+in+the+bloom+of +health+A+year+after+diagnosis%2C+reporter+is+cancer-free (accessed January 21, 2008).

Chapter 5: How to Become an Instinctive Eater

1. Joseph Christiano, *Seven Pillars of Health* (Lake Mary, FL: Siloam, 2000), 43–47.

Chapter 6: Diet and Nutrition

1. Weissberg and Christiano, *The Answer is in Your Bloodtype*, 119; further expanded with information from Bio-Foods, Inc., Santa Barbara, California.

2. Weissberg and Christiano, *The Answer is in Your Bloodtype*, 125–127.

3. Ibid., 127.

4. Ibid., 154.

5. Ann Louise Gittleman, MS, with James Templeton and Candace Versace, *Your Body Knows Best* (New York: Pocket Books, a div. of Simon and Schuster, Inc., 1996), 126–127.

6. Weissberg and Christiano, *The Answer is in Your Bloodtype*, 155.

7. Gittleman, *Your Body Knows Best*, 127.

8. Weissberg and Christiano, *The Answer is in Your Bloodtype*, 128.

9. Ibid., 127.

10. Ibid., 124.

11. Ibid.

12. Ibid., 155.

Chapter 12: Pick-a-Meal Recipes

1. Molly O'Neill, *New York Cookbook* (N.p., N.d.), 326–327.

2. The Moosewood Collective, *Moosewood Restaurant Low-Fat Favorites* (N.p., 1996), 289.

3. Adapted with slight changes from *Prevention's the Healthy Cook* by the editors of *Prevention Magazine* Health Books (Emmaus, PA: Rodale Press, Inc., 1997), 255.

4. Adapted with slight changes from *The Kripalu Cookbook* by Atma Joanne Levitt (Lee, MA: Berkshire House Publishers, 1995), 30.

5. Adapted with slight changes from *Vegetarian Times Complete Cookbook* by Vegetarian Times, Inc. (New York: Macmillan, 1995), 403.

6. Adapted with slight changes from *The Kripalu Cookbook*, 291.

7. Adapted with slight changes from *The Self-Healing Cookbook*, 7th edition, by Kristina Turner (Vashon Island, WA: Earthtones Press, 1998), 113.

Chapter 14: Nutrition Support Ideas

1. Dr. A. F. Beddoe, *Biologic Ionization As Applied to Human Nutrition* (N.p.: Whitman Publications, 1984, 2002), 239.

Nutrition Support Ideas

Colon Health

INNER OUT: 14-DAY COLON CLEANSING AND DETOXIFYING SYSTEM

The Inner Out Colon Cleansing and Detoxifying System is designed to generate a progressive cleansing effect on your body for fourteen days. It does this in three phases: Phase 1, preparation, kills parasites and breaks up mucus buildup. Phase 2, cleansing, scrubs and cleans the colon. Phase 3, restoration, restores normal colon function with added probiotics.

Enzymes

DIGESTIVE ENZYMES

This digestive enzyme matrix is loaded with a complete line of enzymes to meet any shortage of enzyme production that may be missing in your digestive system. Each capsule contains a matrix of enzymes that provide the specificity of enzymatic action for every food group, creating a greater capacity for better digestion, assimilation, and uptake of nutrition from the foods you eat.

Vitamins

A.M./P.M. MULTIVITAMINS

This is a daily multivitamin supplement for blood types A, B, AB, and O. Each formula contains vitamins, minerals, antioxidants, and herbs specifically formulated to meet the nutritional requirements of each blood type.

Trace Minerals

CONCENTRACE

These are liquid trace minerals. Our bodies do not manufacture them! One of the secrets to good health and longevity is found in the soil—trace minerals! This source of organic trace minerals has a similar complement of precious organic trace minerals. We are made from dust of the earth, and this dust, our own soils, is greatly depleted. ConcenTrace liquid trace mineral supplementation is a very necessary and healthy choice.

Calcium

CORAL CALCIUM

Calcium is a priceless organic mineral and essential for the function of every organ and gland. It is also imperative for balancing the blood and tissue pH in the body. Calcium is the major mineral our body needs in abundance, yet it is the most difficult mineral to absorb. Coral calcium, marine grade, imported from Okinawa, Japan, with magnesium and vitamin D_3 (cholecalciferol) is formulated to promote proper assimilation in the body.

Protein

BODY GENETICS PROTEIN SHAKES AND
THIN TASTIC PROTEIN BARS

Protein is essential for your body. Your body could not function without it. You need enough protein on a daily basis. Other than food sources, you should supplement your diet with a shake or bar as an afternoon pick-me-up or midmorning grab-and-go. Whatever your preference, be certain to include enough protein throughout every day.

Water

ALKALINE WATER

You can go without eating for days, even weeks, but you cannot go very long without water. Every cell in your body is craving the quenching effect of hydration. Revitalize your cellular strength, bring more life into your skin, and supply your body with organic minerals that protect it from disease and chemical imbalance with every ounce of water you drink—drink alkaline water.

Antiaging

HOMEOPATHIC HGH, ORALLY ABSORBED

To roll back the clock is impossible, but to slow down or reverse the negative effects associated with the aging process is possible. By supplementing with HGH, replacing what time and nature can no longer produce, you can enjoy sleeping better, more energy, smoother-looking skin, lower cholesterol, lower percent of body fat, and feelings of youthfulness. You once had enough HGH; now be certain that you still do through supplementation.

For further information on ordering these and other Body Genetics products, contact us at:
Body Redesigning by Joseph Christiano
www.bodyredesigning.com
800-259-2639

Thermoblast Weight-Loss Meal Replacements

BODY GENETICS MEAL REPLACEMENT BAR

Body Genetics Meal Replacement Bar creates a thermoblast when it comes to losing weight. It is formulated to increase the body's ability to burn calories. It comes in delicious dark chocolate and serves as the perfect meal replacement for weight-loss enhancement. It is loaded with over seventy antioxidants for cellular and cardiovascular protection.

Benefits: It stimulates the metabolism and enhances weight loss, causing the body to use fat for energy. It is filling, delicious, it cuts sugar cravings, and it is satisfying. It keeps you from skipping meals, which is detrimental to basal metabolic rate (BMR).

BODY GENETICS STRAWBERRY-FILLED COOKIES

Body Genetics Strawberry-Filled Cookies have been formulated to serve as a meal replacement or snack. The awesomely delicious taste makes weight loss fun, tasty, and satisfying. Each cookie is naturally prepared and has a unique proprietary blend of natural ingredients that work synergistically to stimulate the metabolism for weight loss.

Benefits: The cookies aid the metabolism for additional calorie burning and satisfy cravings for sweets. They are a good fat-burning meal replacement or snack.

BODY GENETICS ENERGY BOOSTER/FAT BURNER CAPSULES

Body Genetics Energy Booster/Fat Burner capsules are a nonephedrine thermogenic supplement designed to enhance weight loss. Each tablet has a unique proprietary blend of natural ingredients that work synergistically to stimulate the metabolism for weight loss and increased energy. Tablets cause no adverse side effects commonly associated with weight loss and energy products that use ma huang and ephedra.

Body Genetics Trim—a fat calorie–metabolizing supplement without caffeine.

Benefits: The capsules burn calories, suppress appetite, improve performance, and increase energy and mental alertness.

For further information on ordering these and other Body Genetics nutritional products, contact us at:

Body Redesigning by Joseph Christiano
www.bodyredesigning.com
(800) 259-2639

Body Type Workout Video/DVD

BODY TYPES—THE PEAR, APPLE, OR BANANA

This twenty-minute body-type workout video is designed to target problem areas specific for your particular body type while providing a total body workout in less time. Dr. Joe, world-acclaimed personal trainer, counts cadence and keeps you motivated throughout each workout. Enjoy the "pop-ups" in each video with interesting and helpful tidbits of information. All you need are dumbbells and a flat bench.

Choose the workout video that best fits your body type. These videos are compatible for the beginner level but can be advanced to intermediate and advanced levels.

BODY TYPES—THE PEAR, APPLE, OR BANANA (DVD)

This DVD has all three body-type workouts. It allows you to select the correct body type workout that is most compatible to your figure. All three workouts are included so you may be accurate in selecting the correct workout for your body type.

DRESS UP, SLIM DOWN VIDEO

This video accompanies any of the body-type workout videos. It is designed to help you appear taller and slimmer instantly by dressing according to your body type. A nationally renowned high-fashion and model consultant works with Dr. Joe to show you how to transform your figure into an hourglass immediately. Learn tips on what jewelry, shoes, and colors to select. This video is the perfect complement while you are getting your body in shape.

For further information on ordering these and other Body Genetics nutritional products, contact us at:

Body Redesigning by Joseph Christiano
www.bodyredesigning.com
(800) 259-2639

Thermoblast Twelve-Week Weight Loss Program

JUMP-START COMPONENTS

- Thirty-two-page booklet that includes the weight-loss concept; instructions; and seven varieties of breakfast, lunch, dinner, and snacks that are compatible for ALL blood types
- Thirty-day progressive walking program for gradual fitness conditioning
- One box (14) Thermoblast Strawberry cookies
- One box (14) Thermoblast Chocolate Meal Replacement Bars
- Thermoblast Energy/Metabolism Booster (60 caps) or TRIM (caffeine free)
- French Vanilla or Dutch Chocolate Protein Shake (30 servings)

Home Blood Typing Kits are also available. All weight-loss products are available individually.

For further information on ordering these and other Body Genetics Nutritional products, contact us at:

Body Redesigning by Joseph Christiano
www.bodyredesigning.com
(800) 259-2639

Health and Fitness Coaching and Services

FORK IN THE ROAD—THE ROAD MAP TO REDESIGNING A NEW YOU

Fork in the Road is a dynamic motivational Health and Fitness Life Coaching DVD series designed to assist the individual who is ready to make healthy lifestyle changes. Professional health and fitness trainer and life coach Dr. Joseph Christiano implements three fundamental components—attitude, diet, and exercise—for successfully reaching your fullest potential.

As your life coach and personal trainer, Dr. Joe teaches you how to overcome negative influences, make positive decisions, and rediscover your personal worth by challenging your mental attitude. While developing the correct mental attitude you will learn how to reach your physical genetic potential for weight loss, disease-free living, and maximum health. Dr. Joe teaches how to individualize and be most accurate with food and exercise by factoring in your unique genetic individuality.

Included in the series are the following DVDs:

- DVD 1 - Introduction to Series
- DVD 2 - Redesigning Your Attitude
- DVD 3 - Redesigning Your Diet
- DVD 4 - Redesigning Your Exercise
- DVD 5 - Redesigning Your Shape (Women)
- DVD 6 - Redesigning Your Workout (Men)
- Mapping Journal
- Food Cards
- Live online monthly coaching for teaching, motivation, and accountability with Dr. Christiano (optional)

For further information on ordering these and other Body Genetics products, contact us at:
Body Redesigning by Joseph Christiano
www.bodyredesigning.com
800-259-2639

Services and Benefits

PIP—Personalized Illness Profile
"Eliminate Illness by Eradicating the Root Cause!"

PROBLEM: ILLNESS

If you are like most people, you may very well be dealing with some sort of health issue that is disrupting your state of well-being and robbing you of the quality of life you are seeking. And you are probably very frustrated by the lack of results. This is true because you have been shown how to treat the symptoms, not the root causes.

Addressing illnesses has become a vicious cycle of identifying symptoms, symptom stomping with medications, and continued poor health...until now!

SOLUTION: ERADICATION

Once an illness, disorder, or sickness has been determined, the next step is to identify and eradicate the root cause of the condition. Seek and destroy the root cause of your illnesses, and you will restore your health.

PIP is an extensive health evaluation, which includes all ten body systems. The evaluation will expose which system(s) in your body is compromised and by what root cause. Some of these root causes can be anything from a parasite such as mold, fungus, slime mold, or worms, or environmental toxins such as chlorine, dyes, or other solvents. Other root causes may be food allergies and/or hormonal imbalances.

Healthy Partner

Being a health-conscious person makes becoming a Healthy Partner a natural fit at www.bodyredesigning.com. As a Healthy Partner you receive 30 percent off of all purchases, as well as additional benefits such as our e-newsletter, savings on shipping and handling costs, plus free access to our online Health and Fitness Coaching sessions with Dr. Christiano. Visit our Web site at www.bodyredesigning.com for more information about PIP and/or becoming a Healthy Partner.

Emotional Food Triggers Questionnaire

Answer each question using a scale of 4 (to indicate the most important or most descriptive of your personality), all the way down to a 1 (to indicate it's not really important or is the least descriptive of your personality). Remember, you need to rank each of the four choices to every question from most to least following this scale. You will be assigning a number to each option below the question, leaving none blank.

Scoring

4 = highly important or highly descriptive of your personality or values
3 = important to you or somewhat descriptive of your personality or values
2 = neutral or depends on the situation and doesn't describe much of your personality
1 = not important in relation to the other options listed; doesn't describe you at all

1. How do you respond when someone at work regularly brings in sweets?

____ You try to distract yourself to avoid the sweets by just focusing more on your work.

____ You thank them and just eat a little bit so they don't get their feelings hurt.

____ You eat it but feel angry inside because you think they are trying to wreck your diet.

____ You don't feel tempted to eat the sweets yet are glad that others seem to enjoy them.

2. Which situations below might cause you to overeat?

____ Trying to calm down or escape the stress and pressure of daily life

____ Celebrating a special occasion or holiday with friends or family members

____ Feeling lonely, empty, or upset inside over not performing up to your potential

____ You rarely overeat because of your personal beliefs about managing food in a healthy way.

3. What factors are most likely to cause you to just sit and watch TV?

____ Trying to prevent feeling boredom by channel surfing just to see what's on

____ Wanting to see certain shows so you can intelligently discuss with others later

____ Interested in learning how the characters rapidly solve problems or stay in control

____ Experiencing different cultures or personalities to better understand their point of view

4. Which approach is most common for you to take when you are involved in a confrontation?

___ Directly expressing what you see happening around you to quickly calm things down

___ Trying to prevent the other people involved from ending up with hurt feelings

___ Actively avoiding the conflict to protect your own feelings from being hurt

___ Stepping back to quietly figure out what the root issues are that led to the conflict

5. Which of these actions is most likely to give you the greatest energy boost?

___ Doing something you really enjoy

___ Talking with someone you really like

___ Thinking about a positive experience from your past

___ Reflecting on your life purpose and personal mission statement

6. Describe your typical experience with managing daily responsibilities:

___ Feeling distracted, stressed, or overwhelmed from having too much to do

___ Wanting to discuss and review your options with someone you trust

___ Detaching or pulling away from a situation to figure out what's best for you

___ Using a disciplined and structured process to stay on task with personal priorities

7. How do you like to spend your free time?

___ Planning or participating in activities that are fun and enjoyable to you

___ Connecting with friends or family you never get to spend enough time with

___ Studying or learning new things now to improve your life in the future

___ Quietly resting and recharging your energy without distractions

8. When facing a problem, do you:

___ Take immediate action to solve the problem

___ Ask others for their opinion or ideas

___ Think about which option feels right for you

___ Quietly pray about what to do next

9. What factors would be most important to you if considering buying a pet?

___ Pet ownership keeps you active because it involves some low-impact exercise.

___ Companionship from pet ownership means you would never feel lonely again.

___ Caring for the needs of the pet actually makes you feel better inside.

___ It gives you the opportunity to provide the pet a good home in a peaceful environment.

10. Which approach would you take if you had extra money in your budget?

___ Race to your favorite store and spend it on whatever looks interesting to you

___ Thoughtfully select a gift to share with someone you care about

___ Buy something you have wanted for a long time and feel excited about owning it

___ Put the extra money into savings for a future "rainy day" when you might need it

11. What describes your greatest desire in close relationships?

___ To get to know other people involved in similar activities so you can do them together

___ To compassionately listen to the needs of others to better support or encourage them

___ To communicate effectively so others really understand how you feel inside

___ To teach or share your insights with others so they can find deeper meaning in life

12. Indicate your typical response during extremely hectic or stressful times:

___ Always feeling busy from trying to get it all done without burning out in the process

___ Trying to not bother others with your problems since they are having a hard time too

___ Feeling frustrated or confused with questions about why life seems so unfair

___ Resting in your personal belief that things always happen for a reason

13. How would you describe your beliefs about exercise and personal fitness?

___ An important habit that reduces daily stress and improves overall health

___ An important way to stay healthy that is easier to maintain when joined by others

___ A necessary but painful part of life best reflected in the phrase "no pain, no gain"

___ A rewarding personal discipline that develops physical wellness and strength

14. How do you first react when hearing about a tragic situation in the news?

____ Interested in hearing how the people involved reacted in case it ever happens to you

____ Feeling hurt or sad for the people involved and wondering who is going to help them

____ Worried or anxious about the possibility of the same thing happening to you

____ Silently praying for the people involved to be safe while hoping that things work out

15. What do you think about most when planning holidays or vacation time?

____ Finishing up home or work projects you never seem to have time to complete

____ Having special times together with friends or family while at home or on trips

____ Taking time off from the hectic pace of life to relax, unwind, and have some fun

____ Spending quiet time journaling, reading, in meditation, or in mapping out future goals

16. How do you usually respond when forced to make a quick decision?

____ Look at the situation and go with your gut instinct about what you think will work best

____ Think about what the people you respect and trust the most would advise you to do

____ Take the path of least resistance and agree in order to avoid arguments or more conflict

____ Filter the decision through your core values and priorities to reach the right decision

17. How do you react when forced to make a major change at work or at home?

____ Focus on what you can control and begin to anticipate and plan about what comes next

____ Ask others what they are planning to do as part of considering all of your options

____ Get mad at the people or circumstances that seem to be forcing this change on you

____ Accept the reality of the situation as just another part of life and try not to dwell on it

18. What approach do you take when you begin to feel hungry inside?

____ Eating anything as fast as possible in order to quickly get back to the activity at hand

____ Preparing enough for you and others since it's likely they are hungry too

____ Look for snack foods to make you feel better until you have time to prepare a meal

____ Stop what you are doing to prepare and eat a healthy meal and then get back to work

19. How would you most likely define a healthy and successful lifestyle?

____ Being self-disciplined, organized, and structured to successfully manage daily activities

____ Feeling connected to the people you care about and having regular times together

____ Feeling in control of your choices and having freedom to decide what is best for you

____ Living in harmony with your personal beliefs in a simple and peaceful way

20. What are you the most passionate about accomplishing in your life?

____ Enjoying a long and healthy life full of meaningful experiences and fun memories

____ Staying close to people by patiently providing love and acceptance no matter what

____ Personal and professional success that brings the respect and admiration of others

____ Living wisely and well to reflect God's love to others in all that you say, think, or do

Scoring Your Totals to Determine Your Food Triggers:

Now that you have indicated how important each element is to you, it's time to go back and add up your total score by category to get your final result. Here's how it works! Each question above has four types of responses, which follow an exact format to reveal four different quadrants that influence our health and can trigger the appetite for food, which can be fueled by Behavioral, Relational, Emotional, or Spiritual factors.

- The first response is always going to reflect your "B" score for Behavioral motivation.
- Your second response will always reflect your "R" score for Relational motivation.
- Your third answer will show your "E" score for Emotional motivation.
- Your final answer will reflect your "S" score for Spiritual motivation.

Here's an example of how to add up your food trigger scores using the first question on the evaluation to show how to record and tabulate the numbers in each of the four quadrants.

1. How do you respond when someone at work regularly brings in sweets?

__3__ You try to distract yourself to avoid the sweets by just focusing more on your work.

__4__ You thank them and just eat a little bit so they don't get their feelings hurt.

__2__ You eat it but feel angry inside because you think they are trying to wreck your diet.

__1__ You don't feel tempted to eat the sweets yet are glad that others seem to enjoy them.

Using this example, the BRES scores for this question are:

- B = 3
- R = 4
- E = 2
- S = 1

This example revealed that the "R" quadrant was highest. This answer indicates that relationship factors were the underlying food trigger that motivated eating food to make someone else feel better instead of eating food to fuel the body. Now add up all of the numbers from each question to discover your total Food Trigger quadrant score.

Remember, the responses will always follow the same BRES pattern on all twenty questions. Your score could range from as low as 20 up to a maximum of 80 in these four key areas to show your underlying motivations regarding the use of food, importance of exercise, and rest as well as maintaining a healthy lifestyle inside and out.

Your personalized BRES scores go here:

B (Behavioral quadrant)   =   ___
R (Relational quadrant)   =   ___
E (Emotional quadrant)   =   ___
S (Spiritual quadrant)   =   ___

Now that you have added up your total BRES scores, it's time to map out your numbers in each category on the food trigger grid on page 38. This will help you to gain a visual understanding of which quadrant is most likely driving you toward making unhealthy choices with food.